浙江省社科联社科普及课题成果

郑红莲◎著

越州印记

绍兴民俗文化双语解码

YUEZHOU IMPRINT

BILINGUAL DECODING OF SHAOXING FOLK CULTURE

中国出版集团有限公司

研究出版社

图书在版编目（CIP）数据

越州印记：绍兴民俗文化双语解码：汉英对照 /
郑红莲著. -- 北京：研究出版社，2025.4. -- ISBN 978-7-5199-1820-0

Ⅰ. K892.455.3

中国国家版本馆 CIP 数据核字第 20257R714Q 号

出 品 人：陈建军
出版统筹：丁　波
责任编辑：张　璐
助理编辑：王　玲

越州印记
YUEZHOU IMPRINT
绍兴民俗文化双语解码

郑红莲　著

研究出版社 出版发行

（100006　北京市东城区灯市口大街100号华腾商务楼）
北京建宏印刷有限公司印刷　新华书店经销
2025年4月第1版　2025年4月第1次印刷
开本：710毫米×1000毫米　1/16　印张：18.75
字数：248千字
ISBN 978-7-5199-1820-0　定价：78.00元
电话（010）64217619　64217652（发行部）

Contents 目录

第一章　Chapter 1

岁时节日篇
Festivals and Occasions in Different Seasons

贺岁 Chinese New Year's Greeting　//　003

数罗汉 Counting the Arhats　//　008

清明上坟鹅 Tomb Sweeping Goose Meat　//　012

立夏尝新 Tasting New Food at the Start of Summer　//　016

七夕食巧果 A Popular Snack on the Qixi Festival　//　020

插地藏香 Incense Burnt for Ksitigarbha　//　024

中秋拜月 Moon Worship on Mid-Autumn Festival　//　027

看大潮 Watching the Tide　//　031

冬至大如年
The Winter Solstice as Significant as the Chinese New Year　//　036

分岁与守岁 Dividing and Observing the Year　//　039

第二章　Chapter 2

日常生活篇
Daily Life

乌毡帽 Black Felt Hat　//　045

乌篷船 Black Awning Boat   //   050

老街台门 Water Town Gatehouses   //   055

渔舍瓜铺 Fisherman's Hut and Melon's Shed   //   061

长衫和短衣 Long Gown and Short Jacket   //   065

饮茶 Tea Drinking   //   070

水泡饭 Water-Soaked Rice   //   075

断发文身 Hairdressing and Tattooing   //   079

霉干菜、霉苋菜梗和其他

Molded Dried Vegetables, Molded Amaranth Stems and Others   //   083

埠船和航船 Dock Boats and Navigation Ships   //   089

第三章　Chapter 3

人生礼仪篇
Etiquette Norms

称谓 Appellations   //   095

女儿酒 The Wine for Daughter's Wedding   //   101

花轿与发轿 Bridal Sedan Chair   //   106

拜堂 Worship at the Hall   //   111

抢亲 Marriage by Capture   //   117

做舍姆 Doing Shem   //   120

满月与得周 Baby's Full Month and One Year's Birthday   //   124

做生日与做寿 Birthday and Longevity Celebration   //   129

第四章　Chapter 4

社会规约篇
Social Convention

施善 Benevolence Practice　//　135

尊师重教 Respect Teachers and Value Education　//　140

桥俗 Bridge Customs　//　147

酒俗 Wine Customs　//　152

坐茶店 Sitting in a Tea House　//　156

曲水流觞
Drinking Wine and Composing Poetry Beside a Meandering Stream　//　161

水龙会 Water Dragon Association for Firefighting　//　165

施茶会 Tea Offering Association　//　169

第五章　Chapter 5

生产商贸篇
Production, Commerce and Trade

养蚕 Sericulture　//　175

稻作文化 Rice-Planting Culture　//　182

幌子招牌青龙匾 Signboards, Banners and Dragon Plaques　//　187

酒业会市 Wine Industry Fair　//　193

锡箔锻制 Production Process of Tinfoil　//　198

市集 Markets　//　202

当铺与当票 Pawnshops and Pawn Tickets　//　209

供奉行业祖师
The Worship of Ancestral Masters of Various Professions　//　213

第六章　Chapter 6

游艺娱乐篇
Entertainment and Amusement

社戏 Community Opera　//　219

赛龙舟 Dragon Boat Race　//　224

斗鸡 Cockfighting　//　228

猜谜 Riddle-Guessing　//　234

斗蛐蛐 Cricket Fighting　//　238

猜拳 Finger-Guessing Game　//　241

目连戏 Mulean Opera　//　245

放风筝 Kite Flying　//　250

第七章　Chapter 7

民间信仰篇
Folk Beliefs

大禹祭典 The Ceremony of Worshiping Dayu　//　257

祭祖 Ancestral Worship　//　264

炉峰香市 Lufeng Incense Market　//　267

地方神祇 Local Deity　//　272

请龙晒龙 Praying to and Sun-Drying Dragon　//　278

放湖灯 Lantern Floating Festival　//　282

求签祈梦 Divination and Dream Seeking　//　285

三茅菩萨 Three Mao Bodhisattvas　//　290

Chapter 1 第一章

岁时节日篇

Festivals and Occasions in Different Seasons

贺岁
Chinese New Year's Greeting

　　绍兴历来重视农历正月初一这个岁首之日，民间流传了许多贺岁活动，年长月久，还形成了不少颇有特色的贺岁习俗。初一当天，人们都早早起来，穿上最漂亮的衣服，打扮得整整齐齐。清早开门之前在院子中间燃放爆竹，取"早升早发"之意。一般的单门独户人家，只能先开门再放爆竹，俗称"开门爆仗"。大门打开后，家家户户首先焚香接神，以茶、酒、点心、佳肴和水果迎接福神，以汤圆数盅祭祀祖先，祈求神灵和祖先的保佑。从正月初一到正月十八，每家每天还有在祖宗神像前点一对蜡烛的习俗。

　　As an ancient city, Shaoxing always attaches great importance to the first day of the first lunar calendar, which marks the beginning of the year. Many New Year's activities have been passed down from generations to generations here, and as time goes by, a lot of distinctive customs have been developed. On the first day of the Lunar New Year, Shaoxing people always get up early, put on their best clothes and dress neatly. Before opening the door, people set off firecrackers in the middle of the yard, because there is an old saying in China that early rise would bring early fortunate. Ordinary individual households always open the door first and then set off firecrackers, which was well known as opening the gate of fortune on the first day of the Lunar New Year. After that, every household burned incense to welcome gods, greeted them with tea, wine, snacks, delicacies and fruits, and sacrificed ancestors with glutinous rice balls to pray for the blessings of gods and ancestors. From the first day to the 18th day of the first lunar month, there was also a custom of lighting candles in front of the ancestral shrine every day.

汤圆是绍兴人家大年初一早上必吃的食物，里面通常加上少许年糕丁，表示"团团圆圆""高高兴兴"。吃完早餐，全家出门走街，俗称"走喜神方"。走的方向，一般以万年历所书为准，如果万年历上写"大利西南"，就向西南方向行走，以此来确保一年好运。走完回家后，人们相互贺年，俗称"拜岁"。每个家庭按照长幼顺序，依次向长辈跪拜。受拜者连说："恭喜恭喜"。对婴幼儿童，则说"聪明智慧，易长易大"等祝福语。大户人家在这一天还有大开祠堂之门、燃香点烛、祭拜列祖列宗等习俗。这天凡是在路上遇到熟人或长辈，都需要拱手拜年，否则会被认为没有礼貌。

Glutinous rice balls, also called Tangyuan in Chinese or sweet dumpling, is a must eat food for natives on the morning of the first day of the Lunar New Year. A small amount of diced rice cake is usually added symbolizing "reunion" and "happiness". After breakfast, the whole family would go out to the streets, commonly known as "walking with the God of Fortune". The direction of the walk was generally determined by the Chinese almanac. If it said that southwest was auspicious, people walked in the southwest direction to ensure good luck for the whole new year. After returning home, people sent best wishes to each other, commonly known as "paying New Year's greetings". Each family member is required to kneel or bow to their elders in the order of seniority. And the worshiped would repeatedly say, "May you happy and prosperous." Blessings, such as "becoming smart and growing up quickly", are always given to infants and young children. In old days those wealthy families had the custom of opening ancestral halls' doors, burning incense and candles, and worshiping their ancestors on the first lunar day. Besides, it was considered impolite if one did not bow to acquaintances or elders encountered on the road.

图1　绍兴汤圆 郑红莲摄 Shaoxing Tangyuan PHOTO: Z.H.L.

　　正月初一，凡邻居、朋友登门拜访，一定先是相互祝贺新年吉祥，主人以"撮泡茶"招待客人，里面一般放入两颗橄榄或金桔，俗称"元宝茶"。这一天家家户户都会赶早睡觉，称为"赶鸡睡"，因为头一天除夕守岁熬夜需要及时休整。在嵊州，旧时还有正月初一给女子敬茶的习俗。这一天早上，等到女主人起床梳妆打扮好，男主人便要端上一杯糖茶，以示敬意。早餐吃汤圆时，第一碗也要先盛给女主人。平时由女主人做的所有家务活，如烧茶做饭、喂养牲口等，这一天全部都由男主人承担，女主人可以茶来伸手、饭来张口，俗称"敬女日"。在新昌一带，正月初一有不把水泼在地上、不动刀斧、不点灯火等风俗习惯。

In the past, on the first day of the first Lunar month, when neighbors and friends came to visit, people always wished one another happy and prosperous in the coming year. The host served green tea to guests with two olives or kumquats, commonly known as "tea of fortune". Almost every household went to bed early in the evening, which was called "chasing chicken sleep", because they need a big rest after staying up late on Lunar New Year's Eve. In Shengzhou, a county of Shaoxing, there used to be a custom of serving tea to women on the first day of the lunar new year. When the hostess was dressed up, the host would serve her a cup of sweet tea to show his respect and gratitude. The first bowl of glutinous rice balls for breakfast was also served to the hostess. All the household chores that were commonly done by the hostess, such as making tea, cooking, feeding livestock, etc., were all taken care of by the host on the first day. This was known as "Women's Respect Day" in Shaoxing. In the area of Xinchang, there were also some special customs on the first day, such as no water splashed on the ground, no knives and axes used, and no lights allowed.

初二至初八，一些家庭妇女开始穿街走巷到各寺院烧香拜佛，俗称"烧八寺香"。她们认为，在这一期间去绍兴的八个寺院烧香礼佛，便可以求得一年吃穿不愁、万事顺意。正月初二到十五，亲戚朋友也会相互邀请吃饭喝酒，俗称"做人客"。做客往往先近亲，后远亲，由亲及疏。做客时客人须带上一些礼物和蜡烛。如果送长辈，绍兴的风俗多送白糖、桂圆、莲子等，送小辈多用糕点、糖果。

From the second day to the eighth day of the Lunar New Year, local ladies started to walk around streets and alleys to burn incense and worship Buddha at various temples, commonly known as "burning incense" from eight temples. They believed that during the period, visiting the eight temples in Shaoxing to burn incense and worship Buddha can bring adequate food and clothing for the whole year, and everything does smoothly. From the second day to the fifteenth day of the Lunar New Year, relatives and friends often invite one another to have meals and drinks together, commonly known as "be a guest". When visiting relatives, it is often customary to visit close relatives first and then distant ones, proceeding from the closest to the most distant. It was also a tradition for people to bring some gifts and candles when they visited others, like white sugar, longan and lotus seeds to elders, and pastries and candies for younger generations.

数罗汉
Counting the Arhats

　　绍兴旧时拥有众多寺院，每个寺院都塑有罗汉佛像，除了开元寺专门设有罗汉堂，塑有五百罗汉外，其他寺院均在大殿两侧塑十八罗汉像。罗汉，是梵文阿罗汉的简称，是小乘佛教修行四果位的最高果位，据说通过修行，以达到了断贪、嗔、痴等一切烦恼，应受人天供奉，永远进入涅槃，不再生死轮回的修学顶端。因此，每年正月初一，数罗汉便成了善男信女、老老少少，去寺院祈求平安、占卜问卦的传统习俗。

　　Shaoxing used to have many temples, and each temple had statues of Arhats. In addition to Kaiyuan Temple, which once possessed a special Arhat Hall with 500 Arhats, the other temples had 18 Arhat statues on both sides of the main hall. Arhat is the abbreviation of the Sanskrit word arahant. It is the highest level of the four stages of practice in the Hinayana Buddhism. It is said that through practice, all afflictions such as greed, anger, and ignorance can be eliminated, and they should be worshiped by humans and gods. They could enter Nirvana forever and would not be reincarnated in the cycle of life and death. Therefore, on the first day of the first lunar month every year, counting the Arhats became a traditional practice for men and women, old and young. They visited temples to pray for peace and seek fortune-telling.

绍兴开元寺始建于后唐长兴元年（930），据新编《绍兴市志》载：清"道光十三年（1833）僧越慧筹资重修。……寺右树罗汉堂，陈五百罗汉"。开元寺罗汉堂位于大殿西侧，占地甚广。堂内建曲折长廊，罗汉像高1米左右，均为坐式，依次序分别放在长廊的两侧。五百尊罗汉高低不一、表情各异。有的粉脸年少、稚气未脱，有的老态龙钟、白眉盈尺。千姿百态，栩栩如生。

Kaiyuan Temple in Shaoxing was first built in the first year of Changxing of the Later Tang Dynasty(930). According to the newly compiled *Shaoxing City Chronicles,* "In the 13th year of Daoguang(1833), the monk Yue Hui raised funds to renovate it. On the right side of the temple, there was an Arhat Hall with 500 Arhat statues. " The Lohan Hall of Kaiyuan Temple was located on the west side of the main hall and covered a large area. Inside the hall, there were winding corridors, and the Arhat statues were about one meter high, all sitting in order on both sides of the corridor. The five hundred Arhat statues had different heights and facial expressions. Some were youthful and immature with pink faces and were young, while others were old with long white eyebrows. They were in various poses and looked lifelike.

数罗汉时，应以跨进罗汉堂大门门槛的第一只脚为准，如果是左脚先跨进门槛，则以左边的第一尊罗汉数起；如果是右脚先跨进门槛，则数右边罗汉，一直数到与自己年龄相同的那尊罗汉，观察他的容貌、表情、姿态，以占卜一年的福祸吉凶。但多数寺院的罗汉只有十八尊，这样，数的时候就要重复计数，以数到与自己年龄相符的罗汉为止。

图2 罗汉佛像 郑红莲摄 Statue of Arhat PHOTO: Z.H.L.

When counting the Arhats, one should base it on the first foot that crosses the threshold of the Arhat Hall. If it is the left foot that enters first, start counting from the first Arhat on the left side; if it is the right foot, start counting from the right side. Continue counting until one reaches the Arhat who corresponds to one's age, and observe its appearance, expression, and posture to divine the good or bad fortune, and auspicious or inauspicious events for the coming year. Because there are only eighteen Arhat statues in most temples, one needs to repeat the counting until reaching the Arhat statue that matches with his or her age.

数罗汉除了少数年长的善男信女较为虔诚，在数到的罗汉前点烛焚香、祈求保佑外，多数人数罗汉不过是作为新年里的一种乐趣而已，所以不管数到的罗汉法相如何，大多一笑了之，真正当作一回事的人是很少的。抗日战争时候，绍兴一度沦陷，开元寺罗汉堂被毁，从此绍兴就没有五百罗汉了。从20世纪80年代起，有些寺院虽然重塑了十八罗汉，但绍兴正月数罗汉的风俗在慢慢消失。

Apart from a small number of devout male and female followers who were older in age, most people who count the Arhats only do it as a form of entertainment during the Chinese New Year. They may light candles and burn incense to pray for blessings in front of the Arhats they count, but for the most part, they do not take it seriously. During the War of Resistance Against Japanese Aggression, Shaoxing was occupied and the Arhat Hall of Kaiyuan Temple was destroyed. As a result, Shaoxing no longer had five hundred Arhats. Since the 1980s, although some temples rebuilt the eighteen Arhats, the tradition of counting the Arhats during the first month of the lunar year in Shaoxing has been slowly disappearing.

清明上坟鹅
Tomb Sweeping Goose Meat

绍兴人把扫墓称作上坟。清明节前后，正是风和日丽、柳绿花红的日子，除了上坟还可以踏春游玩，所以上坟往往是全家出动。绍兴水网交错、河道纵横，这个时候河里船只密集，路上行人如织，处处热闹非凡。因此，绍兴人把清明前后称作上坟市。

Shaoxing people refer to tomb sweeping as going up to the tomb. Around the Qingming Festival, the weather is usually sunny and warm, with willows turning green and flowers blooming. In addition to tomb sweeping, people also go out for spring outings, so it's often a family affair. Shaoxing has a network of waterways and rivers crisscrossing the city, and during Qingming, boats are densely packed in the river, and pedestrians are everywhere on the streets, making it very lively. Therefore, Shaoxing people call the period around the Qingming Festival the season for going up to the tombs.

与别处不同，绍兴人上坟时必有一碗鹅肉，俗称"上坟鹅"。这是因为绍兴沿门绿水，草料丰富，所以农村家家都养鹅。另外，鹅体肥大，杀一只鹅，可以分装成许多碗，俗称"鹅十八"，用作祭祀祖先或其他婚丧事宜的时候，比较划算。再者，清明时节的鹅肉格外油润，令人垂涎欲滴。清朝绍兴人金埴在描写绍兴养鹅习俗时写道："凡飨神饷客，庆祭婚丧，以及节岁礼馈，在在必设之。……上坟曰'坟鹅'，庆岁曰'年鹅'，祀田曰'田鹅'。盖至今越风盛行而他处弗尚也。"

Unlike other places, Shaoxing people always bring a bowl of goose meat when they go tomb sweeping, which is commonly known as tomb-sweeping goose meat. This is because Shaoxing has abundant grass and water resources, so every rural family raises geese. In addition, geese are large in size and one goose can be divided into many bowls of meat, commonly known as "eighteen bowls of goose meat". It is more cost-effective when used for ancestor worship or other wedding and funeral ceremonies compared with other poultry. Moreover, the goose meat during the Qingming Festival is particularly oily and delicious. Jin Zhi, a Shaoxing fellow from the Qing Dynasty, wrote about the custom of raising geese in Shaoxing, saying that, "Whenever there are banquets for

图3　绍兴白切鹅郑红莲摄 Shaoxing boiled goose meat PHOTO: Z.H.L.

gods, celebrations for weddings and funerals, or gifts for festivals, it is necessary to have geese. ... Goose meat is called 'tomb-sweeping goose' for tomb sweeping, year goose for 'New Year's celebrations goose', and field goose for field worship. This custom is popular in the Yue region (Shaoxing), but not in other places."

除鹅肉外，艾饺、艾糕也是清明上坟的必备点心。取洗干净的艾叶稍微煮一下，加入糯米粉，以鲜笋、咸菜为馅的咸味艾饺是绍兴的一大特色。清明之后，天气转暖，绍兴多雷阵雨，当地谚语有"清明吃艾饺，不怕阵雨浇"的说法。

Besides goose meat, artemisia dumplings and artemisia cakes are must-have snacks for tomb sweeping during the Qingming Festival. Cleaned artemisia leaves are boiled briefly and mixed with glutinous

图4 绍兴艾饺
郑红莲摄 Shaoxing
artemisia dumplings
PHOTO: Z.H.L.

rice flour. The salty artemisia dumplings with fresh bamboo shoots or pickled vegetables as filling are a major specialty of Shaoxing. After the Qingming Festival, the weather turns warmer and there are often thunderstorms in Shaoxing. There is a local saying that goes "An individual who eats artemisia dumplings during the Qingming Festival will not be afraid of being caught in a thunderstorm".

立夏尝新
Tasting New Food at the Start of Summer

立夏是中国二十四节气之一，也是当地樱桃、豌豆等水果蔬菜开始上市的日子，绍兴人喜欢在这一天品尝新上市的樱桃和豌豆。绍兴人习惯把豌豆称为蚕豆，一般在清明前后落花结荚，到立夏的时候开始成熟，所以绍兴本地有"清明见荚，立夏好吃"的谚语。而立夏吃竹笋，民间认为可以健脚、有腿劲。周作人在《立夏》一诗中写道："新装杠秤好称人，却喜今年重几斤。吃过一株健脚笋，更加蹦跳有精神。"一般的做法是把整株笋带壳放进炉灶里面煨熟，剥壳后让家里的小孩子整株吃，俗称"健脚笋"。

Lixia is one of the 24 solar terms in China, and it is also the day when local fruits and vegetables such as cherries and peas begin to hit the market. Shaoxing people like to taste the newly available cherries and peas on the day. Shaoxing people are accustomed to calling peas broad beans. They generally start to mature around Lixia after blooming during the Qingming Festival. Therefore, there is a saying in Shaoxing that goes "Seeing the pods during Qingming, tasting the peas during Lixia". Eating bamboo shoots during Lixia is believed by the folk to be beneficial for strengthening the legs. In his poem *Lixia*, Zhou Zuoren wrote, "It's good to weigh people with a new scale, and I'm happy to see how heavy they are this year. After eating a plant of 'leg-strengthening bamboo shoots', I can jump and bounce with more energy." A typical way is to put the whole bamboo shoot with its shell into the stove to cook, and then let the children in the family eat the whole bamboo shoot after peeling the shell, which is commonly known as "leg-strengthening bamboo shoots".

图5 绍兴蚕花饭 郑红莲摄 Shaoxing Canhua rice PHOTO: Z.H.L.

在绍兴新昌，立夏这一天人们还有吃蚕花饭的习俗。蚕花饭是用粳米、籼米和糯米三种米加上切成小粒大小的咸肉丁煮成的一种混合饭，当地有"吃了咸肉蚕花饭，一年蚕花勿退板"的俗语。在绍兴嵊州，则有"立夏吃蛋胜吃鸡"的说法，所以立夏这一天，差不多家家户户都要煮上一大锅带壳鸡蛋。有的还专门用彩线编成小网袋，把蛋放进去，挂在小孩的脖子上。小孩之间常用它们玩斗蛋的游戏，在这一游戏中，谁的鸡蛋最硬，谁就是赢家。

In Xinchang, the southern part of Shaoxing, there is a custom of eating Canhua rice on the day of Lixia. Canhua rice is a mixed rice dish made with three types of rice: sticky rice, idica rice, and glutinous variety, as well as small diced salted pork. There is a local saying that goes "Eating salted pork Canhua rice on Lixia, silkworms will not leave their trays for the whole year". In Shengzhou, the northern part of Shaoxing, there is an old saying that, "Eating eggs on Lixia is better than eating chicken". Therefore, almost every household cooks a large pot of eggs with shells on the morning of that day. Some even weave small net bags with colorful threads, put eggs in them, and hang the bags around the necks of children.

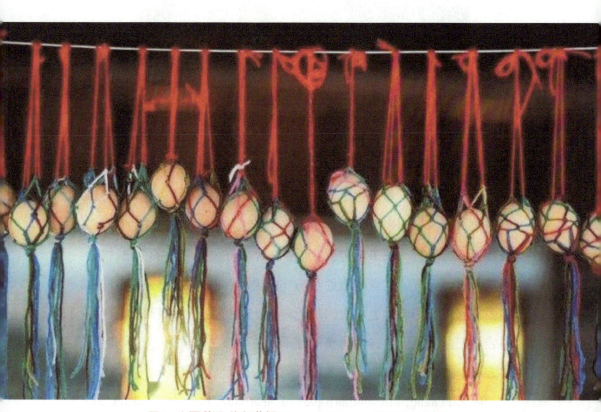

图6　立夏彩蛋　郑红莲摄 Lixa colorful eggs PHOTO: Z.H.L.

One of the most popular games among kids at that time is egg-fighting game, in which the person who has the hardest round end of egg is the winner.

在绍兴，立夏还有称娃的风俗。工具用的是一种扛秤，秤钩上挂着一只大竹篮，方便被称的娃娃坐。称的时候还有些讲究，例如秤砣只能由内向外移动，不能从外向内移动。因为民间认为如果把秤砣先放在较重的斤两上，后面发现不够重量，再把秤砣向内移动，这样可能会影响被称的娃娃的生长发育。称完后，家长一般把孩子的重量记录下来，以便与下一年做比较。以上立夏尝新、立夏称娃等风俗至今在绍兴还广为流传。

In Shaoxing, there is also a custom of weighing babies during Lixia. The tool used is a type of scale, with a large bamboo basket hanging from the hook to allow the baby to sit comfortably. There are some specific rules when weighing babies, for example, the weight should be moved from the inside to the outside, and not from the outside to the inside. This is because people believe that if the weight is first placed on the heavier side, and then moved inward if it is not enough, it may affect the growth and development of the baby who is weighed. Parents usually record their children's weight to compare it with the next year's weight. The customs of tasting new food and weighing babies during Lixia are still widely spread in Shaoxing today.

七夕食巧果
A Popular Snack on the Qixi Festival

农历七月初七，称为七夕节，也叫乞巧节。《牛郎织女》是我国的四大民间故事之一。相传这一天夜晚是牛郎织女鹊桥相会的佳期。

The seventh day of the seventh lunar month is known as the Qixi Festival, also called Qiqiao Festival. *The Cowherd and the Weaver Girl* is one of China's four major folktales. Legend has it that this is a great time for the Cowherd and the Weaver Girl to meet on the Magpie Bridge.

传说，有一位老实勤恳的小伙子，名叫牛郎，在他照顾多年的老黄牛的帮助下，和天上下凡的一位名叫织女的仙女结为夫妻。婚后两人男耕女织，生活幸福，还生下一儿一女。可是不久就被玉皇大帝知道了，立刻派了天兵天将下到人间捉拿私自下凡的织女。当牛郎赶到时，织女已被天兵抓走。他在老黄牛的帮助下，用箩筐挑着一双儿女去追赶天兵。眼看快要追到时，不料王母娘娘用玉簪在空中一划，划出来一条天河把牛郎和织女隔开了。喜鹊知道这事，便自动集合起来，在每年的七月初七搭起一座"鹊桥"，让牛郎织女渡河相会。

According to legend, there was a hardworking and honest young man named the Cowherd. With the help of an old ox he had cared for many years, he married a fairy named the Weaver Girl who had descended from the heavens. After marriage, they lived a happy life together, with the man farming and the woman weaving, and they even had a son and a daughter. However, soon after, the Jade Emperor found out and immediately sent heavenly soldiers down to capture the Weaver Girl, who had come to earth without permission. When the Cowherd arrived, the Weaver Girl had already been taken away by the heavenly soldiers. With the help of the old ox, he carried his two children in a basket and chased after the heavenly soldiers. Just as he was about to catch up, Queen Mother used a jade hairpin to draw a line in the sky, creating the Milky Way and separating the Cowherd and the Weaver Girl. The magpies knew about this and automatically gathered together to build a magpie bridge every year on the seventh day of the seventh lunar month, allowing the Cowherd and the Weaver Girl to cross the river and meet each other.

在绍兴，七夕节人们常用白糖和面粉为原料，做成一种花式面点，菱形状，被扭成结，小巧玲珑，是极薄极脆的油炸面皮片，被称为"巧果"。《越谚》描写道："巧果，七夕油焯粉果，样巧味脆，即乞巧遗意。"巧果是七夕应节食品，至今在绍兴一些农村还有七夕炸巧果的风俗。这一天，妇女们挎篮背筐到处采摘槿杞柳叶，把它们放在水里揉搓后，用汁水洗头发。据说洗后发泽光亮，发际生香。

In Shaoxing, people often use sugar and flour as raw materials to make a fancy pastry on the Qixi Festival. It is diamond-shaped, twisted into knots, small and exquisite, and extremely thin and crispy fried dough flakes, called "Qiao Guo". *The Yue provevb* is described as, "A fried pastry made of oil and flour on the Qixi Festival, which is delicate and crispy, symbolizing the pursuit of love." Qiao Guo is a traditional food for the Qixi Festival, and the custom of making fried Qiao Guo on the day still exists in some rural areas of Shaoxing. On the day, women used to carry baskets and go pick honeysuckle and willow leaves everywhere, put them in water, rub them, and use the juice to wash their hair. It was said that after washing, the hair would be shiny and fragrant.

图7　七夕巧果
郑红莲摄 Qixi Qiao
Guo PHOTO: Z.H.L.

据说七夕节晚上，如果到丝瓜棚下，可能听到牛郎织女的丝丝窃语。又传说，七夕节晚上如果下雨，那雨水是牛郎和织女相会时流下的眼泪。宋朝时候绍兴还有立乞巧竿、祭牛女的习俗。在七夕节当天，将一根顶着莲花的长竹竿放在院子里，被称为"巧竿"，人们用水果、点心和茶酒祭祀牛郎织女。

It was also said that on the night of the Qixi Festival, if you go under the luffa trellis, you may hear whispers from the Cowherd and the Weaver Girl. There is a legend that if it rains on the night of Qixi, the raindrops are the tears shed by the Cowherd and the Weaver Girl when they meet each other. During the Song Dynasty, there were also customs in Shaoxing to set up Qiqiao poles and offer sacrifices to the Cowherd and the Weaver Girl. To be more specific, a long bamboo pole topped with a lotus flower was placed in the courtyard, called the Qiao Pole, and people offered fruit, snacks, and chartreuse to worship the Cowherd and the Weaver Girl.

插地藏香
Incense Burnt for Ksitigarbha

农历七月三十，据说是地藏菩萨诞生的日子，绍兴民间有插地藏香的习俗。这天晚上，不论城乡，地上到处都插满棒香，光亮闪烁，十分壮观。地藏菩萨和文殊、普贤、观音并称为中国佛教四大菩萨。佛经上说他曾受释迦牟尼佛的嘱咐，在释迦既灭，弥勒未生之前，现身六道，救度天上以至地狱的一切众生。相传他显灵说法的道场在安徽九华山，因此每年农历七月三十，朝拜九华山，成为流行甚广的信仰习俗。

On the thirtieth day of the seventh lunar month, it is said to be the birthday of Ksitigarbha Bodhisattva, and there is a custom in Shaoxing to burn incense for Ksitigarbha. On that night, regardless of urban or rural areas, incense sticks are inserted all over the ground, shining brightly and spectacularly. Ksitigarbha, along with Manjusri, Samantabhadra, and Avalokitesvara, are known as the Four Great Bodhisattvas of Chinese Buddhism. According to Buddhist scriptures, he was instructed by Sakyamuni Buddha to appear in the six realms to save all sentient beings from heaven to hell before the Buddha's passing and Maitreya's birth. It is said that his place of manifestation and preaching is at Jiuhua Mountain in Anhui Province. Therefore, the worship of Jiuhua Mountain on the thirtieth day of the seventh lunar month has become a popular religious custom in China.

但是，绍兴离九华山路途遥远，所以在农历七月三十的晚上，绍兴人一般都是在自家门口的路上或天井里燃香礼拜。相传地藏菩萨不住天庭而是住在地下，所以人们都直接把香插在地上。城里天井多用青石板铺砌，香就插在石板的缝隙里。这种香的下半截是染成红色或绿色的细竹棒，俗称"棒香"。在绍兴，这种香一般不在寺院里使用，香烛店也只是在农历七月三十前生产供应。棒香燃烧完之后，竹棒还在，因此第二天孩子们以收集红红绿绿的竹棒为乐。

However, Jiuhua Mountain is far away from Shaoxing, so on the night of the thirtieth day of the seventh lunar month, Shaoxing people usually burn incense and worship on the road in front of their own houses or in their courtyards. According to legend, Ksitigarbha does not reside in the heavenly palace but underground, so people directly insert incense sticks into the ground. The courtyards in the city are mostly paved with green slabstone, and the incense sticks are inserted into the gaps between the stones. The lower half of this type of incense is a thin bamboo stick dyed red or green, commonly known as "stick incense". In Shaoxing, this type of incense is generally not used in temples, and incense and candle shops only produce and supply it before the thirtieth day of the seventh lunar month. After stick incense is burned out, the bamboo sticks are still there, and children have fun by collecting colorful bamboo sticks the next day.

图8　燃香礼拜地藏菩萨 郑红莲摄 Burning stick incense to worship Ksitigarbha PHOTO: Z.H.L.

　　绍兴地区，除了插棒香礼拜地藏菩萨，还有供奉一碗清水的习俗。供奉完后，常使用这碗里的清水擦洗眼睛，认为这样可以让眼睛更明亮。

　　In addition to the custom of burning stick incense to worship Ksitigarbha in Shaoxing, there is also a tradition of offering a bowl of clear water. After offering it, people often use the water to wash their eyes, believing that it can make their eyes brighter.

中秋拜月
Moon Worship on Mid-Autumn Festival

农历八月十五是我国传统的中秋节。这天晚上，绍兴各地历来有赏月、拜月的习俗。根据古代的阴阳五行之说，月为"太阴"，女子也属阴，所以人们习惯称呼月亮为"月亮婆婆"。中秋之夜，绍兴人有供月、拜月、摸秋等习俗，它们与女性也密切相关。

The fifteenth day of the eighth lunar month is China's traditional Mid-Autumn Festival, also called Moon Festival, and there is a long-standing custom in Shaoxing of admiring and worshiping the moon on that night. According to the ancient theory of yin-yang and five elements, the moon is "Tai Yin", and women also belong to yin, so people are used to calling the moon Grandma Moon. On the night of the Mid-Autumn Festival, Shaoxing people have customs such as offering to the moon, worshiping the moon, and touching the autumn, which are closely related to women.

中秋节当晚，绍兴人家必须在庭院或者屋外场地上，放置一张八仙桌，上面供奉着素月饼、水果、老南瓜和一碗凉白开，同时燃香数支，点上一对蜡烛，称为"供月"。供祭一会儿后，妇女、儿童轮流对着天空的月亮跪拜行礼，叫作"拜月"。周作人在《中秋》一诗里写道："红烛高香供月华，如盘月饼配南瓜，虽然吃惯红绫饼，却爱神前'素夹沙'。"这首诗把孩子们拜月亮时的开心和喜悦，描绘得淋漓尽致。

On the night of the Mid-Autumn Festival, every household in Shaoxing must place a table of Eight Immortals in the courtyard or outdoor space, with vegetarian mooncakes, fresh fruits, old pumpkins, and a bowl of cold boiled water offered on it. At the same time, several incense sticks and a pair of candles are lit, which is called "Offering to the Moon". After offering for a while, women and children take turns kneeling down and paying respects to the moon in the sky, which is called "Worshiping the Moon". In his poem *Mid-Autumn Festival*, Zhou Zuoren wrote, "The red candles and high-incense are offered to the moon, mooncakes as round as plates paired with pumpkins. Although used to

图9　中秋供月　郑红莲摄 Offering to the moon PHOTO: Z.H.L.

eating red silk cakes, we love 'fine sand' in front of the gods." The poem vividly depicts the joy and happiness of children when they admire the moon.

在绍兴，成年男子必须回避拜月的习俗，俗称"男不拜月"。因为男人属阳性，月亮上面的嫦娥是绝色仙女，男子敬而远之，可以避免不必要的麻烦。拜完月亮后，女子们常常用手指蘸着供月亮的凉白开，涂在自己和孩子的眼睛上，一边涂一边默念道："眼目清亮，眼目清亮。"据说，这样可以让眼睛炯炯有神。

In Shaoxing, adult men must avoid the custom of worshiping the moon. This is because men are considered to be yang, and it is also said that Chang'e on the moon is a beautiful fairy. Men keep their distance to avoid unnecessary trouble. After worshiping the moon, women often dip their fingers in the cold boiled water offered to the moon and apply the water to their own and their children's eyes while silently reciting "clear and bright eyes". It is believed that this can make their eyes clear and bright.

有新娶媳妇的人家，中秋夜当婆婆的必将供完月亮的那个长南瓜抱走，塞到新媳妇的被窝里，图个吉利。民间对此有两种说法：一种是南瓜多子，与绍兴人祈求多子多福的传统观念有关；第二种是长南瓜酷似男根，具有繁衍子孙的功能。按照绍兴风俗，旧时中秋之夜人们还可以到别人的田里、园中任意摘取瓜类蔬菜，主人不会怪罪生气，育龄女子多在此夜偷摘南瓜，作为生育子女的好兆头，俗称"摸秋"。

In the past in Shaoxing, when a new daughter-in-law was married, on the Mid-Autumn Festival night, the mother-in-law would take away the long pumpkin offered to the moon and stuff it into the new daughter-in-law's bedding for good luck. There were two folk beliefs about the tradition: one was that pumpkins bore many offspring, which was related to the traditional concept of seeking blessings for many children in Shaoxing; the second was that the shape of the long pumpkin resembled a male genital, which had the function of reproducing offspring. According to Shaoxing customs, people used to be able to freely pick melon vegetables in other people's fields and gardens on the night of the Mid-Autumn Festival, and the host would not blame or get angry. Many women at the age of childbearing would secretly pick pumpkins on that night as a good omen for giving birth to children, which was called "Touching Autumn".

看大潮
Watching the Tide

　　农历八月十八，绍兴历来有看大潮的习俗。这一天，全城百姓聚集在沿塘三江、镇塘殿、后桑盆，人山人海、盛况空前。附近住户还会提前几天邀请亲戚朋友，杀鸡宰鹅，设宴待客，就像过节一样，所以人们又把这一天称为"观潮节"。

　　On the 18th day of the eighth lunar month, there is a tradition in Shaoxing to watch the large tide. On that day, people from all over the city gather at the three rivers along the embankment, Zhentang Temple, and Housang Pen, forming a sea of people, with an unprecedented grandeur. Nearby residents always invited relatives and friends a few days in advance, slaughtered chickens and geese, and hosted banquets like a festival, so people called that day "Tide-watching Festival".

　　绍兴沿海一带是钱塘江与曹娥江的汇合处，所以每到农历八月十八左右，潮汐特别壮观，潮头也格外整齐，形成了内陆地带无法看到的独特景观。古时，人们由于缺乏科学知识，对许多自然现象缺乏正确的认识，而将一切归之于神灵，所以一直认为潮汐是涨潮神和退潮神发怒与和解所造成的。并把农历八月十八看作是潮神的生日。因此，绍兴当地人年年相约去看大潮、祭潮神。

The coastal area of Shaoxing is the confluence of the Qiantang River and the Cao'e River, so around the 18th day of the eighth lunar month, the tides are particularly spectacular, and the tide heads are also particularly neat, forming a unique landscape that cannot be seen in inland areas. In ancient times, due to the lack of scientific knowledge, people lacked the correct understanding of many natural phenomena and attributed everything to gods and spirits. Therefore, they always believed that the tides were caused by the anger and reconciliation of tide gods. They also regarded the 18th day of the eighth lunar month as the birthday of tide gods. Therefore, the locals in Shaoxing gather every year to watch large tides and offer sacrifices to tide gods.

这一天，在三江至镇塘殿、后桑盆一线的海塘上，红男绿女、老人小孩，熙熙攘攘、摩肩接踵。塘上商贩的叫卖声、殿内老人的念佛声，吵吵嚷嚷、不绝于耳。大概下午一点钟，人们能从西边江面上看到淡淡的一条白线，这叫"潮头"。潮头一出现，观潮的人群立刻安静下来，一一踮起脚尖，伸长脖子张望。绍兴沿海的潮水都是从西往东奔腾而下，这时如果遇上东风，潮水被风力阻隔，潮汐就更壮观威猛。

On that day, on the seawall from Sanjiang to Zhentang Temple and Housang Pen, there were crowds of people, including men and women, young and old, bustling and jostling. The cries of vendors on the embankment and the chanting of the elderly in the temple were constantly heard. At around one o'clock in the afternoon, people can see a faint white line on the river surface from the west, which was called the tide head. When the tide head appeared, the crowd watching tides immediately quieted down, tiptoeing and craning their necks to look. The tides along the coast of Shaoxing flew from west to east. If an easterly wind blew at that moment, the tides were even more spectacular and mighty as they were blocked by the wind.

这个时候，被请来演戏感谢潮神的戏班演员都忙碌起来，准备着在潮水到达时"落地请寿"。"落地请寿"是指演员们必须穿上戏服，下台来到海塘上临江演出，以此为潮神祝寿。这是多年以来形成惯例，每个戏班都会遵照执行。否则，就会受到看潮人群的指责甚至唾骂。一旦潮头出现，停歇在江边的几艘蜑船开始发动，缓缓开向江心去搏击怒涛，俗称"接潮头"。船身时而被浪潮抛向浪尖，时而跌入浪谷。岸上看大潮的人们个个都紧张得屏住呼吸，而船上艄公都不慌不忙、镇定自若。渔夫们则扛着网兜，迎着潮水前进，瞅准被潮水冲得头昏脑涨的海鳗、海蜇，随手一兜就迅速跑上岸来。鲁迅在他的作品中把这些艄公和渔夫叫作"弄潮儿"。

At that time, the theater troupe actors who were invited to thank tide gods were busy preparing a performance called "landing and offering birthday wishes" when tides arrived. All actors must put on their costumes, come down from the stage, and make performance by the river on the embankment to wish tide gods a happy birthday. It became a tradition over the years, and every theater troupe followed it. Otherwise, they would be criticized or even spat on by the crowd watching tides. Once the tide head appeared, several sampans moored by the riverbank started up and slowly headed towards the center of the river to fight against the raging waves, which was commonly known as "meeting tide heads". The boats were sometimes thrown onto the crest of the waves and sometimes fell into the troughs. The people on the shore watching large tides were all nervous, holding their breath, while the boatmen on board remained calm and composed. The fishermen carried their net bags and advanced against the tide. Spotting the moray eels and jellyfish that were dizzy from the tide, they scooped them up with a flick of the hand and quickly ran ashore. Lu Xun referred to these boatmen and fishermen as "tide fighters" in his works.

以前看大潮还有一件开心的事就是能在这天品尝海螺蛳。只要花上几角钱，便能买到一大包的海螺蛳。每个海螺蛳，长约半寸，像颗钉子，只需要磕去它的尾部，轻轻一吸，慢慢细嚼，味道鲜美。所以人们在等候观潮时，常以海螺蛳为休闲零食。八月十八看大潮的习俗，至今仍流传不绝。

Another happy thing about watching the large tide in the past was being able to taste small sea snails on that day. Just with a few cents, you could buy a large bag of small sea snails. Each sea snail is about half an inch long, like a nail. You just need to crack off its tail, gently suck it, slowly chew, and the taste was delicious. Therefore, people often used small sea snails as a leisure snack while waiting to watch the tide. The custom of watching the large tide on the 18th day of the eighth lunar month still continues today.

图10 海螺狮 郑红莲摄 Sea snails PHOTO: Z.H.L.

冬至大如年
The Winter Solstice as Significant as the Chinese New Year

在绍兴，冬至是二十四节气中最重要的节气之一，民间有"冬至大如年"的说法。这一天，家家户户都要祭祀祖先，有的甚至到祠堂家庙里去祭祖。祭祖之后，全家团聚在一起吃饭喝酒，俗称"冬至酒"，也称"做冬至"。

In Shaoxing, the winter solstice is one of the most important solar terms among the 24 solar terms, and there is a saying in folk culture that the winter solstice is as significant as the Chinese New Year. On the day, every household worshiped their ancestors, and some even went to ancestral temples to pay respects. After the ancestor worship, the whole family gathered together to have a big meal with alcohol, which was commonly known as "Winter Solstice Wine" or "Winter Solstice Making".

冬至日前后，绍兴人过去喜欢用石臼将一年要吃的大米全部提前舂好，称为"冬舂米"。一是因为过了冬至，再过一个月左右的时间就"着春"了，人们到时得忙着各种农活，准备春耕，没有时间去舂米。二是因为春天来了，天气越来越潮湿，米粒没有冬令时候的坚实，"冬舂米"就可以避免米粒易碎，减少粮食的耗损。

During the period of winter solstice, people in Shaoxing used to like to use a stone mill to grind all the rice they would eat for the year in advance, which was called "Winter Grinding Rice". One reason was that after the winter solstice, it would be about a month before spring plowing begins, and people would be busy with various farming activities and preparing for spring plowing, leaving no time to grind rice. Secondly, as spring approached, the weather became increasingly humid, and the rice grains were not as solid as they were in winter. "Winter Grinding Rice" can prevent rice grains from becoming fragile and reduce food waste.

绍兴人大多喜欢喝酒，并且家家都会酿酒。绍兴人家中酿酒，一般都爱在冬至前下缸，酿好后香气扑鼻、特别诱人，此时酿酒用的鉴湖水还属于冬天的水，一般酿出来的酒易于保藏，不会变质。冬至时期人们还用特别的酿酒技术酿成"酒窝酒""蜜殷勤"给老人食用，或者当作礼物送给亲朋好友。

Most people in Shaoxing like to drink and almost every household knows how to brew wine. Generally, they like to put the wine into the fermentation jar before the winter solstice. After it is brewed, the aroma is very fragrant and tempting. At that time, the water used for brewing the wine is still winter water from Jianhu Lake. Hence, the wine brewed during this period is easy to preserve and would not spoil. During the winter solstice period, people also use special brewing techniques to make "Jiuwo wine" and "honey wine" for the elderly to drink, or as gifts for relatives and friends.

按照绍兴民俗，冬至这天还有很多禁忌，例如不许说不吉利的话，不许争吵殴打，不许打破碗盆，妇女不许回娘家，如果已经在

图11　黄酒酒缸 郑红莲摄
Yellow wine jars in Shaoxing
PHOTO: Z.H.L.

娘家的，在冬至这天前必须回到婆家，不许打骂孩子，即使是最调皮的学生，在冬至日也可以免受责罚，学堂里的先生只能举着戒尺愤愤地警告说："账，给你记到明日再算！"

According to the folk customs of Shaoxing, there were many taboos on the day of the winter solstice. For example, it was not allowed to say unlucky words, not allowed to quarrel or fight, not allowed to break bowls or pots, women were not allowed to return to their parents' home, and if they were already there, they must return to their husband's family before the winter solstice. It was not allowed to beat or scold children, even the most mischievous students can escape punishment on the day of the winter solstice. Teachers in school can only warn them angrily with a ruler, saying that, "I'll remember your mistake until tomorrow!"

分岁与守岁
Dividing and Observing the Year

　　分岁与守岁，是除夕夜的一种岁时习俗。绍兴当地全家团聚吃年夜饭，称为"分岁"，谚语有"三十日夜吃，正月初一穿"的说法，所以分岁的菜肴都特别丰盛。有二十碗、十六碗的，碗数必须成双数，而且每碗菜都有一个吉利的名称。

　　Dividing and observing the year is a traditional custom on the Lunar New Year's Eve. In Shaoxing, the whole family gather together to have a reunion dinner, which is called dividing the year. According to a proverb, "Eat on the night of the 30th and wear new clothes on the first day of the lunar new year." Therefore, the dishes for dividing the year are particularly sumptuous. There are twenty or sixteen dishes, and the number of dishes must be an even number, and each dish has an auspicious name.

　　例如鲞冻肉上面盖一个白鲞头，称为"有想（鲞）头"。一碗煎鱼，头尾都翘出碗外，称作"元宝鱼"，而这碗鱼在除夕分岁时是不准吃的，以讨"吃过有余"的彩头。以莲藕切块，加红枣、荸荠一起煮，称作"有富"，寓有"富贵"的意思。盐煮花生称为长生果，煮熟的栗子称"轰轰烈烈"。分岁时，还要吃年糕、粽子，取"年年高中"的意思。另外，还有一盘不可或缺的"八宝菜"，是将腌菜切丝，与千张丝、冬笋丝、黄豆芽、黄花菜等一起炒。上虞等地分岁时如有家人在外无法赶回一起团聚时，餐桌上必须配置碗筷，以表示阖家团圆。

For example, putting a white fish head on top of the braised pork jelly is called "You Xiang Tou", homophonous with prosperity. A bowl of fried fish with the head and tail sticking out of the bowl is named "Yuanbao Fish", but this fish cannot be eaten during the Lunar New Year's Eve dinner to signify having "more than enough" in the coming year. Cutting lotus roots into pieces, and cooking them with red dates and water chestnuts is called "You Fu", which means wealth and prosperity. Boiling peanuts with salt is called "longevity fruit", and cooked chestnuts is called "booming and prosperous". During the period of dividing the year, people also eat rice cakes and Zongzi, which expresses a best wish of achieving "higher scores in the coming new year". In addition, there is an indispensable dish called "Eight Treasure Vegetables", which is made by cutting pickled vegetables into shreds and stir-frying them with shredded tofu skin, bamboo shoots, mung bean sprouts, and daylily flowers. In places like the district of Shangyu in Shaoxing, if some family members cannot go back home and gather together for the reunion dinner, their utensils still need to be set on the table to represent the reunion of the family.

分岁之后，便到门外燃放爆竹，俗称关门爆仗。门外点着的蜡烛被移到室内，称为"守岁蜡烛"。孩子们将所得的压岁钱放在枕头底下，长辈们还要在孩子床头边塞些柑橘、荔枝等物，称作压岁果子。除夕夜，除了孩子，大人们都围炉团坐，饮茶谈笑，有的到

图12　八宝菜 郑红莲摄
Eight Treasure Vegetables
PHOTO: Z.H.L.

半夜才睡，还有的甚至通宵达旦，称为"守岁"。古时，在绍兴，读书人家在除夕这天还要祭祀书神。如今，这一习俗已经消失不见，但分岁与守岁的风俗仍延续至今。

After dividing the year, people set off firecrackers outside the door, commonly known as closing the door with firecrackers. The candles lit outside the door were moved indoors and called year-observing candles. Children put their lucky money under their pillows, and elders also put tangerines, lychees, and other fruits at the head of their beds, which were called lucky fruit. On Chinese New Year's Eve, except for children, adults sat around the stove, drank tea, chatted, and laughed. Some stayed up until midnight, while others even stayed up all night, which was called "observing the year". In ancient times, in Shaoxing, families of scholars also offered sacrifices to the god of literature on Chinese New Year's Eve, which disappeared in later years. But the traditions of dividing and observing the year still continue to this day.

Chapter 2 第二章

日常生活篇

Daily Life

乌毡帽
Black Felt Hat

　　乌毡帽，作为绍兴独有的民俗文化之一，是一项极具地域特色的文化遗产，承载着绍兴的文化底蕴，也是绍兴人审美情趣的表达。在绍兴柯岩风景区，有一座独特的亭子，整体造型是由几只大小不等的酒坛托起一项巨大的乌毡帽，令游客惊叹设计者别出心裁的创意。

　　Black felt hat, as one of the unique folk cultures in Shaoxing, is an extremely characteristic cultural heritage, carrying the cultural connotations of Shaoxing and expressing the aesthetic taste of Shaoxing people. In the Keyan Scenic Area of Shaoxing, there is a unique pavilion whose overall shape is supported by several barrels of different sizes, forming a huge black felt hat, which amazes tourists with the designer's original and creative idea.

　　绍兴作为旅游城市，乌毡帽是游客了解绍兴文化的重要载体。北方的毡帽大多是白色的，而绍兴的毡帽则是黑色。这与绍兴人自古以来崇尚黑的审美密切相关。一方面是受到越地文化的影响，另一方面还与绍兴当地的风俗习惯不可分割，绍兴人只有在办丧事时会佩戴白帽，而平时生活中非常忌讳戴白色的帽子。旧时，不论农

图13 "乌毡帽"亭子 郑红莲摄 "Black felt hat" pavilion PHOTO: Z.H.L.

民、渔民、船工、箔工，以及一些木匠、石匠等手工业工匠，都有戴乌毡帽的习惯。因此，乌毡帽是劳动人民的一个鲜明标志。

As a tourist city, Shaoxing's black felt hat is an important carrier for tourists to understand Shaoxing culture. While most northern felt hats are white, Shaoxing's felt hats are black. This is closely related to the aesthetic of black that Shaoxing people have admired since ancient times. On one hand, it is influenced by the culture of the Yue state, and on the other hand, it cannot be separated from the local customs and habits of Shaoxing. Shaoxing people only wear white hats when they hold funerals, and they are very taboo about wearing white hats in daily life. In the old days, whether farmers, fishermen, boatmen, foil workers, or some handicraft workers such as carpenters and stonemasons, they all had the habit of wearing black felt hats. Therefore, the black felt hat is a distinct symbol of the laboring people in old days.

在他乡异地，乌毡帽成了绍兴人的一个重要标志。鲁迅在他的作品里，多次写到乌毡帽。例如在《故乡》中写到闰土，形容他"紫红的圆脸，头戴一顶小毡帽"。在《阿Q正传》中提到："阿Q没有现钱，便用一顶毡帽做抵押。"有人说，不论你在天南地北，只要看到戴乌毡帽的，十有八九是绍兴人。

Black felt hats have become an important symbol of Shaoxing people. Lu Xun wrote about the black felt hat many times in his works. For example, in *My Old Home*, he described Run Tu as "having a purple-red round face, wearing a small felt hat on his head". In *The True Story of Ah Q*, it was mentioned that, "Ah Q didn't have cash, so he used a black felt hat as collateral". Some people say that no matter where you are in the world, if you see someone wearing a black felt hat, there is a high chance that they are from Shaoxing.

乌毡帽内外乌黑，圆顶，卷边，前段呈现畚斗形。它的制作工艺相当复杂，一般经过挑毛、脱脂、压制成胚、染色等72道工序。制作乌毡帽的主要步骤包括挑选羊毛、处理羊毛、制作毛坯、碾制毛坯、揉搓毛坯、毛坯定型、染色和毡帽定型。由于乌毡帽坚实耐用，具有保暖防水的功能，所以除了夏季，其他季节都有很多人戴着。有时也有人将乌毡帽倒转过来作为篮子使用。

The black felt hat is black both inside and out, with a round top, rolled edges, and a front that resembles a dustpan shape. Its production process is quite complex, generally involving 72 steps such as selecting wool, defatting wool, pressing into wool blanks and dyeing. The main steps in making a felt hat include selecting wool, processing wool, making wool blanks, rolling wool blanks, kneading wool blanks, shaping wool blanks, dyeing, and shaping the black felt hat. Because the felt hat is solid and durable, with functions of warmth and waterproofing, many people wear it in all seasons except for summer. Sometimes, people also invert the black felt hat and use it as a basket.

图14　带着乌毡帽的农民 郑红莲摄 A farmer with black felt hat PHOTO: Z.H.L.

乌毡帽由纯羊毛制作，并且做工复杂，所以价格不菲。从前，农民、手工业者收入微薄，买一顶乌毡帽被看作是一件大事。如果有一顶新毡帽戴在头顶上，身边的人常会投来羡慕的目光。一顶乌毡帽通常可以戴七八年甚至十来年，即使戴久了也被看作是一份家产，所以阿Q能把它当作抵押物来换酒喝。

The black felt hat is made of pure sheep wool and the workmanship is complex, so the price for it is not cheap. In the past, farmers and craftsmen had meager incomes, and buying a black felt hat was considered a big event. If someone wore a new black felt hat on their head, people around them would often look at them with envy. A black felt hat can usually be worn for seven or eight years, or even ten years. Even if it was worn for a long time, it was considered as a family asset, so Ah Q could use it as collateral to exchange for drinks.

斗转星移，随着社会的发展，除了一些老年农民、渔民和工匠，戴乌毡帽的绍兴人越来越少。但作为一种具有浓厚地方特色的产品，乌毡帽登上了众多绍兴旅游商店的柜台，特别是外地游客，喜欢租一件长衫、一顶乌毡帽来拍照留念。2007年，绍兴乌毡帽作为绍兴一种民俗文化被浙江省人民政府列入第二批浙江省非物质文化遗产名录。

With the passage of time and the development of society, fewer and fewer Shaoxing people wear black felt hats, except for some elderly farmers, fishermen, and craftsmen. However, as a product with strong local characteristics, the black felt hat has appeared on the shelves of many Shaoxing tourism shops. Especially among tourists from other places, they like to rent a long gown and a black felt hat to take pictures and keep memories. In 2007, the Shaoxing black felt hat was listed as a second batch of Zhejiang Province's intangible cultural heritage by the Zhejiang Provincial Government, as a representative of Shaoxing's folk culture.

乌篷船
Black Awning Boat

乌篷船是绍兴一带的特色水上交通工具，因竹篾被涂成黑色而得名，一般有脚划船和明瓦船两种。脚划船比较小，它的特点是船工还能用双脚划桨。明瓦船除了固定的乌篷外，还有几道用河蚌壳薄片制作的可移动的船篷。这种河蚌壳薄片既可遮阳避雨，又能采光，所以俗称明瓦。

The black awning boat is a characteristic water transportation in the Shaoxing area, named for its black painted bamboo strips. There are generally two types: the foot-paddled boat and the Mingwa boat. The foot-paddled boat is relatively small, and its feature is that the boatman can also row with their feet. The Mingwa boat has not only a fixed black awning but also several movable boat awnings made of thin slices of river mussel shells. These river mussel shell slices can not only shade from the sun and rain but also allow light to pass through, so they are commonly known as Mingwa (clear tiles).

脚划船由于空间有限，所以仅用于载客，不装运货物。船手坐于船尾，备有一片划楫和一支长桨，划船时，船手既用手划楫，又以脚踩桨。当船行驶到空阔笔直的河面时，船工常把划楫放在腋下作舵，仅用双脚划桨。这种用脚划桨的方式，据说在全国各地很难

图15　绍兴脚划船
郑红莲摄 Shaoxing
foot-rowing boat
PHOTO: Z.H.L.

见到，可以说是绍兴一种特有的交通习俗。

　　Foot-rowing boats are only used for carrying passengers due to limited space and not for transporting goods. The boatman sits at the stern with a paddle and a long oar. When rowing, the boatman uses both hands to paddle and also uses his feet to push the oar. When the boat travels on a wide and straight river surface, the boatman often places the paddle under his arm to steer and only uses his feet to row. This way of rowing with feet is said to be rare throughout the country and can be considered a unique transportation custom in Shaoxing.

　　当船手划船时，乘客一般坐在船的中舱，舱里铺有木板，板上备有草席、枕头。乘客累了就可以躺下休息一会儿。中舱的船篷可以移动，方便乘客上下船和观赏水上的风景。这种船既可以用作交通，也可以观光游览。例如邀请几位好友，带上一些酒菜，租上一条脚踏船，让船夫慢慢划桨，泛舟水上，既能欣赏远山近水的美景，又能和好友把酒畅谈，不亦乐乎！又如一个人在船上闭目养神，静听潺潺流水声，也会让人忘记尘世烦恼，身心愉悦。

When the boatman rows the boat, passengers usually sit in the middle cabin of the boat, which is covered with wooden boards and equipped with straw mats and pillows. If passengers get tired, they can lie down and rest for a while. The canopy in the middle of the boat can be moved to facilitate passengers getting on and off the boat and enjoying the scenery on the water. This type of boat can be used for transportation as well as sightseeing. For example, you can invite a few friends, bring some food and drinks, rent a foot-rowing boat, let the boatman row slowly, drift on the water, enjoy the beautiful scenery of mountains and rivers, and have a good time with your friends. Or, if you are alone on the boat, you can close your eyes and listen to the sound of flowing water to forget the troubles of the world and feel happy and content.

明瓦船的船身更大，其大小一般以明瓦篷的片数来区分，片数越多，船身就越大，比如有三明瓦、四明瓦、五明瓦等。明瓦船上的油漆装饰都非常讲究，船头上刻有巨大的鹢首。民间传说鹢居住在海上，连蛟龙见了都害怕，所以人们认为把鹢首刻在船头可以保证船只的出行安全。船身上，用彩色油漆绘画出各种各样的传说故事。因为船身足够大，乘客可以自由地走来走去。船的中舱备有桌椅，人们可打牌作乐，也可饮酒赏景。后舱备有藤床、被褥，乘客可躺下休息。舱内还有炉灶，可炒菜做饭。过去，一般人家常租一条明瓦船用于迎亲、上坟或游玩等活动，而豪门大户或官宦人家大多有自家的船只。

The hull of a Mingwa boat is large, and its size is generally distinguished by the number of Mingwa canopies. The more canopies there are, the larger the hull, for example, three clear tiles, four clear tiles, five clear tiles, and so on. The paint decoration on the Mingwa boat is very exquisite, and a huge egret head is carved on the bow. Folklore has it that egrets live on the sea and even dragons are afraid of them. Therefore, people believe that carving an egret head on the bow can ensure the safety of the boat's journey. On the hull, various legendary stories are painted with colored paint. Because the hull is large enough, passengers can walk around freely. The middle cabin of the boat is equipped with tables and chairs for playing cards and enjoying the scenery while drinking. The rear cabin is equipped with rattan beds and bedding for passengers to lie down and rest. There is also a stove in the cabin for cooking. In the past, ordinary families often rented a Mingwa boat for activities such as welcoming relatives, visiting graves, or sightseeing, while wealthy households or officials usually had their own boats.

图 16 绍兴
明瓦船 郑红莲摄
Shaoxing Mingwa
boat PHOTO: Z.H.L.

民国后期，战乱不断，经济萧条，百姓生活穷困潦倒，明瓦船渐渐退出人们的视野。但乌篷的脚划船作为一种便利灵活的水上交通工具却一直保留下来，并且数量越来越多。20世纪80年代，绍兴纺织业蓬勃发展，柯桥一百多条脚划船船主，各拿一本纺织布料样品，在介绍绍兴纺织产品中，发挥着重要的作用，被人们称为水上布市。其后随着旅游业的发展，脚划船逐渐遍布绍兴各处的旅游景点。许多外地游客以坐这种乌篷的脚划船作为到绍兴旅游的一大快事。一些旅游部门还将脚划船作为小型纪念品广为宣传，而明瓦船基本消失在人们的记忆里，不但外地人不知道，就连本地人知道的也不多。

In the late period of the Republic of China, there were constant wars, economic depression, and the people's lives were poor and miserable. The Mingwa boat gradually disappeared from people's sight. However, the foot-rowing boat with a black awning as a convenient and flexible water transportation tool has always been preserved and its numbers have increased. In the 1980s, the textile industry in Shaoxing was booming. More than 100 foot-rowing boat owners in Keqiao each took a sample of textile fabrics, which played an important role in introducing Shaoxing textile products and were called Cloth Market on Water. With the development of tourism, foot-rowing boats gradually spread to various tourist attractions in Shaoxing. Many tourists from other places enjoy riding on black canopy foot-rowing boats as a fun activity when visiting Shaoxing. Some tourism departments also promote models of foot-rowing boats as small souvenirs. On the other hand, the Mingwa boat has almost disappeared from people's memory, not only unknown to outsiders but also not well-known by locals.

老街台门
Water Town Gatehouses

　　台门是绍兴当地具有地域性特色的居住建筑，也是绍兴民居中的上等建筑。"绍兴城里五万人，十庙百庵八桥亭，台门足有三千零"，形容绍兴古城里老台门数量之多。台门一般深藏在古城水乡的小巷深处，一座座都幽静别致，白墙黑瓦，飞檐翘角。

　　Gatehouses are a style of residential architecture with local characteristics in Shaoxing and are also considered as high-level buildings among Shaoxing's residential houses. It is said that in the past "there were as many as 3,000 gatehouses although there were just 50,000 people, ten temples, one hundred shrines, and eight pavilions in Shaoxing city". The saying describes the large number of gatehouses in the ancient city of Shaoxing. Gatehouses are generally hidden deep in the alleys of the ancient water town, each with its own unique charm, white walls and black tiles, and flying eaves.

　　台门的由来主要有两种说法。一是高台说。高台说认为，台门源自战国到西汉时期的古老建筑形式"高台建筑"，以"台上筑屋"表达求神庇佑、与神沟通的原始情怀，同时绍兴潮湿天气较多，台门具有防潮功能。二是府第说。台字有高、稳之义，同时也有尊敬的意思。绍兴住宅入口的典型做法是台门、前院、二门，二

图17　绍兴老台门
郑红莲摄 Shaoxing
ancient gatehouse
PHOTO: Z.H.L.

门又叫仪门，前院一般很小，相当于现代住宅的"玄关"。典型的台门，会有一个"台门斗"的空间，台门斗比实际地面要高一些，用台阶联系，这样，门的起步有高度又有空间，实现了"台"（高、基础、支撑等）的意义。

There are mainly two versions about the origin of gatehouses. The first version is the high platform, which believes that gatehouses originated from the ancient architectural form of "high platform architecture" during the Warring States period to the Western Han Dynasty. The construction of "houses on high platform" is used to express the primitive feelings of seeking divine protection and communicating with gods. At the same time, Shaoxing has a humid climate, and gatehouses have a moisture-proof function. The second version is the official residence. The Chinese character of gatehouses means high and stable, as well as respect. The typical entrance of a Shaoxing residence consists of a gate, a front courtyard, and a second door, which is also called the ceremonial door. The front courtyard is usually very small, equivalent to the "modern foyer". A typical gatehouse maximize the use of space, with a "higher gate" than the actual ground level and connected by steps. This way, the starting point of the door has both height and space, realizing a unique and charming aesthetic that is in harmony with the surrounding waterways and landscape.

台门占地较多，小的数亩，大的数十亩。整座台门都是外筑高墙，内部分为成进建筑厅堂和楼屋两部分，前者有五进、七进甚至有九进多的。达官显贵们还喜欢在楼屋后面建个花园。整个台门建筑气势恢宏、庄严典雅。绍兴城里这类官宦台门有上百处，其中最有名的有吕府台门、孙府台门和伯府台门。

A gatehouse occupies a relatively large area, ranging from a few acres to tens of acres. The entire gatehouse is surrounded by high walls, and the interior is divided into two parts: the building halls and the tower houses. The former has five, seven, or even nine sections, while the latter is often accompanied by a garden behind it. The entire gatehouse is magnificent, solemn, and elegant. There are hundreds of such official gatehouses in Shaoxing city, among which the most famous ones are the gatehouse of the Lü Family, Sun Family, and Count (Bo) Family.

吕府台门是明代嘉靖年间礼部尚书吕夲的府邸，位于绍兴城区新河弄169号，占地约29.8亩，坐北朝南，共有13座厅堂。台门内所有建筑按照三条纵轴线和五条横轴线设计布局。整体结构简朴，用工精细。孙府台门则位于偏门直街31号，是明代正德、嘉靖年间孙氏的官邸。孙氏六代有"祖孙父子叔伯兄弟尚书"的美名，当时家世显赫，府第规模宏大，后来曾改作家族祠堂。

The gatehouse of the Lü Family is the mansion of Lü Yan, the Minister of Rites during the Jiajing reign of the Ming Dynasty. It is located at No. 169 Xinhe Lane in the urban area of Shaoxing and covers an area of about 29.8 acres. It faces south and sits north, with a total of 13 halls. The layout of all buildings inside gatehouses follows three vertical axes and five horizontal ones. The overall structure is simple and the craftsmanship is exquisite. The gatehouse of the Sun Family is located at No. 31 Pianmen Straight Street and was the official residence of the Sun family during the Zhengde and Jiajing reigns of the Ming Dynasty. The Sun family had a prestigious reputation that "grandfathers, fathers, sons, uncles and brothers all were ministers". At that time, their family was prominent and their mansion was large in scale. Later, it was used as a ancestral hall for the family.

绍兴谚语有"吕府十三厅，不及伯府一个厅"的说法，谚语中的伯府，就是明代王守仁的豪宅。王守仁在正德年间因为平定江西的宸濠之乱被封为新建伯，所以绍兴当地把他的府邸叫作伯府台门。可惜的是，伯府台门毁于一场大火，只留有泥石堆砌的山坡和一方水池，但也足以想象出它当日的宏大规模。

图18 吕府
台门 郑红莲摄
The gatehouse
of the Lü Family
PHOTO: Z.H.L.

There is an old saying in Shaoxing that goes, "The gatehouse of the Lü Family has 13 halls, which are not as good as one hall of the Count (Bo) Family". The Count (Bo) Family referred to in the proverb is the mansion of Wang Shouren, a prominent figure in the Ming Dynasty. During the Zhengde reign, Wang Shouren was enfeoffed as the New Jian Bo for suppressing the Chen Hao Rebellion in Jiangxi Province. Therefore, his mansion in Shaoxing was called the Count (Bo) Family gatehouse. Unfortunately, the Bo Family gatehouse was destroyed in a fire and only a pile of rubble and a water pool remain, but it is still enough to imagine its grand scale in the past.

这些台门设有正门和边门，平日一般人员进出只走边门，只有贵宾驾到或重大事宜时，才大开正门。台门里的正厅为第二厅，也叫大厅。各进之间以天井相隔，内屋多为楼房。台门的正门后面，还有一道仪门，仪门上常悬挂着一些反映该台门地位的牌匾，如状元第、探花第等。除了官宦台门，绍兴还有不少台门为乡绅富家所建。这类台门面积不大，楼房也较少，通常建在小街僻巷中。例如蔡元培故居，就是蔡元培祖父购置，原来只有两进，后来因为房屋不够居住，又在后面增加了一进。现在经过修葺，仍然保存完好。

A gatehouse has a main gate and a side gate. In the past, ordinary people usually entered and exited through the side gate, and the main gate was only opened for VIPs or major events. The main hall in the gatehouse is the second hall, also known as the grand hall. There are courtyards between each section, and most of the interior rooms are tower houses. Behind the main gate of the gatehouse, there is also a ceremonial door, on which some plaques reflecting the status of the gatehouse are often hung, such as Top Scholar or Third Place in the highest imperial examination. In addition to official gatehouses, there are also many gatehouses built by wealthy local gentry in Shaoxing. These gatehouses are not large in size and have fewer tower houses, usually built in small streets and alleys. For example, the former residence of Cai Yuanpei was purchased by Cai's grandfather, originally consisting of only two sections. Later, due to insufficient housing, an additional section was added to the back. After renovation, it is still well-preserved today.

历经历史的变迁，许多老街台门都已经年久失修，目前一部分被列为各级文物保护单位加以保护，一部分被列为拆建对象。

After experiencing the changes of history, many gatehouses on old streets have been left in disrepair for many years. Currently, some of them have been listed as cultural relics protection units at all levels and are being protected, while others have been listed as objects to be demolished and rebuilt.

渔舍瓜铺
Fisherman's Hut and Melon's Shed

在绍兴众多的水面、田野上，散落着以竹子为材料搭建的两种简易房舍，俗称"渔舍瓜铺"，这些小小的建筑物为绍兴水乡增添了浓郁的民俗风韵。

Among the numerous waters and fields of Shaoxing, there are two types of simple houses built with bamboo materials scattered around, commonly known as Fisherman's Hut and Melon's Shed. These small buildings add a strong folk flavor to the water towns of Shaoxing.

渔舍一般建在水面宽阔的鱼塘上，首先用六或八根毛竹夯入河底作为柱子，接着用竹篾或粗铁丝横着绑几根稍细的毛竹作为横档，铺上竹栅，上面覆盖有箬叶的大竹篷，形状像个高大的船篷，篷后以竹簟遮拦，篷前悬挂草帘作为进出的门帘。渔舍有大有小，小的是正方形，仅仅够一个人躺卧，大的是长方形，草帘前留有些空间，方便守渔舍的人白天活动。渔舍一般高出水面一米多。从远处看，它就像建在水上的小窑洞。夜晚渔舍里点着的小油灯，在夜雾朦胧的水面上闪烁着微微灯光，为水乡的夜色增添不少诗情画意。

Fisherman's huts are generally built on wide fish ponds. First, six or eight bamboo poles are pounded into the river bottom as pillars, and then several slightly thinner bamboo poles are tied horizontally with bamboo strips or thick iron wire to serve as crossbars. Bamboo fences are laid on top, covered with large bamboo awnings with palm leaf coverings on top, shaped like a tall boat awning. There is a bamboo mat barrier behind the awning, and a grass curtain hanging in front as an entrance. Fisherman's huts vary in size, with small ones being square and only enough for one person to lie down, and larger ones being rectangular with some space in front of the grass curtain for the fishermen to move around during the day. The fisherman's hut is generally more than one meter above the water surface. From a distance, it looks like a small cave built on the water. At night, the small oil lamp lit inside the fisherman's house flashes a faint light on the misty water surface, adding a lot of poetic and picturesque charm to the night scenery of the water town.

愿意守渔舍的人们往往是一些历尽沧桑的老人，他们熟谙水性，也善于捕鱼，一年四季几乎都生活在渔舍，有些甚至大年三十都在渔舍里度过。夏天，渔舍里蚊子特别多，最担心的还是怕鱼儿生病，一听到有鱼儿直往上窜跳的声音，他们就得想办法寻找对策，防止鱼儿大面积生病。冬天，水面上寒风料峭，但也不能待在渔舍里不出去，得站在风口留意过往的船只。

The people who are willing to guard the fisherman's huts are often elderly people who have experienced many hardships. They are familiar with water and good at fishing. They live almost all year round in the fisherman's huts, and some even spend the Chinese New Year's Eve in the hut. In summer, there are many mosquitoes in the fisherman's huts, but their biggest concern is the possibility of the fish getting sick. Once they hear the sound of fish jumping up, they have to find ways to prevent widespread illness among the fish. In winter, the cold wind on the water surface is piercing, but they cannot stay in the fisherman's huts all day. They have to stand at the windward side and pay attention to passing boats.

旧时，绍兴沿海一带有很多瓜田。瓜的品种也丰富，有西瓜、黄金瓜、梨头瓜、马铃瓜，等等。瓜果成熟的季节，处处飘香，十分诱人。按照绍兴风俗，在炎炎夏日，过路人经过瓜田，是可以摘瓜解渴的，但不允许摘了带走。晚上看瓜园，主要防止野猪、野猫等动物来糟蹋瓜田，所以人们把瓜铺搭建在瓜田上。由于守瓜只需要瓜成熟时才去看管，所以瓜铺的结构比渔舍简单得多。一般只是盖个草棚，在里面放一张床铺，有的连床铺也没有，只是在地面上铺上稻草或一两张旧草席。相较而言，守瓜铺比守渔舍轻松得多，所以常常由一些小孩子来守着瓜地。

In the past, there were many melon fields along the coast of Shaoxing. The variety of melons was also rich, including watermelons, cantaloupes, pear-shaped melons, and muskmelons, etc. During the season when the melons were ripe, the fragrance was everywhere, very tempting. According to the Shaoxing customs, passers-by can pick melons for thirst-quenching when passing by the melon fields on hot summer days, but they were not allowed to take them away. For watching the melon fields at night, it was mainly to prevent wild boars, wild cats, and other animals from damaging the melon fields, so people built melon sheds on the melon fields. Since guarding the melons only required supervision when they were ripe, the structure of the melon sheds was much simpler than that of fishing huts. Generally, it was just a thatched shed with a bed inside. Some didn't even have a bed, just a few old straw mats on the ground. Compared with fishing huts, guarding melon sheds was much easier, so they were often guarded by some children.

孩子们看瓜地有不少趣事。他们常约上邻居家的娃娃们一起，唱唱歌，讲讲故事，有时与隔壁瓜铺的孩子聊天玩耍。玩累了口渴了，他们就摘上几个瓜解乏解渴。家长们总会让看瓜田的孩子带上一小包蒸熟的梅干菜，如果一旦发现吃瓜太多肚皮发胀时，就嚼上一些梅干菜，便可以起到消食的效果。据说这是绍兴本地世代相传的一个偏方。

There were many interesting things when children watched the melon fields. They often invited their neighbors' children to sing songs, tell stories, and sometimes chatted and played with the children in the neighboring melon sheds. When they were tired or thirsty from playing, they picked a few melons to quench their thirst and refresh themselves. Parents always let the children who watched the melon fields bring a small bag of steamed pickled vegetables. If they ate too many melons and felt bloated, they can chew some pickled vegetables to help digestion. It is said that, that is a folk remedy passed down from generation to generation in Shaoxing.

长衫和短衣
Long Gown and Short Jacket

　　长衫和短衣都是旧时绍兴男子的传统服饰。在绍兴，长衫历来被认为是一种高贵身份的象征，穿着长衫的人都是有一定社会地位的豪门大户或书香世家的成员。短衫则是劳动者身份的象征，因为劳苦百姓穿的都是粗布短衫。

Both the long gown and short jacket are traditional clothing for men in old Shaoxing. In the past, the long gown was always considered a symbol of high status. People who wore long gowns were members of wealthy households or literati families with certain social status. The short jacket, on the other hand, was a symbol of working-class identity, as ordinary people who worked hard usually wore rough cloth short jackets.

　　长衫，又称大衫，是一种离地略高于脚背的大襟长衣，有领，在右开襟，从领口起，自右而下，缝有一排纽扣。长衫的面料，随季节而不同。夏季多是用布或绸做的单衫。但绸长衫一般只有大户人家才穿。春秋两季，人们改穿夹衫，又称夹袍。到了冬天，则穿棉袍。有钱的大户人家以羊皮或牛皮，制成皮袄穿着。由于棉袍不耐脏，也不方便清洗，所以人们常在外面套一件罩衫。这种罩衫常用一种经过上浆、砑光的平面棉布制作，这种布料，绍兴人称为

"竹布"，因此用它来缝制的长衫也就叫作"竹布长衫"。

The long gown, also known as the big gown, is a long coat with a high hem that slightly exceeds the ankle. It has a collar and opens to the right, with a row of buttons from the collar down to the right. The fabric of the long gown varies with the season. In summer, it is usually made of cloth or silk as a single layer. However, silk long gowns were usually worn only by wealthy families in the past. In spring and autumn, people wore padded jackets, also known as padded robes. In winter, they wore cotton-padded gowns. Wealthy families wore fur coats made of sheepskin or cowhide. Since cotton-padded gowns were not resistant to dirt and were not easy to clean, people often wore a covering coat outside. This type of covering coat was usually made of a flat cotton fabric that was starched and polished. Shaoxing people call this fabric "bamboo cloth", so the long gown made of it is also called "bamboo cloth long gown".

图19 长衫样衣 郑红莲摄
Long gown sample clothing
PHOTO: Z.H.L.

在鲁迅的众多照片中，他几乎全部都是穿着长衫。即便他从日本留学回国，在绍兴府中学堂任教，以及后来去北京、上海等地工作生活，也都身穿长衫。有些读书人，即便家境贫寒，出门也非要穿长衫不可。所以在绍兴，常出现父子俩或兄弟俩共穿一件长衫。又如鲁迅笔下的孔乙己，虽然穷苦潦倒，身上的长衫已经又脏又破，也还是要穿在身上，不肯脱下来。

In almost all of Lu Xun's photos, he was wearing a long gown. Even when he returned to China after studying in Japan and taught at the Shaoxing Prefectural School, and later worked and lived in Beijing, Shanghai, and other places, he still wore a long gown. Some scholars, even if they were poor, had to wear long gowns when they went out. Therefore, it was common in Shaoxing for fathers and sons or brothers to share a long gown. For example, although Kong Yiji was poor and his old long gown was dirty and torn, he still wore it and refused to take it off.

在绍兴，凡是祭祀、结婚等重大场合，穿长衫的男子们还必须在外面再套一件马褂。绍兴谚语"大衫马褂子"就是指这个。马褂原是清代满族男子的一种上衣，长不过腰，士庶都可穿。后来，马褂更逐渐演变为一种礼仪性的服装，不论身份，都以马褂套在长袍之外，显得文雅大方。民间马褂的颜色多为深色，有黑色、深褐、藏青等色，绍兴人习惯把黑色称为玄色，所以当地人所穿的马褂以玄色居多。

In Shaoxing, on important occasions such as sacrificial ceremonies and weddings, men wearing long gowns must also wear a jacket outside, which is called "Dashan Majia" in the local proverb. The jacket was originally a type of upper garment worn by Manchu men during the Qing Dynasty, which was no longer than the waist and could be worn by both officials and commoners. Later, the jacket gradually evolved into a ceremonial dress, and regardless of their status, people wore the jacket outside the long gown to appear elegant and graceful. The color of the folk jacket is mostly dark, such as black, dark brown, and dark blue. Shaoxing people are accustomed to calling black Chih-Hei color, so the jackets worn locally are mostly Chih-Hei color.

短衣，也叫短衫，旧时有大襟和对襟两种。大襟为右边开襟，而对襟则把襟开于中间。大襟短衫在民国期间除一些年长男子还会穿之外，已经非常少见了。但对襟短衫至今还有人穿。短衫因季节不同样式也不同，夏天穿单衫，春秋穿夹衫，冬天穿棉袄。短衣的面料也有布有绸两种，有钱人家一般在家中穿着绸衫，而普通百姓只能穿得起布衫。有时一些农民、工匠会在腰间扎上一根腰带，既方便劳动，在冬天也有御寒保暖的作用。

The short jacket, also known as the short shirt, had two styles in the old days: a large lapel and a straight lapel. The large lapel has a right-opening, while the straight lapel splits the front in the middle. Large lapel short jackets are now very rare, except for some elderly men who still wear them during the Republic of China period. However, straight lapel short jackets are still worn by people today. The style of short jackets varies with the season. In summer, people wear single-layered shirts, while in spring and autumn, they wear padded jackets, and in winter, they wear cotton-padded jackets. The fabric of short jackets also varies, with both cloth and silk options. Wealthy families usually wore silk shirts at home, while ordinary people can only afford cloth shirts. Sometimes, some farmers and craftsmen tied a belt around their waist, which was not only convenient for work but also kept them warm in winter.

旧社会，在绍兴穿长衫和穿短衣，实际上反映了两种不同的阶层和社会地位。所以出门办事，出门购物，着衫不同会受到截然迥异的接待方式。

In the old society, wearing long gowns and wearing short jackets in Shaoxing actually reflected two different classes and social statuses. Therefore, when going out for errands or shopping, people would receive completely different reception depending on their clothing.

饮茶
Tea Drinking

　　绍兴人不仅喜欢喝酒，也喜欢饮茶。以茶待客、以茶会友，是绍兴的传统习俗。关于茶的专著，唐代陆羽的《茶经》是世界上第一部关于茶的著作。唐宋时期，绍兴已形成饮茶的习惯，当时越州日铸茶在江南小有名气。陆羽在《茶经》中品尝浙东各种茶叶时，给出"越州上，明州、婺州次，台州下"的评价。

　　Shaoxing people not only like to drink alcohol but also enjoy drinking tea. Serving tea to guests and meeting friends over tea is a traditional custom in Shaoxing. The first book in the world about tea was *The Classic of Tea* by Lu Yu, a Tang Dynasty author. During the Tang and Song dynasties, the habit of drinking tea had already formed in Shaoxing, and at that time, Yuezhou's daily-cast tea was somewhat famous in the south of the Yangtze River. When Lu Yu tasted various teas from eastern Zhejiang Province in *The Classic of Tea*, he gave the evaluation that "tea in Yue State is the best, tea in Ming and Wu States ranks the second, and tea in Tai State is the worst".

　　著名诗人欧阳修在《归田录》里写道："草茶盛于两浙，两浙之品，日注第一。"日注即日铸，是指绍兴县平水王化、宋家店一带山谷间所产的茶叶，宋代的吴处厚在《青箱记》中也说："越州日铸茶，为江南第一。"到明清时期，饮茶成为绍兴人日常生活中不可缺少的习俗。

The famous poet Ouyang Xiu wrote in his book *Gui Tian Lu*, "The herb tea flourishes in Zhejiang. Among the products, Rizhu tea ranks first". Rizhu tea refers to the tea produced in the valleys between Pingshui Wanghua and Songjiadian in Shaoxing County. Wu Chuhou of the Song Dynasty also mentioned in his book *Qingxiang Ji* that, "Yuezhou's daily-cast tea is the best in the south of the Yangtze River". By the Ming and Qing dynasties, drinking tea had become an indispensable custom in the daily life of Shaoxing people.

图20　日铸茶叶 郑红莲摄 Rizhu tea leaves PHOTO: Z.H.L.

因此，绍兴人家几乎家家户户都备有一个茶桶，桶内用棉絮焐一把瓷茶壶或锡茶壶，壶里是每天一大早泡好的茶水，以方便随时饮用。但这种茶一般不用来招待客人，当有客人来家，特别是远道而来、或者平时不常来的客人，必须是现烧现泡。有的还会在绿茶中加入白糖，以表示尊重。按照绍兴风俗，"茶洒八分，酒斟十分"，倒茶时不能倒满杯子。如果客人着急离开，没有时间留下来喝茶，主人一定要心怀歉意地说一声："茶水不荐"，作为待客不周的自责。

Therefore, almost every household in Shaoxing had a tea bucket, in which a porcelain or tin teapot was kept warm with cotton, and filled with tea brewed early in the morning for easy drinking at any time. However, this kind of tea was generally not served to guests. When guests came to the house, especially those who came from afar or do not usually visit, tea

图21 茶水和茶点 郑红莲摄 Tea and refreshments PHOTO: Z.H.L.

must be freshly brewed. Some people even added white sugar to green tea as a sign of respect. According to Shaoxing customs, tea should be poured to fill 80% of the cup, while wine should be poured to fill 100%. When pouring tea, the cup should not be filled to the brim. If a guest was in a hurry and did not have time to drink tea, the host must say apologetically, "I regret that I cannot offer you tea", as a self-reproach for not being a good host.

农历正月期间有客人到访，通常会在茶水里面加一颗橄榄或者金橘，民间称为"元宝茶"，认为喝完后可以保佑一年都吉祥如意。在夏天，因为天气炎热，人们常常会在茶叶中加入金银花或白菊花一起泡，达到祛暑解热的功效。

During the first lunar month, when guests came to visit, it was customary to add an olive or kumquat to the tea, which was called Yuanbao Tea in folk culture. It was believed that drinking this tea would bring good luck and fortune throughout the year. In summer, because of the hot weather, people often added honeysuckle or white chrysanthemum to the tea leaves for a cooling effect.

早时没有自来水，绍兴人通常取河水烧水泡茶。后来，有些河水被污染，于是人们在家中天井处放置水缸用来收集雨水，俗称"天落水"。有些商贩，机灵得很，他们用大船从农村的江河中运水到城里来卖，人们买来后再放在水缸里沉淀，称作"澄过水"。普通人家以"天落水"或"澄过水"烧水饮茶，而有钱人家就讲究多了，有的专门在冬天储存雪水，还有的专门到山里面去取山泉水。他们不光讲究水质，对烧水的燃料和泡茶的水温也非常讲究。

例如，烧水的柴火中，认为用青炭最好，松子次之，杂柴最次。

In the past, there was no tap water, so people in Shaoxing usually boiled river water to make tea. Later, some rivers became polluted, so people placed water tanks in their courtyards to collect rainwater, which was called "Tian Luo Shui" in Chinese. Some clever vendors transported water by boat from rural rivers to sell in the city. People would buy it and let it settle in their water tanks, which was called "Cheng Guo Shui". Ordinary households used "Tian Luo Shui" or "Cheng Guo Shui" to boil water for tea, while wealthy families paid more attention to water quality. Some stored snow water in winter, while others went to the mountains to fetch spring water. They not only cared about water quality but also the fuel used for boiling water and the temperature of the water for brewing tea. For example, when using firewood to boil water, green charcoal was considered the best, pine nuts were second, and miscellaneous firewood was the worst.

饮茶的习俗，至今在绍兴仍广为流行。近年来，在绍兴城里还开了不少茶馆，饮茶不仅是人们提神解渴的享受，也成为人们谈论生意、沟通感情的一种方式。

The custom of drinking tea is still popular in Shaoxing today. In recent years, many tea houses have opened in the city, and drinking tea has become not only a way to refresh oneself but also a way for people to discuss business and communicate their feelings.

水泡饭
Water-Soaked Rice

水泡饭是大多数绍兴人习以为常的早餐类型。绍兴是有名的鱼米之乡，人们以米饭为主食。虽然绍兴本地没有闹过饥荒，但当地人一日三餐，常常提醒自己"有时要作无时想，丰年还须防饥年"。所以为节省粮食，绍兴人喜欢用蔬菜煮饭吃。谚语"一年烂饭买条牛，三年烂饭起高楼"，反映了绍兴人在日常生活中崇尚节俭、珍惜粮食的美德。

Water-soaked rice is a common type of breakfast for most people in Shaoxing. Shaoxing is known as the land of fish and rice, and people mainly eat rice as their staple food. Although Shaoxing has never experienced famine, locals remind themselves to prepare for hard times during good times with their three meals a day. To save food, Shaoxing people like to cook rice with vegetables. The proverb "Buy a cow with bad rice for one year, build a tall building with bad rice for three years", reflects the virtue of frugality and cherishing food in the daily life of Shaoxing people.

水泡饭的做法很简单，就用头一天的剩饭放入锅中，加入水煮一会儿就好了。许多绍兴人即便去了外地学习、工作或生活，都还保持着吃水泡饭的习惯。另外，早上吃水泡饭，可以把剩饭吃完，

图22 水泡饭
郑红莲摄 Water-soaked rice PHOTO: Z.H.L.

不至于坏掉而浪费。

The method of making water-soaked rice is very simple. Leftover rice from the previous day is put into a pot with water and boiled for a while. Many people from Shaoxing still maintain the habit of eating water-soaked rice even when they study, work or live outside their hometown. In addition, eating water-soaked rice in the morning can help to finish off the leftover rice and prevent it from going bad and being wasted.

除了水泡饭，绍兴人还爱把南瓜、芋头、青菜、豆类、萝卜、番薯等和大米一起熬成粥。这种和蔬菜、杂粮煮成的粥，古时称为"焦粥"。南宋著名诗人陆游是绍兴本地人，他在《寺居睡觉》里写道："披衣起坐清羸甚，想像云堂焦粥香。"该诗句足以证明绍兴人爱吃菜粥的习俗在南宋时期就已经有了。把新摘的罗汉豆放在米里煮成饭，煮熟后加上一点盐，就叫作"豆饭"。豆饭味道鲜美，既耐饿又可以节省主粮。但吃的时候必须细嚼慢咽，谚语"螺蛳过豆饭，要紧逾须慢"说的就是这个意思，不然吃快了容易噎到，也不容易消化。

In addition to water-soaked rice, people in Shaoxing also like to cook pumpkin, taro, greens, beans, radishes, sweet potatoes, and other vegetables with rice to make porridge. This kind of porridge cooked with vegetables and grains was called "Fou Porridge" in ancient times. The famous poet of the Southern Song Dynasty, Lu You, was a native of Shaoxing. In his poem *Sleeping in the Temple*, wrote, "Sitting up in clothes, I smell the fragrant Fou Porridge in the cloud hall". This line is sufficient to prove that the custom of eating vegetable porridge in Shaoxing existed during the Southern Song Dynasty. Rice cooked with freshly picked broad beans and a little salt is called "Dou Rice". Dou Rice is delicious, filling, and can save on main grain consumption. However, when eating it, one must chew slowly and carefully. The proverb "When eating Dou Rice, it's important to chew slowly like a snail, otherwise it will be difficult to digest" means just that. Otherwise, eating too quickly may cause choking and indigestion.

秋末冬初的季节正是白菜快速生长的时间，打过霜的白菜也清甜可口，这个时候绍兴人喜欢做菜沃饭吃。把剩饭放入锅中加水煮，等到水沸时把切好的白菜放进去，煮片刻后放入少量油、盐、味精就可以出锅了。菜沃饭作为冬天的早餐，既味道可口，又能暖和身体，得到绍兴老老少少的喜爱。

Late autumn and early winter is the time when Chinese cabbage grows rapidly, and the cabbage that has been frosted is also sweet and delicious. At this time, people in Shaoxing like to make Cai Wo Rice to eat. Leftover rice is put into a pot with water and boiled. When the water boils, chopped Chinese cabbage is added and boiled for a while. Then, a small amount of oil, salt, and MSG is added before serving. Cai Wo Rice is a popular winter breakfast among people of all ages in Shaoxing as it is not only delicious but also warms the body.

断发文身
Hairdressing and Tattooing

农历谷雨，一年一度的公祭大禹陵典礼在绍兴大禹陵祭祀广场举行（大禹，上古传说时代的第三位帝王，划定九州）。在祭祀活动中，总能看到一群披发过肩，上身裸露，并在身上绘有各种图案的男子。他们的发式打扮，来源于古代越族先民的断发文身的习俗。

During the solar term of Grain Rain in the lunar calendar, the annual ceremony to worship Dayu, (the third of the three legendary emperors who created the Chinese state) takes place at the Dayu Mausoleum. During the ceremony, you can always see a group of men with long hair, bare upper bodies, and various patterns tattooed on their bodies. Their hairstyle and appearance come from the custom of hairdressing and tattooing of the ancient Yue tribe ancestors.

根据史料记载，断发文身的习俗最早出现在夏周。断发，就是将头发剪短，或披散于后，或略加绑束。文身，也称为文身或刺青，是用带有墨的针刺入皮肤底层而在皮肤上制造一些图案或文字出来。关于断发文身的起源，有多种说法，有婚姻说、避害说、华美说等不同的观点。是文化和信仰相结合的产物。婚姻说基于一个美丽的传说，据说古代有一块巨石，后变成兄妹俩，虽然两人相爱，但因兄妹同祖，不能结婚。后来经神仙指点，他俩用墨汁涂脸。兄妹俩再次相遇时，也互相不认识，于是结成夫妻。

According to historical records, the custom of hairdressing and tattooing first appeared during the Xia and Zhou dynasties. Hairdressing means cutting the hair short, or letting it hang loose, or tying it up slightly. Tattooing is also known as body art or body painting, which involves using a needle with ink to puncture the skin and create patterns or text on the skin. There are various opinions on the origin of the custom of hairdressing and tattooing, including marriage, avoiding harm, and beauty. It is a product that combines culture and belief. The marriage version is based on a beautiful legend. It is said that there was a huge rock in ancient times that turned into a brother and a sister. Although they loved each other, they couldn't get married because they had the same ancestor. Later, they were guided by immortals and used ink to paint their faces. When they met again, they didn't recognize each other, so they got married.

古籍大多持避害说。例如《汉书·地理志》写道：越"其君禹后，帝少康之庶子也，封于会稽，文身断发，以避蛟龙之害"。《礼记·王制》里也有相关记载，如"越俗断发文身，以避龙之害，故刻其肌，以丹青涅之"。因古代越族先民居地多处沼泽潮湿地带，他们常常在水中耕田劳作，为了躲避蛟龙等蛇虫的百毒入侵，所以断发文身，看来是比较合理的说法。

Most ancient books hold the viewpoint of avoiding harm. For example, *Geography in Han Shu* wrote, "The king of Yue, Yu Hou, who was a son of Emperor Shaokang, was enfeoffed in Kuaiji. He tattooed his body and shaved his head to avoid the harm of dragons." There are also relevant records in *The Book of Rites: The Regulations of the King*, such as "The Yue people cut their hair and tattoo their bodies to avoid the harm of dragons. Therefore, they carve their skin and color it with red ink". As the ancestors of the ancient Yue tribe lived in many swampy and humid areas, they often worked in water for farming. In order to avoid the invasion of poisonous snakes and insects, hairdressing and tattooing seem to be a reasonable explanation.

华美说则认为，断发文身可以保持青春美貌，因为文身后，刺青的部位基本不会长毛，也不会生皱纹。相传唐朝时期，文身非常流行，许多人崇尚文身之美。当时不但有专门的刺青师，在集市上还有刺青用的工具和文身图案销售。

The beauty theory believes that hairdressing and tattooing can maintain youth and beauty because the tattooed area is less likely to grow hair or wrinkles. Legend has it that during the Tang Dynasty, tattooing was very popular, and many people admired the beauty of tattoos. At that time, there were not only specialized tattoo artists, but also tools and tattoo patterns for sale in the markets.

海水桑田，历史上许多越族后裔逐步迁徙到台湾、云南、海南等一些百越地区。这些断发文身的习俗，继续在这些地方的少数民族中传承下来。例如台湾的少数民族普遍以文身为美；海南的黎族女性在婚姻的不同阶段都要在身体的不同部位进行文身；云南的傣族则不论男女，在身上文上花草、鸟兽、虫蛇、星辰等图案。有些傣族女性甚至还保留着古代越族妇女"磨齿"的习俗。而在吴越地区，新中国成立前，文身被一些封建帮会利用，演变成某些帮会的标志。解放后，断发文身的习俗在绍兴已经荡然无存。

Due to the changes in land and sea, many descendants of the Yue tribe gradually migrated to other Baiyue areas such as Taiwan, Yunnan, and Hainan. The custom of hairdressing and tattooing has been passed down among ethnic minorities in these regions. For example, tattoos are common among ethnic minorities in Taiwan, and Li women in Hainan have tattoos on different parts of their bodies at different stages of marriage. The Dai people in Yun nan, regardless of gender, tattoo flowers, birds, animals, insects, stars, and other patterns on their bodies. Some Dai women even retain the ancient Yue women's custom of tooth grinding. In the Wu and Yue regions, before the founding of the People's Republic of China, some feudal gangs used tattoos as their symbols. After liberation, the custom of hairdressing and tattooing disappeared in Shaoxing.

霉干菜、霉苋菜梗和其他
Molded Dried Vegetables, Molded Amaranth Stems and Others

民以食为天。在饮食习惯上，绍兴人一直以来保持自己独有的口味爱好和烹饪方法。由于当地崇尚节俭，人们喜欢把食物存储起来慢慢食用，如春天晒笋干、干菜，冬天腌白菜。农历新年前，杀猪肉除了留小部分现吃，大多数都是用盐腌起来。打捞起来的鲜鱼和家里养肥的家禽，基本上都是晒成鱼干、酱鸡、酱鸭，留到过春节或来年再吃。另外，由于绍兴梅雨季节较长，阴雨连绵、高温湿热的天气比较多，食物容易自然发酵发霉，所以绍兴的霉制品也特别多。

Food is the paramount necessity of the people. In terms of dietary habits, Shaoxing people have always maintained their unique taste preferences and cooking methods. As local people value thrift, they like to store food for later consumption, such as drying bamboo shoots and vegetables in spring, and pickling cabbage in winter. Before the lunar New Year, after slaughtering pigs, most of the meat is salted for preservation except for a small portion that is consumed fresh. Freshly caught fish and fattened poultry raised at home are usually dried into sauce fish, sauce chicken, and sauce duck, and saved for the coming

Spring Festival or next year. Additionally, due to the long rainy season in Shaoxing, with many days of continuous rain and high temperature and humidity, food is prone to natural fermentation and mold growth. Therefore, there are many molded food products in Shaoxing.

霉干菜，以春菜腌制晒干做成的绍兴特色菜，在绍兴一年四季的菜肴里都可以见到它。一般的做法是，把霉干菜放在碗底，上面铺上一层五花肉或金华火腿，再放上几片鲜笋，洒上几滴绍兴黄酒，上锅蒸熟。摆上桌来，夹上一筷子，肉的香味、笋的爽口和霉干菜的咸香如同魔法一样把味蕾激活，能让你一顿吃上三碗米饭。霉干菜在夏天最常见的做法是做成干菜汤，据说有消食解暑的功效。所以夏天丝瓜干菜汤、卜子干菜汤都是绍兴人餐桌的常客。另外，还有干菜包子、干菜烧饼、干菜蒸豆腐、干菜烧鱼等等，都鲜美可口。

Molded dried vegetables, made from pickled and dried spring vegetables, is a specialty dish in Shaoxing cuisine that can be found throughout the year. The general method of preparation is to place the molded dried vegetables at the bottom of a bowl, cover them with a layer of fatty pork or Jinhua ham, add a few slices of fresh bamboo shoots, sprinkle with a few drops of Shaoxing local wine, and steam until cooked. When served, the aroma of the meat, the crispness of the bamboo shoots, and the salty fragrance of the molded dried vegetables activate the taste buds like magic, making you able to eat three bowls of rice in one meal. In summer, the most common way of preparing molded dried vegetables is to make them into dried vegetable soup, which is said to have the effect of aiding digestion and relieving heat. Therefore, in summer, dried vegetable soup with silk gourd and dried vegetable soup with burdock are regulars on the tables of Shaoxing people. In addition, there are also steamed buns with molded dried vegetables, baked cakes with molded dried vegetables, steamed tofu with molded dried vegetables, and baked fish with molded dried vegetables, all of which are delicious.

图23 绍兴霉干菜
郑红莲摄 Shaoxing molded dried vegetables PHOTO: Z.H.L.

霉苋菜梗是最典型的绍兴霉制菜。霉制菜一般用蔬菜或豆制品为原料，经过浸泡或蒸煮，冷却后装入容器密封，等它自然发酵而成。常见的有霉苋菜梗、霉菜头、霉毛豆、霉千张、霉面筋、霉笋等。因为霉苋菜梗的保存时间比较长，菜梗吃完还可以用它的卤汁继续浸泡其他菜，所以绍兴人特别喜欢吃霉苋菜梗。

Molded amaranth stems are the most typical Shaoxing molded vegetable. Molded vegetables are generally made from vegetables or soy products, soaked or steamed, cooled, and then sealed in a container to ferment naturally. Common molded vegetables include molded amaranth stems, molded cabbage, molded edamame, molded tofu skin, molded gluten, molded bamboo shoots, etc. Because molded amaranth stems have a relatively long shelf life, the brine can also be used to soak other vegetables after the stems have been eaten, so Shaoxing people especially like to eat molded amaranth stems.

图24 绍兴霉苋菜梗
郑红莲摄 Shaoxing molded amaranth stems PHOTO: Z.H.L.

每到秋末冬初的时候，白菜大量供应上市，绍兴每家每户就开始腌制腌菜。将买来的白菜在太阳下暴晒几天，直到叶子变黄，再将它们整齐地堆在一边，等到外面的菜叶开始发黄，就可以下缸了。下缸前先把腌菜缸洗干净晾干，再把白菜的根部一颗一颗地切掉，然后一层白菜一层盐放入缸中。由男子用力踩实，当踩到有些菜汁出来时，再继续放一层白菜一层盐，再继续踩实。过上一周左右，还要再踩一遍，然后压上几块平整的大石头，使腌菜少与空气接触，这样即便时间长了，也不容易变质。腌上一个月左右，脆嫩爽口的腌菜就做好了。

Every late autumn and early winter, when there is a large supply of Chinese cabbages on the market, every household in Shaoxing starts to pickle vegetables. The bought Chinese cabbages are sun-dried for a few days, then neatly stacked to one side until the outer leaves begin to turn yellow, indicating that it is ready to be put into the pickling jar. Before putting the cabbages into the jar, the pickling jar is washed and dried, and the root of each cabbage is cut off one by one. Then, a layer of cabbages and a layer of salt are alternated to fill the jar. A man would then use force to press down on the cabbages until some juice comes out. Another layer of cabbages and salt are added, and the process is repeated. After about a week, the cabbages are pressed again, then a few flat stones are placed on top to reduce the contact with air, which helps prevent spoilage even if it is stored for a long time. After being pickled for about a month, the crispy and tender pickled vegetables are ready to eat.

与别处喜欢煎炒的烹饪方式不同，绍兴人特别喜欢蒸、焐的方法。最简单的蒸菜方法就是煮饭的时候把菜碗放在饭架上，等到饭煮好了，菜也熟了。这种烹饪方式，省时省力省柴火，一举多得。对于长时间才能蒸熟的菜，采取隔水蒸煮的方法，也叫清蒸。焐就更简单，把菜直接放在米上面煮熟，绍兴俗称饭焐，有饭焐南瓜、饭焐萝卜、饭焐茭白及饭焐猪肉，等等。

Unlike other regions' preference for frying and stir-frying, Shaoxing people particularly like steaming and simmering. The simplest way to steam vegetables is to place the vegetable bowl on top of the rice cooker while cooking rice, so that the vegetables can be cooked when the rice is ready. This cooking method saves time, effort, and firewood, killing two birds with one stone. For dishes that take a long time to steam, the water steaming method is used, also known as clear steaming. Simmering is even simpler—just put the vegetables directly on top of the rice to cook. Shaoxing locals call it rice simmering, and popular dishes include rice-simmered pumpkin, rice-simmered radish, rice-simmered water bamboo, and rice-simmered pork, among others.

图25　霉苋菜梗
蒸豆腐　郑红莲摄
Steamed molded
amaranth stems and
Tofu PHOTO: Z.H.L.

埠船和航船
Dock Boats and Navigation Ships

绍兴是有名的水乡和船乡，被称为"东方威尼斯"。旧时绍兴出行的主要交通工具就是船只。短途乘坐埠船，长途乘坐航船，是绍兴的传统交通习俗。

Shaoxing is a famous water town and boat town, known as the Venice of the East. In the past, the main means of transportation in Shaoxing was boats. Short trips were taken on dock boats, and long-distance trips were taken on navigation ships, which are traditional transportation customs in Shaoxing.

绍兴埠船以其优良的造船工艺和独特的造型，成为中国南方内河航运的代表之一。绍兴埠船的船底和侧壁采用垫板结构，船体中部宽大、两头尖细，船体底部呈弧线形，可以让船在水中流线型更加优美。船只的尾部还装有突出的竿头，可以配合橹桨使用，让船在水中更加平稳。绍兴埠船的船长有12—20米之间，被称为"十三簇车，十七步船"。

With its excellent shipbuilding craftsmanship and unique design, Shaoxing dock boat has become one of the representatives of inland water transportation in southern China. The hull and side walls of a dock boat are constructed with cushion plates, the middle of the hull is wide while both ends are pointed, and the bottom of the hull is curved, which makes the boat streamlined in the water more beautiful. The stern of the boat is also equipped with protruding poles, which can be used with oars to make the boat more stable in the water. The length of a dock boat is between 12—20 meters and is known as "a thirteen-cart and seventeen-step boat".

绍兴埠船具备一定的运载能力，可以载人载货，常用于大肚茶叶、花果木材、绸缎等货物的运输。同时，由于其造型优美，绍兴埠船也经常作为旅游观光船使用，在绍兴市的运河、小东海等水域中载客观光，成为绍兴的一道美丽风景线。

Shaoxing dock boat has a certain carrying capacity and can be used for both passenger and cargo transportation. It is commonly used for transporting large-bellied tea, flowers and fruits, wood, silk, and other goods. Additionally, due to its beautiful design, a dock boat is also frequently used as a tourist sightseeing boat. It carries passengers for sightseeing in many canals, small eastern sea, and other water areas, becoming a beautiful scenery line of Shaoxing.

绍兴航船是中国历史上最古老的商船之一，也是绍兴民俗文化的重要组成部分。相比较而言，航船的空间要大，航线也比埠船更远。它的特点是船头高翘、船尾细长，可在浅水或弱流区域顺利行驶。

Shaoxing navigation ship is one of the oldest merchant ships in Chinese history and an important part of Shaoxing's folk culture. Compared to dock boats, navigation ships have more space and are able to travel longer distances. Its characteristic features include a high and raised bow and a slender stern, which allows it to smoothly navigate in shallow water or weak current areas.

绍兴航船的相关故事丰富多彩，其中最著名的是《红楼梦》中的"航船洞"一章。该章描述了宝钗、黛玉等人乘坐绍兴航船游览西湖，欣赏美景，品尝绍兴黄酒，并在航船上吟诗作画，享受美好时光。这一段描写也成为了中国文化的经典之一。

The stories related to Shaoxing navigation ship are rich and colorful, among which the most famous one is the chapter Navigation Ship Cave in the novel *Dream of the Red Chamber*. This chapter describes several young people, like Baoyu, Daiyu and others, taking a Shaoxing navigation ship to tour West Lake, appreciating the beautiful scenery, tasting Shaoxing yellow wine, writing poems and painting pictures on the ship, and enjoying a wonderful time. This description has also become one of the classics of Chinese culture.

另外绍兴航船还曾经在中国抗日战争中发挥过重要作用。因为绍兴航船可以在江河的浅滩和曲流中穿行，军队和抗日组织利用这一特点，将军火和物资运往前线，支援中国军队的抗战。现在，绍兴航船已成为绍兴市的旅游特色之一，每年吸引大量游客前来体验。

In addition, Shaoxing navigation ship played an important role in the War of Resistance Against Japanese Aggression. Because navigation ships could navigate through shallow rapids and winding rivers, the military and anti-Japanese organizations utilized that feature to transport weapons and materials to the front lines, supporting the Chinese army's resistance against Japan. Nowadays, Shaoxing navigation ship has become one of the tourism highlights of Shaoxing city, attracting a large number of tourists to experience it every year.

Chapter 3 第三章

人生礼仪篇

Etiquette Norms

称谓
Appellations

　　绍兴是一个历史文化名城，素闻其礼仪之风，其中的称谓礼仪也是绍兴地方特色文化之一。称谓，即称呼，是人们交往中极其重要的组成部分，适当的称谓往往能够反映出个人的礼貌、尊重和社交能力。称谓礼仪指的是在交际往来中使用的一套礼节性称谓，对于守礼、尊重等方面，起到一种规范的作用。绍兴人非常注重家庭和亲情，所以在称呼亲戚时都相对细致和严谨，每一种亲戚之间的称呼都有各自的习惯和规范，这也反映了绍兴人注重尊老爱幼和家庭和睦的传统价值观念。

　　Shaoxing is a historic and cultural city well-known for its etiquette culture, including the etiquette of addressing people, which is one of the distinctive local cultural features of Shaoxing. Addressing people, or appellations, are an extremely important part of interpersonal communication. Appropriate appellations can often reflect an individual's politeness, respect, and social skills. The etiquette of addressing people refers to a set of ceremonial appellations used in social interaction, which plays a normative role in maintaining politeness and respect. Shaoxing people attach great importance to family and kinship, so when addressing relatives, they are relatively meticulous and rigorous. Each type of relative has its own habits and norms for addressing, reflecting Shaoxing people's traditional values of respecting the elderly, loving the young, and promoting family harmony.

在绍兴，家庭成员之间的称呼分为父系和母系两个方面。在父系方面，曾祖父和曾祖母称呼为太爷爷和太奶奶，祖父和祖母称呼为爷爷和奶奶。祖父的兄弟按照年龄大小依次称为大爷爷、二爷爷或小爷爷，祖父的姐妹也依次称大姑婆、二姑婆、小姑婆，而姑婆的丈夫称为姑丈。过去，父亲和母亲通常称呼为爹爹和姆嬷，而如今的称呼则改为普通话中的爸爸和妈妈。父亲的哥哥依次称大伯伯、二伯伯，而父亲的弟弟则称为叔叔。

In Shaoxing, the appellations between family members are divided into two aspects: patrilineal and matrilineal. In the patrilineal aspect, great-grandfather and great-grandmother are called Tai Yeye and Tai Nainai, respectively, while grandfather and grandmother are called Yeye and Nainai. Grandfather's brothers are called Da Yeye (the eldest), Er Yeye (the second eldest) or Xiao Yeye (the youngest) in order of age, while his sisters are called Da Gupo, Er Gupo or Xiao Gupo in the same order. The husband of a Gupo is called Guzhang. In the past, father and mother were usually called Baba and Muma, but nowadays they are commonly referred to as Baba and Mama in Mandarin. Father's elder brother is called Da Bobo, Er Bobo, while his younger brother is called Uncle.

夫妻之间习惯性地称呼对方为老公和老婆，而妻子对丈夫的父母则称呼为公公和婆婆。公婆对于儿子的妻子则称呼为媳妇或媳妇大娘，有些地方也会简称为大娘。弟弟和妹妹通常会称兄长为哥哥。对于叔伯的孩子，一般称呼为堂兄弟或堂姐妹。父亲的姐妹可以称呼为姑母或依次称大姑母、二姑母、小姑母，而姑母的丈夫称作姑爹。弟妹对兄长的妻子则称呼为嫂嫂，而对于姐姐的丈夫则称呼为姐夫。妻子对丈夫的哥哥通常称作阿伯，对于丈夫的弟弟则称作阿叔，而对于丈夫的姐妹，则可以称呼为姑娘或小姑。

Husbands and wives habitually call each other Lao Gong (husband) and Lao Po (wife), while wives call their husbands' parents Gong'gong (paternal grandfather) and Popo (paternal grandmother). Parents-in-law call their son's wife Xifu or Xifu Da'niang and sometimes abbreviated as Da'niang. Younger brothers and sisters usually call their elder brother Gege (elder brother). The children of uncles and aunts are generally called Tang Xiong'di (male cousins) or Tang Jie'mei (female cousins). Father's sisters can be called Gu'mu, or in the order of age, Da Gu'mu, Er Gu'mu, Xiao Gu'mu, while the husband of the Gu'mu is called Gu'die. Younger siblings call their elder brother's wife Sao'sao (sister-in-law), while they call their elder sister's husband Jie'fu (brother-in-law). Wives usually call their husband's elder brother A'bo and younger brother A'shu, while they can call their husband's sisters Gu'niang (elder sister) or Xiao Gu (younger sister).

在母系方面，母亲的父母称作外公和外婆，曾祖父母则称作外太公和外太婆。母亲的兄弟被称为舅舅，按照年龄大小依次可以称呼为大舅舅、二舅舅或小舅舅，舅舅的妻子则被称为妗姆。舅舅对于姐妹的子女称为外甥或外甥囡。母亲的姐妹则被称为阿姨，而依次可以称为大阿姨、二阿姨或小阿姨。妻子的父母被称为丈人或丈人阿伯，妻子的兄弟则被称为阿舅或舅佬，而他们的妻子则被称为舅嫂。妻子的姐妹可以称呼为姨妈或小姨。舅舅和阿姨的子女被称为表兄弟或表姐妹。对于儿子的妻子的父母或女儿的丈夫的父母，则被称为亲家公和亲家姆。兄弟之间的妻子相互称为叔伯姆，而姐妹之间的丈夫则被称为连襟。

In the matrilineal aspect, mother's parents are called Wai'gong (maternal grandfather) and Wai'po (maternal grandmother), while great-grandparents are called Wai Tai'gong and Wai Tai'po. Mother's brothers are called Jiu'jiu (uncle), and in the order of age, can be called Da Jiu'jiu, Er Jiu'jiu, or Xiao Jiu'jiu. The wife of an uncle is called Jin'mu (aunt). Uncles call their sister's children Wai'sheng or Wai'sheng Nan (nephew). Mother's sisters are called A'yi (aunt) and in the order of age, can be called Da A'yi, Er A'yi, or Xiao A'yi. Wife's parents are called Zhang'ren or Zhang'ren A'bo (father-in-law), while her brothers are called A'jiu or Jiu'lao (brother-in-law), and their wives are called Jiu'sao (sister-in-law). Wife's sisters can be called Yi'ma (aunt) or Xiao'yi (younger aunt). Children of uncles and aunts are called Biao Xiong'di (male cousins) or Biao Jie'mei (female cousins). The parents-in-law of a son's wife or daughter's husband are called Qin Jia'gong and Qin Jia'mu. The wives of brothers call each other Shu Bo'mu (sister-in-law), while the husbands of sisters are called Lian'jin (brother-in-law).

在民间，早期为了表示对他人亲属的尊敬，在称谓前面常常会加上"令"或"尊"字。例如对他人的父母，可以称令尊和令堂或令大人；对他人的兄弟姐妹则称令兄、令弟、令姐、令妹。对他人的妻子则称尊夫人，对他人的儿女称令郎、令媛。而对于自己的亲属，一般会在称谓前面加上"家"或"舍"字表示谦逊。例如对自己的父母，在他人面前常称家父、家母，对自己的兄姐则称家兄、家姐，对自己的弟妹则称舍弟、舍妹。也有的在他人面前把自己的妻子称为贱内，称自己的儿子为犬子，这种称呼方式现在已经不再被广泛使用。而在绍兴地区，这类传统称谓一直沿袭至今。

In folk culture, in order to show respect for other people's relatives, the words Ling or Zun are often added before the appellations. For example, for someone else's parents, they can be called Ling Zun, Ling Tang or Ling Da'ren. For someone else's siblings, they can be called Ling Xiong (elder brother), Ling Di (younger brother), Ling Jie (elder sister), or Ling Mei (younger sister). Someone else's wife can be called Zun Fu'ren (respectable madam), while their children can be called Ling Lang (son) or Ling Ai (daughter). However, when addressing one's own relatives, the words Jia or She are often added before the appellations to show humility. For example, one may call their own parents Jia Fu and Jia Mu (father and mother of the family) in front of others, call their own elder siblings Jia Xiong and Jia Jie (elder brother and sister of the family), and call their own younger siblings She Di and She Mei (younger brother and sister of the house). Some people used to refer to their own wife as Jian Nei (cheap inside) and their own son as Quan Zi (dog son) in front of others, but this kind of appellations are no longer widely used nowadays. However, in Shaoxing, these traditional appellations have been passed down to this day.

在社会称谓方面，绍兴人常用的有头脑、司务和先生。对一些短衫帮的手工业者，旧时多称呼为头脑或司务，如撑船的，称为船头脑，烧饭的，叫烧饭头脑。对一些木工、石工、抹灰工和锡箔工，则称木作司务、石作司务、泥水司务和锡箔司务。对于一些私塾、学校的老师以及从事账房、行郎、算命、道士、厨师等职业的，都称作先生以表示尊重。

In terms of social appellations, Shaoxing people often use the words Tou Nao, Si Wu, and Xian Sheng. For some craftsmen in the short shirt gang, they were often referred to as Tou Nao or Si Wu in the past. For example, boatmen were called Chuan Tou Nao, and cooks were called Shao Fan Tou Nao. For some carpenters, stonemasons, plasterers, and tin foil workers, they were called Mu Zuo Si Wu (woodwork foreman), Shi Zuo Si Wu (stonework foreman), Ni Shui Si Wu (plastering foreman), and Xi Bo Si Wu (tin foil foreman). For teachers in private and public schools, as well as those who worked in accounting, travel and trade, fortune telling, Taoism, cooking, and other professions, they were all called Xian Sheng to show respect.

总的来说，绍兴人在社交中非常注意礼仪和传统习俗，相对于其他地区，称谓礼仪相对严谨，非常注重称呼的准确性和得体性，这也是绍兴的旧文化遗产，是历史文化的一部分。

Overall, Shaoxing people pay great attention to etiquette and traditional customs in social interactions. Compared with other regions, their appellations and etiquette are relatively strict, and they attach great importance to the accuracy and appropriateness of appellations. This is also a part of Shaoxing's old cultural heritage and an integral part of its historical culture.

女儿酒
The Wine for Daughter's Wedding

绍兴女儿酒以其深厚的历史渊源和独特的文化内涵，在当地人中扮演了重要的角色，成为了一种地方传统文化的重要代表，也为中华民族的婚俗文化贡献了深厚的底蕴。在旧时绍兴，如果家里有女儿出生，便要开始酿制黄酒，也有人家为了方便省事，在当地酒坊定制两坛黄酒。等到女儿出嫁当天，把这两坛黄酒系上红绸，和众多的嫁妆一起送往男家。这种酒，称为女儿酒，是绍兴独有的婚俗文化。

Shaoxing Nu'er Wine plays an important role in the local people's lives due to its deep historical roots and unique cultural connotations. It has become an important representative of local traditional culture and has contributed to the cultural heritage of Chinese wedding customs. In old Shaoxing, when a family had a daughter, they would start brewing yellow wine, or ordered two barrels of yellow wine from local breweries for convenience. On the day of the daughter's wedding, these two barrels of yellow wine were tied with red silk and sent to the groom's family along with other dowries. This wine, called Nu'er Wine, is a unique wedding custom in Shaoxing.

图26 绍兴女儿红
郑红莲摄 Shaoxing
Nu'er Wine PHOTO:
Z.H.L.

　　关于女儿酒作为一种绍兴民俗的完整记载，出现在清代梁绍壬的《两般秋雨庵随笔》中，"浙江绍兴习俗，生女后即酿酒埋藏，待女出嫁时，取以宴客，名为女儿酒。"该文表明绍兴女儿酒在清代时期已经广为流行。与黄酒一样，女儿酒是用上等糯米、优质的酒曲和纯净清澈的鉴湖水酿制而成。酿好后，灌入定制的酒坛中，坛子口上面首先用开水煮过的荷叶包上，再盖上黄沙陶盖，最后用黄泥封住坛口，防止酒气溢出来。

The complete record of Nu'er Wine as a Shaoxing folk custom appeared in Liang Shaoren's essay during the Qing Dynasty, "The custom is to brew wine and bury it after the birth of a daughter in Shaoxing, Zhejiang. When the daughter gets married, it is taken out to entertain guests and is named Nu'er Wine." This indicates that Nu'er Wine was already popular in Shaoxing during the Qing Dynasty. Like yellow wine,

Nu'er Wine was made from high-quality glutinous rice, excellent yeast, and pure and clear Jianhu Lake water. After brewing, it was poured into customized wine jars. The jar mouth was wrapped with boiled lotus leaves, covered with yellow sand pottery lid, and finally sealed with yellow clay to prevent the aroma from escaping.

女儿酒的酒坛非常讲究。因为酒坛是女儿酒的重要组成部分，是为新娘献酒的容器，既寓意深刻，又具有实用价值，也是新人和新家庭的珍贵纪念物。在材质上，女儿酒的酒坛多采用紫砂陶器制成，这种陶器因为其本身良好的保温性质，能够很好地保持酒的温度和口感，使得酒更为美味。在外观上，女儿酒的酒坛通常是红色或者金色的，坛面上绘有龙凤吉祥、八仙过海、龙凤呈祥等图案。酒坛上还经常配有祝福的话语，例如"恭贺新婚，百年好合"，"阖家幸福，永结同心"等，祝福新人幸福和美满。这种酒坛，绍兴当地称作"花雕坛"。

The wine jar used for Nu'er Wine was highly valued. As an important component of Nu'er Wine, the wine jar was not only a container for offering wine to the bride, but also a valuable souvenir for the new couple and their family. In terms of materials, the wine jars were mostly made of red pottery. The good insulation properties of this type of pottery can maintain the temperature and taste of the wine, making it more tasteful. In terms of appearance, the jars were usually red or golden in color, with patterns such as dragons and phoenixes, eight immortals crossing the sea, and dragons and phoenixes presenting auspiciousness painted on the surface. The wine jars were also often accompanied by blessings, such as "Congratulations on your wedding, may you have a hundred years of happiness" and "May your family be happy and united forever", wishing the new couple happy and harmonious. Locally in Shaoxing, this type of wine jar was called Hua'diao Jar.

图27 绍兴花雕坛 郑红莲摄 Shaoxing Hua'diao Jar PHOTO: Z.H.L.

女儿酒的酒坛大小不一，分为50斤、80斤和100斤三种。婚嫁时至少需准备两坛，多的也有8坛以上的。但必须是双数，寓意成双入对、夫妻俩白头偕老之意。酒封好后，放于地窖中储藏，也有藏于夹墙之中。等到女儿出嫁时，取出来作为嫁妆陪嫁，宴请客人。经过十几年的储藏和自然蒸发，坛中的酒基本只剩一半，但打开后酒香扑鼻飘四方。抿一口，芳香醇厚、沁人心脾。

The size of the wine jar used for Nu'er Wine varies, and it is divided into three types: 25 kilos, 40 kilos, and 50 kilos. At least two jars were required for a wedding, and there were also more than eight jars for some families. However, it must be an even number, symbolizing the idea of being paired together and growing old together. After sealing the wine, it was stored in a cellar or hidden in a wall. When the daughter got married, the wine was taken out as part of her dowry and served to guests. After more than ten years of storage and natural evaporation, only half of the wine was left in the jar, but when opened, the aroma of the wine spread everywhere. With just a sip, the wine was fragrant, mellow, and refreshing.

如今，关于女儿酒的习俗在绍兴已经很少见到，但是女儿酒已成为一些酒厂的产品名称在传承沿用，女儿酒、花雕酒成为绍兴名酒。另外，随着陶艺技术的发展，花雕坛作为一种特有的黄酒容器，也成为人们喜爱收藏的雅致工艺品。

Nowadays, the tradition of preparing wine for daughter's wedding is rarely seen in Shaoxing. However, Nu'er Wine has become the product name of some wineries, and it is still inherited and used. Nu'er Wine and Hua Diao Wine have become famous wines in Shaoxing. In addition, with the development of ceramic technology, the jar of Hua Diao Wine as a unique yellow wine container has also become an elegant craft that people love to collect.

花轿与发轿
Bridal Sedan Chair

　　花轿，也叫喜轿，是绍兴地区旧时娶亲的必要运载工具。姑娘出嫁，都把坐花轿看作是一生的一件大事。按照绍兴习俗，寡妇再嫁或大户人家纳小妾都是不能坐花轿的。因此一般女子一生只有一次机会坐花轿，所以民间有歇后语"大姑娘坐花轿——头一回"。

　　A bridal sedan chair was a necessary means of transportation for the traditional wedding procession in Shaoxing area. For girls getting married, riding in a sedan chair was considered a major event in their lifetime. According to the Shaoxing customs, widows remarrying or women of wealthy families taking concubines were not allowed to ride in a sedan chair. Therefore, ordinary women only had one chance in their lifetime to ride in a flower sedan chair, hence the folk proverb "A big girl riding in a bridal sedan chair—the first time in her life".

　　以前，绍兴城里专门从事花轿出租的轿店很多。大一点的店里面，甚至有四五乘花轿供租用。在旧城大坊口就有一家轿店，老板姓车，排行第三，人们便称呼他花轿阿三。这家店生意特别好，许多办婚事的人得提前数月才订得上花轿。

　　In the past, there were many sedan chair shops specializing in renting bridal sedan chairs in Shaoxing City. In large shops, there were

图28 花轿 郑红莲摄
A bridal sedan chair
PHOTO: Z.H.L.

even four or five bridal sedan chairs available for rent. Once there was a sedan chair rental shop at the entrance of the old city, owned by a man whose surname was Che. Che was the third son in his family, hence people called him Bridal Sedan A'san. His shop had particularly good business, and many people who wanted to rent bridal sedan chairs for their weddings had to make reservations several months in advance.

按照习俗，取花轿的当天，要先进行搜轿，请来搜轿的必须是两位夫妻和睦、儿孙满堂的长者。他们一人手里拿着点燃的蜡烛，一人拿着一面镜子，在花轿内上上下下彻底照一遍，再用装满点着檀香的老式熨斗在花轿里熏烫一遍。据说，这样做可以驱散藏在花轿里的鬼怪，保证新娘的安全。

According to tradition, on the day the bridal sedan chair was taken, an "examining the sedan chair" ceremony must be performed first. Two elders who were a harmonious couple with many children and grandchildren were invited to perform this ceremony. One of them held a lit candle, while the other held a mirror, thoroughly shining it up and down inside the bridal sedan chair. Then they used an old-fashioned iron filled with lit sandalwood to fumigate the sedan chair. It was said that doing so can drive away any ghosts or monsters hiding inside the bridal sedan chair, ensuring the safety of the bride.

搜完轿后，就可以出发了。绍兴把花轿抬起出发，称为发轿。这时，鼓乐齐鸣、火铳轰响，新郎着婚礼服护送花轿到大门口，并向花轿作揖三下，俗称送轿。然后就是敲锣打鼓，抬着花轿去女方家接新娘。

After the "examining the sedan chair" ceremony, they can set off. In Shaoxing, when the bridal sedan chair was lifted and set off, it was called "sending off the sedan". At this time, drums and gongs sounded and firecrackers went off. The groom escorted the sedan chair to the front door in his wedding attire and bowed three times to the sedan chair, known as "sending off the sedan". Then, with the sound of gongs and drums, they carried the sedan chair to the bride's house to pick up the bride.

跟在花轿后面的迎亲队伍隆重热闹。有鸣铳的，有手捧迎新贴盒的，有拿着装满红烛提盒的，还有领着彩灯的。彩灯后面是松柏长青担，一头是两棵连根的小柏树和小松树，另一头是一个小木盘，装着五谷杂粮，五谷上有一个彩色的小泥人。寓意新婚夫妇早生贵子、白头偕老。再后面，是两名行郎提着的"厅炉"，有祝婚后生活红红火火的意思。后面还有一挑酒和一头羊，是送给女方家的礼品。最后跟着的是敲锣打鼓的婚庆乐队。

The wedding procession that followed the sedan chair was grand and lively. Some carried firing guns, some held the "welcoming the bride" box, some carried boxes filled with red candles, and others led colorful lanterns. Behind the lanterns was a pine and cypress evergreen carrying pole, with two small cypress and pine trees with roots still attached on one end and a small wooden plate on the other end, filled with grains and a small clay figure in various colors on top of the grains, symbolizing the couple's wish for early birth of a son and happy marriage. Following this are two attendants carrying the "hall stove", which signifies wishing the newlyweds a prosperous life together. There was also a cart carrying wine and a sheep, which were gifts for the bride's family. Finally, there was a wedding band playing gongs and drums at the end of the procession.

按照绍兴习俗，从男方家出发后，一路上花轿必须经过一些名字具有吉祥意义的桥来讨吉利，如大庆桥、五福桥、保佑桥、万安桥、福禄桥等。另外，不管女方家离男方家有多远，花轿中途都不能停下休息，花轿与花轿也不得在路上碰见。因为据说如果两花轿相遇，躲藏在人家花轿中的鬼怪说不定会跑进自家的花轿里来，这样发轿前的搜轿就没有用了。

According to Shaoxing customs, after leaving the groom's house, the bridal sedan chair must pass through some bridges with auspicious names to bring good luck, such as Daqing Bridge, Wufu Bridge, Baoyou

Bridge, Wan'an Bridge, and Fulu Bridge. In addition, no matter how far the bride's house was from the groom's house, the sedan chair cannot stop for rest along the way, and two sedan chairs cannot meet on the road. It is said that if two sedan chairs met, the ghosts and monsters hiding in one of them might run into the other one, rendering the examination of the sedan chair ceremony useless.

图29　绍兴万安桥 郑红莲摄 Shaoxing Wan' an Bridge PHOTO: Z.H.L.

现如今，迎亲用花轿的传统已经越来越少见，新式婚礼多使用轿车来接送新娘。不过，乘坐花轿的风俗在绍兴已然成为风景旅游区的一项人气项目。

Nowadays, the tradition of using bridal sedan chairs to fetch the bride is becoming less and less common, and modern weddings often use cars to transport the bride. However, riding in a bridal sedan chair has become a popular tourist attraction in Shaoxing's scenic areas.

拜堂
Worship at the Hall

　　拜堂作为传统中式婚礼中的一个重要环节，也称为拜天地，新人通过祭拜神明来祈求祝福，同时向双方父母和亲友表达感恩和敬意。在现代婚礼中，拜堂依然是重要的仪式之一，新人仍会向父母行三鞠躬的礼节，新人夫妻互相鞠躬表示敬意与尊重。

　　As an important part of traditional Chinese weddings, worship at the hall is also known as worshiping the heaven and earth. The bride and groom pray for blessings by worshiping the gods and goddesses, while expressing gratitude and respect to their parents and relatives. In modern weddings, worship at the hall is still an important ceremony, and the couple will bow three times to their parents to show respect and gratitude, and to each other as a display of respect and honor.

　　旧时绍兴在举行拜堂仪式前，男女双方还有很多繁琐的习俗，如安床、溻浴、开脸等，一项都不能马虎。安床是指男方根据算命先生选定的日子，在拜堂前，请两位长寿老太太在新房里铺新床。请来的长寿老太太必须是丈夫健在、儿女齐全、手法好的，以此讨个好彩头。为了避免空床，新郎要请一个未婚的小伙子一起睡新床。

Before the worship ceremony in old Shaoxing, there were many complicated customs that both the bride and groom had to follow, such as preparing the bridal bed, ritual bathing, and facial treatments, none of which could be taken lightly. Preparing the bridal bed refers to the groom selecting a day based on the fortune-teller's advice to have two elderly women lay a new bed in the new house before the worship ceremony. The elderly women must be healthy, have their husbands who are still alive, have all their children, and be skilled at laying the bed to ensure good luck. To avoid an empty bed, the groom would invite an unmarried young man to sleep in the new bed with him.

新婚前，新郎、新娘要在各自家中淴浴。淴浴时，在房间里放一个大木盆，盆上放一面筲箕，筲箕里盛着染红的鸭蛋和花生等果品，称作喜果。家人将热水从筲箕淋入木盆，新郎或新娘用木盆里的水擦洗身子，就叫淴浴。淴浴后，筲箕上的鸭蛋、花生等喜果装入盘中，新郎这边一般会把它们分送给亲朋好友，新娘一边的则很少分送。

Before the wedding, the groom and bride would take a ritual bath in their respective homes. During the bath, a large wooden tub would be placed in the room, with a sieve on top containing red-dyed duck eggs, peanuts, and other fruits, known as lucky fruits. Hot water would be poured into the wooden tub from the sieve, and the groom or bride would use the water to wash their body, which is called ritual bathing. After the bath, the lucky fruits on the sieve would be put into a plate. The groom's side would usually distribute them to their relatives and friends, while the bride's side would rarely do so.

此外，新郎还要剃头，新娘还要开脸。新郎剃头一般把剃头师傅请到家里，点上蜡烛，端上茶点，还要多给一些理发费用。所以，对剃头师傅来说，给新郎剃头是个美差。开脸，也叫绞脸，是指用两根红绿线在新娘脸上绞除汗毛。按照习俗，开过脸的女性就表示不是姑娘了。

In addition, the groom would need hairdressing and the bride would need facial depilator. The groom usually invited a barber to come to his home, lighted candles, served tea and pastries, and payed extra for the haircut. Therefore, giving a groom a haircut was a good job for a barber. Facial depilator, also known as wringing the face, referred to using two red and green threads to remove facial hair from the bride's face. According to tradition, women who had facial depilator were no longer considered maiden.

这些繁琐的礼俗完成之后，就是抬花轿接新娘行拜堂之礼。仪式设在大厅堂，墙壁上挂着福禄寿三星画像，旁边配上喜联。桌前摆放大烛台、花筒和香炉。四周挂满亲朋好友送的喜幛贺轴，幛轴上写有"天作之合""佳偶天成""白头偕老"等金字吉语，以表示对新婚夫妇的祝福。等到新娘出轿，大门口顿时响起震耳欲聋的爆竹声，喜气欢快的鼓乐声。这时司仪高声宣布"香烟缥缈，灯烛辉煌，新郎新娘，齐登华堂"，新郎、新娘就在伴郎和伴娘的陪伴下，缓缓走到喜堂中央。接着，在司仪的指令下，新郎、新娘先向外拜天地，再朝向内拜高堂，然后夫妻相对行交拜礼。

After completing the tedious customs, the next step was to carry the bridal sedan chair to welcome the bride to the hall of worship and perform the ceremony of paying respects to the ancestors. The ceremony was held in the main hall, where the walls were decorated with pictures of the three gods of fortune, prosperity, and longevity, accompanied by auspicious couplets. On the table, there were large candlesticks, vases of flowers, and incense burners. The surroundings were adorned with congratulatory scrolls and banners from relatives and friends, with golden words of good wishes such as "a match made in heaven", "perfect match", and "live together until old age" written on them to express their blessings to the newlyweds. When the bride stepped out of the sedan, firecrackers suddenly went off at the door, and the joyful sound of drums and music filled the air. At that point, the master of ceremonies loudly announced, "With the fragrance of incense and the brilliance of candles, the groom and bride ascend to the wedding hall together". The groom and bride then

图30　行交拜礼 郑红莲摄 The ceremony of bowing to each other PHOTO: Z.H.L.

slowly walked to the center of the wedding hall with the company of the best man and maid of honor. Following the instructions of the master of ceremonies, the groom and bride first bowed outward to the heavens and earth, then inward to the parents, and finally faced each other to perform the exchange of marriage vows.

交拜礼之后，一位被称为"寿翁"的长者手拿一根用红纸包着的甘蔗，俗称"福杖"，用它在新娘头上轻轻地敲五下，每打一下，长者就会念一句祝福的话。随后在司仪的主持下，新郎新娘各牵着红绸的一端，由新郎慢慢地把新娘牵入洞房，绍兴俗称"牵红"。

After the exchange of marriage vows, an elder known as Long-life held a sugarcane wrapped in red paper, commonly called Lucky Stick, and gently tapped the bride's head five times. With each tap, the elder recited a blessing. Following that, under the guidance of the master of ceremonies, the groom and bride each held one end of a red silk cloth and the groom slowly led the bride into the bridal chamber, a tradition known as "pulling the red in shaoxing".

"牵红"时，绍兴还有"传盅接袋"的风俗。具体是指在新郎牵着新娘走向新房的路上，人们用五个麻袋铺在地上，再用五只酒盅放在每个麻袋上，等到新郎新娘走过前面的麻袋和酒盅后，人们再把后面的麻袋和酒盅传接到前面，如此反复多次，直到新郎新娘进入洞房为止。因为"传盅接袋"和"传宗接代"谐音，所以绍兴人以此风俗祈愿新婚夫妻早生贵子。

During the "pulling the red" tradition, there is a custom in Shaoxing called passing down cups and sacks. Specifically, as the groom led the bride to the bridal chamber, people lay out five sacks on the ground and placed five wine cups on each sack. When the groom and bride walked over the sacks and cups, people passed them from behind to the front repeatedly until the couple entered the bridal chamber. This is done because in Chinese the homophonic sound of passing down cups and sacks is similar to passing on the family line. Therefore, people in Shaoxing hoped that this custom would bring blessings for the newlyweds to have children soon.

抢亲
Marriage by Capture

一直到清末民初，抢亲在绍兴城乡地区仍流传甚广。抢亲习俗，又叫抢婚，据《中国风俗词典》，起源于原始社会母系氏族向父系氏族过渡时期。当时，由于男性地位的上升，女性地位随着下降。在父系社会形成过程中，男性经常通过掠夺其他部落的女性或是将战争俘虏的女性作为妻子。渐渐地，这种抢亲习俗就流传下来了。

Until the late Qing Dynasty and early Republic of China, the custom of marriage by capture was still widespread in Shaoxing's urban and rural areas. This custom, also known as marriage by abduction, originated during the transitional period from matrilineal to patrilineal societies in primitive society, according to the *Dictionary of Chinese Customs*. At that time, due to the rise of male status, female status declined. During the formation of patrilineal societies, men often took women from other tribes by force or took women who were captured in war as wives. Gradually, this custom of marriage by capture was passed down.

绍兴抢亲习俗，多发生在贫穷人家。有的男女双方虽然早就订好婚约，但因为婚礼手续繁琐，费用开支较大，男女两家都无经济能力承担。于是在女方的默许下，男方和媒人议定好抢亲的时间和地点。一般媒人会想办法让新郎先认识新娘，然后按照抢亲时间，新郎召集一众亲友，摇船或抬轿，来到女方家附近。这时，女方家会有意让姑娘去河边洗菜淘米，新郎看到新娘，立刻从船舱奔出来，用包袱将新娘的头脸蒙住，迅速将其抱入船舱，飞快地把船划走。

The custom of marriage by capture in Shaoxing often occurred in poor families. Although some couples were already permitted to get married by their parents, they were unable to afford the costly wedding procedures. With the consent of the bride, the groom and the matchmaker would agree on the time and place for the marriage by capture. Generally, the matchmaker would find a way for the groom to meet the bride first, and then the groom would gather his relatives and friends, and either row a boat or carry a bridal sedan to the vicinity of the bride's home at the agreed time. At this moment, the bride's family would intentionally let the bride go to the riverbank to wash vegetables or rice. When the groom saw the bride, he immediately rushed out of the cabin, covered the bride's face with a bag, and quickly carried her into the cabin before rowing away swiftly.

在绍兴山区，抢亲的形式多为新郎带人突然闯进新娘家，女方家表面上会左拦右挡，但暗地却配合和支持。有的女方家还会偷偷告诉新郎，新娘躲在哪里，甚至还有将关锁在房中的新娘放出来交给新郎的。新郎便快速把新娘抱入花轿，飞快离开。这个时候，女方家都要故作姿态地呼叫追赶一番，以免邻居闲言碎语。上述两类抢亲，女方家可以不需要准备嫁妆，男方也可因为仓促成亲，免去很多程序和费用。成婚后，男女双方家人依然和好如初，照常走动。

In the mountainous areas of Shaoxing, the form of marriage by capture often involved the groom leading a group of people to suddenly break into the bride's home. The bride's family may resist on the surface, but secretly they cooperated and supported the groom. Some brides' families even secretly told the groom where the bride was hiding, and some even released the locked-up bride to the groom. The groom quickly carried the bride into the bridal sedan and left swiftly. At that time, the bride's family pretended to call for pursuit to avoid gossip from neighbors. In both types of marriage by capture, the bride's family did not need to prepare a dowry, and the groom can avoid many procedures and expenses due to the hasty marriage. After the wedding, the two families remained as close as before and continued their normal interactions.

还有一类抢亲，是因为男方得知女方有赖婚的打算，便突然袭击将新娘抢走。由于女方事先毫不知情，知道时，已经生米煮成熟饭，无可奈何了。此外，在绍兴嵊州、新昌地区，旧时还有强抢寡妇成亲的风俗。到民国后期，抢亲的习俗在绍兴已经逐渐消失，如今已经荡然无存。

There was another type of marriage by capture where the groom learned that the bride planed to marry someone else, so he suddenly appeared and took the bride away. Since the bride was unaware beforehand, she had no choice but to accept the situation. In addition, in the areas of Shengzhou and Xinchang, there used to be a custom of forcibly marrying widows. By the late Republic of China, the custom of marriage by capture gradually disappeared in Shaoxing and is now completely gone.

做舍姆
Doing Shem

绍兴人习惯把妇女生娃叫作"做舍姆"。因为以前的医疗水平较低，医疗条件也相对落后，不少女性因生产而丢掉性命，所以绍兴俗语有言"妇女做产，是一只脚伸在红脚桶里，一只脚伸在棺材里"。做舍姆，就是牺牲性命的意思。

It is a common practice among people from Shaoxing to refer to women giving birth as Doing Shem. This is because in the past, medical technology was really low and medical conditions were also very backward. Many women lost their lives during childbirth. Therefore, there was a saying in Shaoxing dialect that when a woman gave birth, one foot is in the red bucket for happiness and the other foot is in the coffin for danger. Doing shem means sacrificing one's life.

中国传统观念认为，生儿育女是传宗接代的大事。但生产也有不少的风险，所以在绍兴，无论是婆家，还是娘家，对此都十分重视，并有很多的风俗礼数。例如，妇女生产的那一个月，叫作"落月"，娘家要早早送去舍姆羹表达催生之意。按照绍兴风俗，舍姆羹一般包括红糖、鸡蛋、挂面、白鲞、核桃等等，另外还要送去婴儿的衣服，这些衣服必须由手艺好、儿孙满堂的老妪缝制，认为这样可以沾上裁缝的福气，保佑婴儿健康吉祥。

Traditional Chinese beliefs consider giving birth to children as a major event for continuing the family line. However, childbirth also carried many risks in the past. Therefore, in Shaoxing, both the bride's and groom's families attached great importance to this matter and had many customs and rituals. For example, the month after childbirth was called "luoyue" in Shaoxing dialect. The bride's family sent Shem soup early on to express the wish for a safe delivery. According to Shaoxing customs, Shem soup generally included brown sugar, eggs, vermicelli, whitebait, walnuts, and other ingredients. In addition, clothes for the baby must be sent, which were sewn by skilled and experienced elderly women, who were believed to bring good luck to the tailor and bless the baby with health and good fortune.

装运舍姆羹的箩筐或提盒，绍兴人称作"催生担"。在催生担里，还必须有一个红蛋，用红绸包着，用红线绑着，塞在婴儿的衣服里面。到达男方家中，便在孕妇的床上解开红线，提起红绸一角，让红蛋自动滚出来，寓意孕妇顺利生产。

The basket or box used to transport Shem soup was called a birth-inducing carrier by people from Shaoxing. In the carrier, there must also be a red egg wrapped in red silk and tied with red thread, which was stuffed into the baby's clothes. When it arrived at the groom's family, the red thread was untied on the pregnant woman's bed, and the corner of the red silk was lifted to let the red egg roll out on its own, symbolizing a safe delivery for the pregnant woman.

在绍兴，除了送催生担，还有娘家人带鸡来占卜生男生女的习俗。具体做法就是把公鸡母鸡各一只关进笼子里，提着进入女婿家大门，打开鸡笼，如果公鸡先出来，预兆是男娃；如果是母鸡先出来，则预兆是女娃。

In Shaoxing, in addition to sending the birth-inducing carrier, there was also a custom where the bride's family brought chickens to predict the gender of the baby. The specific method was to put a rooster and a hen in a cage, carry them into the groom's family home, and open the cage. If the rooster came out first, it was a sign of a boy; if the hen came out first, it was a sign of a girl.

绍兴把刚生完娃的妇女叫作舍姆娘，舍姆娘为防风寒，应头缠纱巾，在产房内静养一个月。产房也叫暗房，一般都设在楼下，关紧门窗，外人不能进出，即使是自家长辈，也不能进出暗房，房中还忌讳刀斧等利器。婴儿出生时的胎衣，要放进瓦罐中，藏在床底下，等到出月后再土埋。绍兴民间认为婴儿胎衣是命根，与孩子一生的吉凶祸福相关，不能损毁。

In Shaoxing, women who just gave birth were called Shem mothers. To prevent catching a cold, Shem mothers should wrap their heads with a scarf and rest quietly in the delivery room for one month. The delivery room was also called the dark room and was usually located on the ground floor, with windows and doors tightly closed. Even close relatives cannot enter the dark room, and sharp objects such as knives and axes were also forbidden. The baby's umbilical cord and placenta were put into a clay pot, hidden under the bed, and buried in the ground after a month. Folk beliefs in Shaoxing hold that the umbilical cord and placenta are related to the child's destiny throughout their life and must not be destroyed.

婴儿出生三天后，绍兴俗称"三朝"，家人要为其洗浴，叫作"洗三朝"。有些地方，还有谢床公床婆的风俗。就是将一些红蛋放在床前，产妇燃香祈愿，一是感谢床公床婆的保佑，让婴儿顺利生产；二是祈求日后继续保佑婴孩无灾无难，健康成长。同时，还有给邻里街坊送红蛋、挂面，分享添丁的好消息。

Three days after the baby was born, it was called "Three Chao" in Shaoxing, and the family members gave the baby a bath, which was known as "Washing Three Chao". In some places, there was also a custom of thanking the bed god and goddess. Some red eggs were placed in front of the bed, and the mother burned incense to express gratitude for the bed god and goddess's blessing for a safe delivery and to pray for the baby's health and growth in the future. At the same time, neighbors were given red eggs and noodles to share the good news of the new arrival.

满月与得周
Baby's Full Month and One Year's Birthday

满月是指婴儿出生后满一个月，绍兴俗称"弥月"。据说我国古代为婴儿做满月的习俗始于唐朝。按照绍兴的风俗习惯，婴儿满月要办满月酒，邀请亲朋好友，摆宴设席，非常隆重。外婆家需要送外孙穿戴的帽子、抱裙和形如披风的"一口钟"（古代的服装名称，一种无袖不开衩的长外衣），另外还要准备面条、馒头等作为孩子谢神的贡品。

Full month refers to one month after the baby is born, which is called "Mi Month" in Shaoxing. It is said that the ancient Chinese custom of celebrating a baby's full month began in the Tang Dynasty. According to the customs and traditions of Shaoxing, a full-month celebration is held for the baby, inviting relatives and friends to a banquet, which is very grand. The maternal grandmother needs to prepare a hat, an apron, and a "yi kou zhong" (an ancient garment name, a sleeveless long coat without a slit) for the baby to wear. In addition, noodles and steamed buns are prepared as offerings to thank the gods on behalf of the baby.

按照习俗，婴儿在满月这一天第一次剃头，因此满月酒也叫剃头酒。给婴儿剃头时，桌上点香燃烛，奉上10种水果糕点作为贡品，绍兴称之为"十盘头"。剃头时，由一位福寿双全的老人抱着婴儿，端坐在厅堂，手艺高超的剃头司务娴熟地把婴儿的胎发剃掉。剃满月头不仅能得到高出好几倍的剃头钱，而且按照惯例，供奉的十盘头送给剃头司务食用。剃下的胎发，要团成一团，放入桂圆壳中，用细线绑住挂在床头。满月头的发式也有讲究，男孩子一律剃成仅保留囟门的瓦片头，脑后留个"鸭尾巴"；女孩子则只剃脑门周围一圈，保留大部分的胎发。

According to the custom, the baby's first haircut is given on the day of the full month celebration, which is why the full-month banquet is also called the haircut banquet. During the haircut, incense is lit and candles are lit on the table, and ten kinds of fruits and pastries are offered as offerings, which are known as "ten plates" in Shaoxing. An elderly person who is blessed with longevity holds the baby and sits in the hall, while the skilled barber shaves off the baby's fetal hair. The haircut not only earns several times more money than usual, but also according to tradition, the ten plates offered are given to the barber to eat. The shaved hair is rolled into a ball and placed in a longan shell, tied with a thin thread and hung at the head of the bed. The hairstyle for the full-month baby also has its own rules. Boys are shaved with only the fontanelle remaining, leaving a "duck tail" at the back of their head. Girls are only shaved around the circumference of their forehead, leaving most of their fetal hair intact.

得周是指婴儿满一周岁，绍兴人历来对此非常重视，也会大加操办。婴孩周岁当天，往往穿戴一新，绍兴谚语"倌倌得周"就是指这个。按照习俗，这一天婴儿穿戴的衣服鞋帽，必须由外婆家送去，父母则忙于祭祀神灵和祖先。这一天，和许多地方一样，绍兴也有抓周的风俗。所谓"抓周"，是指在婴儿面前，摆上一个盘子，里面盛放文房四宝、珠宝、书籍、算盘等物，任由婴儿自己抓摸。如果孩子抓了文房四宝或书籍，父母亲友都会很高兴，认为孩子长大后肯定聪明有智慧，能读诗从文。

De Zhou refers to the baby's first birthday, and people in Shaoxing always attach great importance to it and would celebrate it grandly. On the first birthday, babies are often dressed in new clothes, which is referred to as "guan guan de zhou" in Shaoxing dialect. According to customs, the clothes, shoes, and hats worn by the baby on the day must be sent by the maternal grandmother, while the parents are busy worshiping the gods and ancestors. Like many other places, Shaoxing also has the custom of Zhua Zhou on the day. Zhua Zhou means to place a plate in front of the baby, filled with writing brushes, jewelry, books, abacuses, and other items, allowing the baby to grab them freely. If the baby grabs

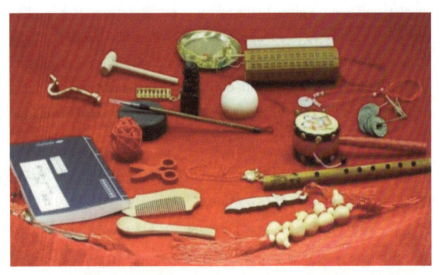

图31　抓周用的道具 郑红莲摄 Props for the one-year-old catch PHOTO: Z.H.L.

the writing brushes or books, the parents and relatives will be very happy, believing that the child will be smart, wise and able to read and write well in the future.

周岁这天，父母也要设宴请客，绍兴叫"办得周酒"。在嵊州、上虞、新昌等地，孩子得周叫作"闹周"，除了抓周和摆酒设宴，还有用白糯米麻糍做许多的闹周果，也叫得周果。果子中间有糖和乌豇豆做成的细沙，香甜可口，父母把闹周果分给亲朋好友品尝。

On the baby's first birthday, parents also host a banquet for guest in Shaoxing. In places such as Shengzhou, Shangyu, and Xinchang, the celebration of a baby's first birthday is called "nao zhou". In addition to Zhua Zhou and banquets, many Nao Zhou fruits are made using sticky rice and sesame paste, which are also called De Zhou pastry. The fillings of the pastry are fine sand made from sugar and black beans, which are sweet and delicious. Parents usually distribute them to relatives and friends to taste.

在绍兴，如果孩子满月或得周，第一次去外婆家，外公外婆、舅舅舅母通常要给男娃送一只未生蛋的母鸡，给女娃送一只小雄鸡。绍兴谚语称它们为"积货兆"。意思是孩子把鸡养大，可以换鹅，把鹅养大可以换猪、羊，这样下去就能积攒钱财用来结婚娶妻。如今，在绍兴乡下一些地区还保持这一风俗。

In Shaoxing, when a baby reaches her first month or first week, they usually go to their maternal grandparents' house for the first time. The grandfather, grandmother, uncles and aunts would usually give a male baby an unhatched hen and a female baby a young rooster. In Shaoxing dialect, they are called "ji huo zhao". This means that the child can raise the chicken up and exchange it for a goose. When the goose is raised, it can be exchanged for a pig or a sheep. With time passing by, the child can accumulate wealth to use for marriage in the future through this way. Nowadays, this custom is still practiced in rural areas of Shaoxing.

做生日与做寿
Birthday and Longevity Celebration

在绍兴，做生日和做寿都是庆祝出生日的习俗，民间通常50岁以下称为做生日，50岁以上才叫做寿，而且都是逢十之年才做。其他岁数，并不讲究。

In Shaoxing, birthday and longevity celebration were both traditional customs to celebrate one's birthday. Generally, the birthday party for people under 50 years old was called birthday celebration, and the party for those over 50 years old was called longevity celebration. Both celebrations were usually held on the decade years such as 50th, 60th, 70th, etc. Other ages were not particularly emphasized.

绍兴俗语"十岁外婆家，廿岁丈母家"指的是做生日的风俗，意思是应该由外婆家给外孙庆祝十岁的生日。旧社会因为男子十八九岁就结婚，所以二十岁生日由丈母娘家操办。这一天，岳母家通常提着生日礼物，到女婿家祝贺生日。

The Shaoxing proverb "A child's 10th birthday should be celebrated at their maternal grandmother's home, while their 20th birthday should be celebrated at their mother-in-law's home", refers to the custom of birthday celebration, which means that grandmothers should hold the 10th birthday for boys, and when they grow up and get married, they could have the 20th birthday party at their mothers-in-law's house. In the old days, men would usually get married early at the age of 18 or 19, so their 20th birthday would be celebrated at their wife's home. On the day, the mothers-in-law would prepare birthday gifts and send congratulations to the sons-in-law on their birthdays.

另外，绍兴还有"三十要做，四十要错"的讲究，意思是三十岁的生日要和家人好好庆祝一番，但绝不能做四十岁的生日。因为绍兴方言"四"和"死"同音，为了忌讳，人们一般不做四十岁生日。也有的把四十岁的生日提前到三十九岁来做，这种方式，绍兴俗称"做九"。做生日一般都是邀请少数亲友参加，规模不大。

In addition, there is an old saying in Shaoxing that one should celebrate at 30 years old, but not at 40 years old. It means that one should celebrate their 30th birthday with their family, but should not celebrate their 40th birthday. This is because in Chinese dialect the pronunciation of four and death are identical, so people generally don't celebrate their 40th birthday to avoid bad luck. Some people choose to celebrate their 39th birthday instead of their 40th, which is known as Zuo Jiu in Shaoxing. Birthday celebration was usually a small-scale event that only a few close friends and relatives were invited.

相较而言，做寿的场面就要大很多。如果是豪门大户，通常都要设置专门的寿堂，大红灯笼高高挂，红毯铺地，张灯结彩，热闹非凡。在寿堂正中，悬挂大幅中堂，内容有"麻姑献寿图""百寿图"或"寿星图"，两旁配以寿联。寿堂上必须供以寿桃和寿面，表示延年益寿的寓意。由于新鲜的桃子不是一年四季都有采摘，所以人们用面粉制成桃形，染成红色替代。寿面是食物中最长之物，以面祝寿，有长寿之意。这些寿桃、寿面有些是家里准备的，还有的来自亲友馈赠。祝寿后，这些食物要分给未能参加寿宴的亲友和邻里街坊。

Compared to birthday celebration, the scene of celebrating longevity was much grander. For those wealthy family, they usually set up a special longevity hall, with red lanterns hanging high, red carpets on the ground, decorations and colorful lights, creating a lively atmosphere. In the center of the longevity hall, there was a large central painting, such as the pictures of *Magu Offering Birthday Wishes*, *Hundred Years of Life* or *The God of Longevity*, with longevity couplets on both sides. Longevity peaches and noodles must be offered in the longevity hall to express the meaning of extending one's life. Fresh peaches were not available all year round, so people used flour to make peach-shaped buns and dyed them red as a substitute. It was also believed that longevity noodles were a kind of food with the longest length, and presenting noodles to celebrate birthday implied the meaning of longevity. Some of longevity peaches and noodles were prepared by the family, while others were gifts from relatives and friends. After the celebration, these foods were distributed to relatives, friends, and neighbors who were unable to attend the banquet.

祝寿这天，寿星盛装打扮，端坐在寿堂之中。这时，点燃大红烛、奏响起鼓乐，晚辈以长幼为序，依次向寿星一一叩拜。亲朋好友来后也一起向寿星道贺。接着，设寿宴款待来宾。按照绍兴习俗，每桌必须上一大盘炒面，客人们一般争先食用，叫作吃寿面。饭后，有钱人家还会请戏班子来演唱堂会。

On the day of the longevity celebration, the elderly whose birthday is being celebrated sat in the longevity hall dressed in his or her best clothing. At that time, red candles lit and drums and music were played. The younger generation would then bow to the elderly in the order of seniority, while relatives and friends would also come to congratulate the god of longevity. Afterwards, a longevity banquet was held to entertain guests. According to traditional customs, a large plate of fried noodles always was served at each table and guests rushed to eat them, which was called eating longevity noodles. After the meal, wealthy families may invite a troupe to perform in the hall.

在绍兴，除了做生日和做寿，还有做女儿的要在父母六十六岁生日时送六十六块肉的习俗。绍兴俗语有云"六十六，阎罗大王要吃肉"，因此女儿送肉，有为父母消灾祈福的寓意。在绍兴，这一风俗习惯流传至今。

In addition to celebrating birthday and longevity, there was also a custom in Shaoxing that daughters need give 66 pieces of meat to their parents as a gift on their 66th birthday. The Shaoxing proverb says "At the age of 66, the king of hell wants to eat meat", so daughters gave meat to their parents as a way to pray for their parents' safety and blessings. This custom has been passed down in Shaoxing to this day.

Chapter 4 第四章

社会规约篇

Social Convention

施善
Benevolence Practice

"美由善心来，心似莲花开"，乐善好施是中华民族的传统美德，绍兴将此美德作为一种风俗习惯践行在生活的方方面面。不管是有钱人还是穷人，都愿意尽自己的努力多做"好事"，帮助有困难、有需要的人们。在绍兴，施善之举有施药、施财、施医、施住处，修路、修桥、修凉亭，照顾老人、收养孤儿等等，数不胜数。

"Beauty comes from a kind heart, and the heart is like a lotus flower in bloom. " Practicing benevolence and generosity is a traditional virtue of the Chinese nation, and Shaoxing takes this virtue as a custom to be practiced in all aspects of life. Both rich and poor people are willing to do their best to do more good deeds and help those in need and difficulties. In Shaoxing, acts of kindness include providing medicine, money, housing, and medical treatment; repairing roads, bridges, and pavilions; taking care of the elderly and adopting orphans, and so on, which are too numerous to mention.

每当遇到天灾人祸老百姓吃不上饭时，总有人自愿出头组织施粥救助等活动。为了筹集救助的物资和款项，他们登门拜访当地的大户人家，劝说他们出钱结善缘。这样，灾民一天三顿可以领白粥充饥。也有一些家底殷实的有钱人家，自发地给穷人提供免费的食物。这样的善举，常常世代传颂。

Whenever there were natural disasters or man-made calamities and the common people cannot have enough to eat in the past, there were always people who volunteered to organize porridge-sharing activity and other relief activities. In order to raise materials and funds for relief efforts, they went door-to-door to visit local wealthy families and persuaded them to donate money to help those disaster victims. This way, the victims could have three meals a day of rice porridge to sustain themselves. There were also some well-to-do families who spontaneously provided free food to the poor. Such acts of kindness are often passed down from generation to generation and are widely praised.

同善局和灵霄社是绍兴当年固定的施医、施药的场所。民国时，陈幼生、曹炳章、胡宝书、何廉臣、裘吉生等绍兴医生都在这里轮流义诊，他们为病人开的药方可到社内局内的药柜配药，不收取一分钱。同善局创办于1792年，而开元寺灵霄社创办于1924年，它们长期为老百姓施药、施医、施材、施衣。灵霄社有时还为无依无靠的老人发放2到4元的每月生活救济。

The Tongshan Bureau and Lingxiao Society were regular places for providing free medicine and medical treatment in Shaoxing in the past. During the Republic of China period, Shaoxing doctors such as Chen Yousheng, Cao Bingzhang, Hu Baoshu, He Lianchen, Qiu Jisheng took turns to offer free medical consultations there. The prescriptions they wrote for patients could be dispensed at the pharmacy in the office, without charging them a penny. The Tongshan Bureau was founded in 1792, while the Lingxiao Society of Kaiyuan Temple was founded in

1924. They had been providing free medicine, medical treatment, basic materials and clothing for the common people for a long time. Lingxiao Society sometimes even granted a monthly living allowance of 2 to 4 yuan for those elderly who had no families to rely on.

　　绍兴水路复杂，形如网状。过去，凡是河面宽阔没有造桥的地方，都设有专门的义渡。义渡的船只有专门的船手为来往过客摆渡，一年四季， 风雨无间。有些渡口过往的人不多，就设有绳渡。绳渡的船较小，呈正方形，上口宽，底部窄。船内相对的船帮两头，钉有一个大铁环，里面系着一根大粗绳，绳子的两头分别系在两岸的石孔上。渡河的人上船之后，只需要慢慢地抓着绳子移动，就可以把船开到对岸。至于义渡和绳渡的修理费用，以及人员开支等费用，一般都是由乐善好施的民众捐款来承担。

Shaoxing's waterways are complex and resemble a web. In the past, wherever there was a wide river without a bridge, a special free ferry was set up. The free ferry ships were manned by fixed boatmen to shuttle back and forth for passengers all year round, rain or shine. Some ferry crossings had few passersby, so rope ferries were set up. The boat of the rope ferry was smaller, with a square shape, and a wide opening on the top and a narrow base at the bottom. The two opposite sides of the boat's side planks had a large iron ring nailed onto each, which was tied to a thick rope with both ends tied to the stone holes on either side of the bank. After the passengers boarded the boat, they only needed to move slowly by grabbing the rope to move the boat to the other side. As for the repair costs and personnel expenses of the free ferry and the rope ferry, they were generally funded by donations from kind-hearted people.

旧时没有电灯，特别是农村地区，如果没有月亮和星星，晚上总是伸手不见五指，走夜路的人很容易掉入河中或坑里。绍兴当地人会沿着河岸或桥墩路上立上一盏盏小灯，俗称"天灯"，为过路的人照亮来去的路。天灯大多是点着蜡烛的灯笼，灯笼外壳上一般写着"天灯代月"几个字。每天晚上一盏天灯得换上好几根蜡烛，这些人力物资也都是由好心人自愿捐助的。

In the old days, there were no electric lights, especially in rural areas. Without the moon and stars, it was always pitch-black at night, and people walking on the road were prone to fall into the river or pits. Local people in Shaoxing would light up small lamps along the riverbank or bridge piers, commonly known as sky lanterns, to illuminate the way for passersby. Sky lanterns were mostly lanterns lit with candles, and the shell of the lantern generally had the words, "sky lantern, an alternative of the moon". Every night, several candles were generally consumed for each sky lantern. Those human and material resources were all voluntarily donated by kind-hearted people.

绍兴南部以及新昌、嵊州一带，以前出门都得翻山越岭，所以一路上有凉亭茅厕，还有为引注溪水山泉而用石板砌成的小水池，供来往的人落脚歇息、避风避雨和解渴避暑。另外，在铜盘湖上，有一条形状像纤道的避风塘，也是老百姓捐款所建。过往船只如果遇到大风大浪，就可靠近避风塘躲避风浪。由于使用时间较长，避风塘常常需要修护，一旦发现问题，人们总是非常自觉地出资或筹资修缮，把做好事当成习惯。

In the south of Shaoxing, as well as in the areas of Xinchang and

Shengzhou, one had to climb over mountains and hills to go outside in the past. Therefore, there were pavilions, thatched restrooms along the way, as well as small pools made of slate to collect creek water and mountain springs for passersby to rest, shelter from the wind and rain, quench their thirst, and escape from the summer heat. In addition, on Tongpan Lake, there was a shelter shaped like a narrow path, which was also built with donations from the common people. If passing boats encountered strong winds and waves, they could rely on it to shelter from the wind and waves. Due to the long period of use, the shelter often needed repair. Once problems were discovered, people were always very conscious of raising funds for repair, regarding doing good as a habit.

我国传统思想认为，"积德增福""善有善报，恶有恶报""积善之家必有余庆""乐善好施能服于人，上善若水厚德载物"。因此乐于助人的美德几千年来代代相传，并不断发扬光大。

Traditional Chinese thinking believes in that "an accumulation of virtues will lead to an increase of blessings", "good deeds will be rewarded and evil deeds will be punished", "a family that accumulates virtues will have good fortune", and "being charitable and benevolent can win people's hearts, and the highest virtue is like water, which carries everything with its profound goodness". Therefore, the virtue of being willing to help others has been passed down for thousands of years and continuously promoted in China.

尊师重教
Respect Teachers and Value Education

尊师重教之风在绍兴几千年来经久不衰。据记载，明清以来，私塾、学堂遍及绍兴各地。崇尚读书成为了一种风俗，所以《嘉泰会稽志》记载，"今之风俗，好学笃志，尊师择友，弦诵之声，比屋相闻。"

The tradition of respecting teachers and valuing education has lasted for thousands of years in Shaoxing. According to records, private schools and study halls have been found throughout Shaoxing since the Ming and Qing dynasties. The pursuit of reading and learning has become a custom, so *The Jiatai Kuaiji Annals* recorded, "Today's customs are to love learning, be diligent, respect teachers and choose good friends. The sound of recitation can be heard from house to house".

绍兴的尊师重教与当地的施善美德密不可分，民间出资办学助学的比比皆是。当时官办的学堂并不多，大量学堂是由民间个人捐款或由家族宗祠拨资建造。早在北宋时期（999年），绍兴新昌两父子石文渥、石待旦两位读书人出钱创办了绍兴地区第一个义塾——石溪义塾。南宋时，嵊州姚崇景出资建造了姚氏义塾。到了清代，当地乡绅出资购地、捐建书堂的风气更为盛行。清末绍兴地区影响较大的义塾就多达47所，还有许多一般的义塾。

The tradition of respecting teachers and valuing education in Shaoxing is closely linked to the virtue of philanthropy. There were many privately-funded schools and scholarship programs in the area in the old days. At that time, there were not many government-supported schools, and a large number of schools were built with donations from private individuals or funding from family ancestral halls. As early as the Northern Song Dynasty (999 AD), two scholars, Shi Wenwo and Shi Daidan, funded the establishment of the first charity school in Shaoxing called Shixi School. In the Southern Song Dynasty, Yao Chongjing funded the construction of the Yao Family School in Shengzhou. In the Qing Dynasty, the trend of local gentry purchasing land and donating to build schools became even more prevalent. In the late Qing Dynasty, there were as many as 47 influential charity schools in Shaoxing, as well as many ordinary ones.

义塾不仅为本家族的孩子提供免费上学的机会，还为家境贫寒的邻里他族的孩子提供免费入学。教材和学习用品等基本上也都是免费提供。有些义塾还为学生提供伙食补贴以及参加乡试和会试的路费。义塾的办学经费主要来自学田的租金收入。例如，敬敷义塾的学田多达3000多亩，一般的义塾也有几百亩学田。

These charity schools not only provided free education opportunities for children of their own families, but also offered free enrollment to children of poor families in the neighborhood who were from other clans. Necessary teaching materials and study supplies were also provided for free. Some charity schools even provided meals and travel expenses for students to participate in the local imperial examinations. The operating

图32 蕺山书院 郑红莲摄 Jishan Academy PHOTO: Z.H.L.

expenses of charity schools mainly came from the rental income of their school fields. For example, the Jingfu School had more than 3,000 mu (1 mu = 0.067 hectares) of school fields, while ordinary private schools also had several hundred mu of school fields.

除了官府办的学堂和民间建的义塾，以前还有老师自办的学堂，一般叫作私塾。当然还有大户人家把老师招到家中设立的家塾。不管是哪种办学形式，教学内容基本相同，都是以《三字经》《百家姓》《千字文》等作为低年级的教材，高年级选读《论语》《大学》《中庸》《孟子》等书。在私塾或家塾里读完书的学生，可以进县学或书院继续读书，也可以直接参加科举考试。

In addition to schools established by the government and charity schools set up by individuals, there were a few schools established by teachers themselves, which were generally known as private schools. Of course, there were also wealthy families who invited teachers to establish family schools in their homes. Regardless of the forms of education, the teaching content was basically the same, using books such as *Three Character Classic*, *Hundred Family Surnames*, and *Thousand Character*

Classic as the textbooks for lower grades, and selecting books such as *Analects of Confucius*, *The Great Learning*, *The Doctrine of the Mean*, and *Mencius* for higher grade students. Those who completed their studies in private schools or family schools could continue their education at county schools or academies, or could directly participate in the imperial examinations.

　　在绍兴，孩子上学是一件非常重要的事情。旧时，上学前需要请算命先生根据生辰八字算出上学的年龄宜单还是宜双。如果是宜单，一般是七岁上学，如果是宜双，则多是六岁，或者八岁。第一次上学，要准备好红蜡烛，带上桂圆、荔枝、馒头、生葱等去学堂举行拜师仪式。桂圆、荔枝用来孝敬老师，馒头是分给同学吃的。生葱取其谐音，意思是聪明智慧。拜师时，先拜孔子的画像，然后再拜老师。如果学生只有乳名，这时学堂的老师就会为学生取一个书名，这个书名就成为学生日后的正式名字。

　　In Shaoxing, sending children to school is a very important matter. In the past, before a child started school, it was necessary to ask a fortune-teller to predict whether the child's age was suitable for starting school in an odd-numbered or even-numbered year, based on the child's birth date. If it was suitable for an odd-numbered year, the child would generally start at seven years old, and if it was for an even-numbered year, the child would start at six or eight years old. For the first day of school, a red candle should be prepared, and longan, lychee, steamed buns, spring onions and other items should be brought to hold a ceremony to pay respects to the teacher at the school. Longan and lychee were used to show respect to the teacher, and steamed buns were distributed among classmates to eat. Spring onions were used for their homophonic meaning, which stood for wisdom. When paying respects to the teacher, students first bowed to Confucius' portrait and then to the teacher. If a student only had an infant name, then the school teacher would give the student a formal name, which would become the student's formal name in the future.

图33　拜师仪式　郑红莲摄
Apprenticeship ceremony PHOTO: Z.H.L.

在绍兴，老师往往被认为是最有学问的人，所以普遍受到人们的尊敬。旧时，老师每天不用做饭，一日三餐都在学生家轮流吃，民间称为"派饭"。轮到派饭的人家时，必定会以家中最好的菜肴招待老师。老师一般也很客气，荤菜一般只吃一半，另一半留到下餐再吃。老师换洗的衣物，除了内裤外，其他的也由派饭的人家帮忙洗好。平时，走在路上，遇见老师，人人都会拱手作揖相让。逢年过节，学生家长要向老师赠送礼物。节日或办喜事，老师也一定被请去当座上宾。此外，结婚用的祝词，祭祀用的祭文，以及墓碑、春联等，也都是请老师来作。甚至，本地的一些大事也会征求老师的意见。

In Shaoxing, teachers are often considered the most knowledgeable people and are therefore widely respected. In the past, teachers did not have to cook their own meals and would take turns eating three meals a day at students' home, which was known as arranged meals in the local dialect. When it was a family's turn to provide meals for the teacher, the host family would always serve the best dishes they had. The teachers were generally very polite and would only eat half of the meat dishes, leaving the other half for the next meal. The host family would also help wash the teacher's clothes, except for his underwear. When walking on the street, people would bow and give way to their teachers as a sign of respect. During festivals or when celebrating a happy event, parents of the students would present gifts to teachers. On holidays or special occasions, teachers were also invited as honored guests. In addition, teachers were asked to write blessings or epitaphs, and to help write couplets for Spring Festival, among other things. Even for important local events, the opinions of teachers were often sought.

清代学者金埴记录了绍兴当地一个尊师的故事。有一户陶姓人家，他有三个孩子，请了一位家庭老师给孩子授课。一天晚上因为讲课口干舌燥，这位老师无意说到："现在，要是有一碗腰花汤润嗓子就好啦！"说者无意，听者有心。没过一会儿，老师就听到院子里传来杀猪的声音，他心想，这么晚了，谁家还在杀猪。正纳闷着，主人竟然派人送来一碗热气腾腾的腰花汤。先生又惊又愧，决心努力教学感谢主人的一番美意。后来，这家的三个孩子个个登第，都因文章写得好而出名。

In the Qing Dynasty, scholar Jin Zhi recorded a story that highlighted the respect for teachers in Shaoxing. There was a family surnamed Tao, who had three children and had hired a family tutor to teach their children. One night, the tutor was lecturing and his throat became dry and he unintentionally said, "It would be nice to have a bowl of soup with pig's kidney to moisten my throat!" His words were unintentional but the listener took note. After a while, the tutor heard the sound of a pig being slaughtered in the yard and wondered which household would still be slaughtering pigs at such a late hour. A few minutes later, the host presented a steaming hot bowl of pig's kidney soup to him. The tutor felt both surprised and ashamed, and determined to work hard and teach the children well in appreciation of the kindness shown by the host family. Later, all the three children in the family achieved success in the imperial examinations and became famous for their well-written essays.

民国时期，绍兴的学塾、书院改建为学堂，尊师重教之风历久弥新。根据《绍兴市志》记载，新中国成立后到20世纪90年代，全市由港澳台同胞和国外华侨出资捐建的学校达到38所。

During the period of the Republic of China, the private schools and academies in Shaoxing were rebuilt into public schools, and the tradition of respecting teachers and valuing education continued. According to *The Chronicles of Shaoxing City*, from the establishment of New China until the 1990s, a total of 38 schools were donated and built by compatriots from Hong Kong, Macao, Taiwan, and overseas Chinese.

桥俗
Bridge Customs

　　"垂虹玉带门前来，万古名桥出越州"，绍兴城内水道交错，有水乡、水城之美誉，有水便有桥，有桥便有景。绍兴有一首流传很广的民谣，"一，大木桥；二，凤仪桥；三，三脚桥；四，螺蛳桥；五，鲤鱼桥；六，福禄桥；七，戢望桥；八，八字桥；九，酒务桥；十，日晖桥"。十座桥组成的民谣足以说明绍兴有很多桥。《绍兴市志》记载，1990年统计显示，绍兴共有桥梁10355座，这些桥梁建造年代不同，建筑风格也各有特色，代表了丰富的文化内涵，也发展形成了独有的桥梁风俗。

　　There is a poem describing the bridges in Shaoxing, "A rainbow arches above the jade belt, and an ancient famous bridge spans the Yue State". The waterways within the city are intertwined, earning it the reputation of being a water town and a water city. Where there is water, there is a bridge, and where there is bridge, there is scenery. Shaoxing has a widely spread folk song that goes, "One, Damu Bridge; Two, Fengyi Bridge; Three, Three-foot Bridge; Four, Snail Bridge; Five, Carp Bridge; Six, Fulu Bridge; Seven, Jiewang Bridge; Eight, Eight-character Bridge; Nine, Wine service Bridge; Ten, Rihui Bridge". The ten bridges in the song are enough to show that there are many bridges in Shaoxing.

According to *The Annals of Shaoxing City*, in 1990 there were a total of 10,355 bridges. The bridges were built at different times and have different architectural styles, representing rich cultural connotations, and developing their unique bridge customs.

图34 绍兴八字桥 郑红莲摄 Shaoxing Eight-character Bridge PHOTO: Z.H.L.

　　古时在绍兴，老百姓非常乐意捐钱修桥修路建凉亭，因为做这些事被认为是行善积德的好事。所以只要有人带头，就会一呼百应。也有的大户人家愿意全部承担造桥的费用，造福身边的百姓。在绍兴还流传着一位医生因修桥而被奉为土地神的故事。清代时期，有一位叫倪涵初的医生住在亭后村，他不仅医术高明，救人无数，还热心社会公益事业。他曾经一人出资在漯山附近建了一座桥让来往行人免于摆渡过河的麻烦。当地老百姓为感谢倪医生的恩情，在他去世后便在江边修建了一座庙，把他当作土地神来供奉，四时祭祀，香火不断。

In ancient times in Shaoxing, ordinary people were very willing to donate money to repair bridges, roads, and pavilions because it was widely believed that good deeds would accumulate good virtues. So as long as someone took the lead, everyone would follow suit. Some wealthy households were also willing to fully bear the cost of building bridges to benefit the local people. In Shaoxing, there is also a story of a doctor who was revered as a local god of the land because of his bridge-building efforts. During the Qing Dynasty, a doctor named Ni Hanchu lived in Tinghou Village. He was not only skilled in medicine and saved countless people, but also actively participated in social public welfare activities. He once financed the construction of a bridge near Luoshan for pedestrians to cross the river without the hassle of ferrying. Local people built a temple by the river after his death to show their gratitude to Doctor Ni, and they worshiped him as a local god of the land, offering sacrifice and burning incense throughout the year.

按照习俗，建桥前需要请风水先生看好位置，算好黄道吉时才能破土动工。开工那天，要准备三牲和香烛祭拜土地神，保佑建桥平安。有的还要敲锣打鼓、张灯结彩，犹如过节一般。建新桥，还需要提前请当地德高望重、知识渊博的长者拟定好桥名。大多数桥名都采用福禄平安、吉祥如意的字眼，如安宁桥、万寿桥、万安桥、五福桥等。在绍兴，正月初一有兜喜神方的民俗，人们都喜欢在这些桥上走一走，以求一年万事顺意、幸福安康。结婚迎亲时，花轿也会被抬上去兜一圈，如果是轿船，就有意从这些桥下通过，祈求婚姻美满。

According to customs, before constructing a bridge, one who practices geomancy need to be invited to carefully observe the location and calculate the auspicious time before starting construction. On the day of the groundbreaking, offerings of three animals and incense are prepared to worship the local land god, praying for the safe construction of the bridge. Some even have the sound of gongs and drums and colorful lanterns to celebrate like a festival. Building a new bridge also requires the local respected elder with high reputation and profound knowledge to choose a name for the bridge in advance. Most bridge names use words such as fortune, happiness, peace, and security, such as Anning Bridge, Wanshou Bridge, Wan'an Bridge, and Wufu Bridge. In Shaoxing, there is a custom of walking on these bridges on the first day of the lunar new year, with the best wishes to have a prosperous and happy new year. During weddings, wedding sedans would be lifted up for a lap on these bridges, and boats would also intentionally pass across these bridges to pray for a happy marriage.

绍兴人还习惯把桥周边一带称为"桥下"，这些地方以往人流船只来往较多，商铺林立，于是人们常来桥下购物，所以有"天上天下，不如大善桥下"的谚语。人们还喜欢在桥头、桥上、桥下谈天说地、休闲纳凉。绍兴有古木桥10座，石梁桥348座，石拱桥241座，均建筑精美。桥上的栏板多为花卉云纹等雕刻图案，望柱顶端有雕莲瓣，也有蹲狮，还有的是"暗八仙"浮雕，就是雕上八仙手上拿的一些物件。还有的在桥洞两侧刻上桥联，如东浦镇的新桥有一幅"浦北中心为酒国，桥西出口是鹅池"的桥联。这些都展现出绍兴丰富多彩的桥梁民俗。

Shaoxing people generally call the areas around the bridge "under the bridge". These places used to have a lot of pedestrian and boat traffic, with many shops around. So people often come to shop under the bridge, hence the saying "Heaven and earth are not as good as under the bridge of Dashan". People also like to chat, relax, and cool off under the bridge, on the bridge, or at the bridgehead. Shaoxing has 10 ancient wooden bridges, 348 stone beam bridges, and 241 stone arch bridges, all of which are beautifully built. The railings on the bridge are mostly carved with floral and cloud patterns, and the top of the pillars are carved with lotus petals or squatting lions. Some have sculpted reliefs of "hidden eight immortals", which are some objects held by the eight immortals in their hands. There are also some bridge couplets carved on both sides of the bridge holes, such as the couplet of Xin Bridge in Dongpu Town, which reads "The Center of northern Pu is wine kingdom, The exit of western bridge is the goose pond". All of these demonstrate the rich and colorful bridge customs of Shaoxing.

酒俗
Wine Customs

绍兴有长达2500多年的酿酒历史，据《吕氏春秋》记载，早在春秋战国时期，这里就酿造精良美酒。绍兴地区土地肥沃，气候温和，日照充足，四季分明，又有鉴湖这一丰沛而优质的水源，酿酒具备得天独厚的环境，因此绍兴享有"酒乡"之誉。

Shaoxing has a history of brewing wine for over 2,500 years. According to *The Annals of Lü Buwei*, as early as the Spring and Autumn Period and the Warring States Period, exquisite wine was brewed here. The land in Shaoxing is fertile, the climate is mild, and there is plenty of sunshine and distinct seasons. With the abundant and high-quality water source of Jianhu Lake, brewing wine has a unique advantage in this region, hence Shaoxing is known as "the hometown of wine".

在绍兴，家家户户都有冬日酿酒的风俗，男男女女都有喝酒的习惯。凡是有亲朋好友来访，都会备以好酒款待；凡是结婚、生娃、祝寿等喜事，都要办酒席庆贺；凡是节日和节气等重要时节，也要用酒祭祀祖先和神灵。因此在绍兴，"无酒不成俗"这话再贴切不过。在战国时期，越王勾践曾用酒作为奖品鼓励生育增加人口。据记载，生男孩奖励两壶酒和一条狗，生女孩奖励两壶酒和一头猪。

In Shaoxing, it is customary for every household to brew wine in winter, and both men and women have the habit of drinking. Whenever relatives and friends visit, they will be treated with good wine; whenever there is a happy event such as a wedding, birth, or birthday celebration, a banquet will be held to celebrate; and whenever there is an important festival or solar term, wine will be used to worship ancestors and gods. Therefore, in Shaoxing, the saying "no custom without wine" is very appropriate. In the Warring States Period, King Goujian of Yue State used wine as a prize to encourage childbirth and increase the population. According to records, giving birth to a boy was rewarded with two pots of wine and a dog, while giving birth to a girl was rewarded with two pots of wine and a pig.

"投醪河"的故事也是绍兴酒俗历史悠久的佐证。公元前473年，越王勾践经过"十年生聚""十年教训"后，亲征伐吴，这时当地的老百姓纷纷献上自家的好酒为越王饯行。勾践谢过乡亲们的情谊，但不愿意独自饮用，于是他把酒投入河中，让将士们共饮。将士们深感恩德，土气大增，一举大败吴国。绍兴城南的投醪河由此得名。

The story of Touzao River is also a testament to the long history and customs of Shaoxing wine. In 473 BC, King Goujian of Yue State launched a military campaign against Wu after "ten years' efforts of gathering strength" and "ten years of education and training". The local people presented their good wine to King Goujian as a farewell gift. Goujian thanked the locals for their kindness, but did not want to drink alone. So he poured the wine into the river and shared it with his soldiers.

The soldiers were deeply grateful and emboldened, and they went on to defeat the State of Wu. Touzao River in the south of Shaoxing got its name from the incident.

图35　绍兴黄酒
郑红莲摄 Shaoxing rice wine PHOTO: Z.H.L.

　　除了在家设酒宴招待客人外，绍兴本地还有很多酒馆，例如创建于清朝、已有一百多年历史的咸亨酒店。也有些小酒馆供人们日常沽酒小酌。相传，南宋时期著名诗人陆游与其前妻唐婉在绍兴沈园邂逅相遇。虽然当时陆游已另娶新妇，唐也改嫁他人，但唐婉念及旧情仍叫人备好酒菜，亲自款待陆游。陆游不禁追忆往事，感慨万分，写下了"红酥手，黄滕酒，满城春色宫墙柳"这首千古绝唱的诗歌。

In addition to hosting guests at home, there are many pubs in Shaoxing, such as Xianheng Hotel, which was founded in the Qing

Dynasty with a history of more than 100 years. There are also some bistros where people can enjoy a drink. Legend has it that during the Southern Song Dynasty, the famous poet Lu You and his former wife Tang Wan met in Shaoxing's Shen Garden. Although both of them had remarried, Tang still prepared food and wine to entertain Lu You out of her nostalgia for the past. Lu could not help but recall the past, feeling emotional, and wrote the immortal poem, "Pink hands so fine Gold-branded wine, Spring paints green willows palace walls cannot confine."

绍兴向来有以酒待客、以酒志庆、以酒祭祀的风俗。光结婚一事，就有定亲酒、正酒、回门酒、谢媒酒等等。为祭祀祖先的备酒就更多了，有上坟酒、夏至酒、端午酒、七月半酒、八月半酒、重阳酒、冬至酒等。祖先的生辰死忌时所供奉的酒菜，叫作忌日酒。此外，民间建房子和入住新房都要办酒席。这些风俗习惯，反映出绍兴鲜明的酒乡特色。

Shaoxing has always had the custom of using wine to entertain guests, celebrate events, and offer sacrifices. Even for weddings, there are different types of wine, including betrothal wine, wedding wine, visiting in-laws wine, and thank-you wine. There are even more types of wine offered for ancestral worship, such as tomb-sweeping wine, summer solstice wine, Dragon Boat Festival wine, Ghost Month wine, Mid-Autumn Festival wine, Chongyang Festival wine, Winter Solstice wine, and so on. Wine offerings for ancestors' birthdays or death anniversaries are called death-day wine. In addition, there are wine banquets when building a new home or moving into a new home. These customs reflect the distinctive characteristics of Shaoxing as a wine town.

坐茶店
Sitting in a Tea House

在绍兴，人们不光喜欢在家喝茶，还喜欢去茶店喝茶。旧时，只要花上几角钱，就可以悠闲地在茶店泡上半天，既可以谈生意，也可以谈天说地、八卦闲聊，俗称"坐茶店"。茶店里常坐满各色茶客，有长衫帮、短衫帮、年轻力壮的、七老八十的，唯独没有女茶客。

In Shaoxing, people not only enjoy drinking tea at home, but also like to go to the tea house. In the past, one could spend a few coins to leisurely spend half a day in the tea house, talking business, gossiping, or just chatting. This was commonly called "sitting in a tea house". The tea houses were often filled with various types of customers, such as those wearing long robes or short shirts, young and strong, and even those in their seventies and eighties, but there were no female customers in tea houses.

茶店一般用松材烧火，设有一座多孔灶，灶上可以同时放五到七把铜壶烧水。灶炉边上安着一个大水缸，里面装满从小河里挑来的清水。茶店里摆放着木桌板凳，茶壶茶碗。茶店里的伙计，绍语称之为"茶博士"，有三个绝活：一是不论客人啥时进店，茶博士总能马上泡好一壶温度适宜的茶水；二是茶博士提着开水壶不停

图36 绍兴茶店
郑红莲摄 Shaoxing
tea shop PHOTO:
Z.H.L.

地在狭小的通道上来回穿梭，为茶客加水，却从不会烫到人；三是当茶博士给客人泡茶时，总来"凤凰三点头"，既表示对客人的敬意，又使茶叶在茶具内均匀受热，茶叶的香味也很快地泡出来。

Tea houses generally used pine wood to burn fire with a multi-hole stove on which five to seven copper pots can be placed to boil water. There was a large water tank next to the stove where clean water was taken from a small river. The tea shop was furnished with wooden tables, benches, teapots, and tea cups. The waiters in the tea shop, referred to as "tea doctors" by colloquial language, had three special skills: First, they could always quickly brew a teapot of water at the appropriate temperature no matter when the customer arrived; second, the tea doctors constantly shuttled back and forth along the narrow passage with the boiling water pot to refill the customers' teapots, but they never scalded the customers; third, when brewing tea for customers, the tea doctors always did "a phoenix bow" to show respect to the customers, and at the same time, the tea leaves were evenly heated in the tea ware, and the fragrance of the tea was quickly extracted.

在绍兴，来坐茶店的茶客只要说声"红的"或"绿的"，茶博士就知道要的是一壶红茶或绿茶。老茶客甚至啥也不用说，因为要红茶还是绿茶，茶博士已经了然于心。茶客一般喜欢坐在固定的位置，如果有他的朋友来了，就招呼茶博士："拿个茶碗来。"如果是来了两个朋友，就要另外泡一壶茶。茶客有时有事需要暂时离开一会儿，就把茶壶盖拿开，把茶碗盖在茶壶上。茶博士一看就明白，不会去收拾茶具让其他人坐空位。

In Shaoxing, tea drinkers who came to the tea house just need to say black or green and the tea doctor immediately knew that they wanted a pot of black tea or green tea. Even old tea drinkers did't need to say anything because the tea doctor already knew whether they wanted black tea or green tea. Tea drinkers usually liked to sit in a fixed position. If their friend came, they would call out to the tea master, "Bring me a tea bowl". If two friends came, another pot of tea was needed to be brewed. Sometimes, if a tea drinker needed to leave temporarily, he would remove the lid of the teapot and place the tea bowl on the top of teapot. The tea doctor understood that and wouldn't tidy up the tea set to let someone else sit in the empty seat.

在绍兴，茶店的营业时间特别长，一般一大早就开店营业，到了傍晚时分喝茶的人才渐渐离开。中午时间，短衫帮多来茶店喝茶解困消乏。民国后期，茶店门口还常贴"莫谈国事"的告示，提醒茶客闲谈不要议论国家大事，以免招来麻烦。所以茶店里谈论最多的是生意上的事或街头巷尾的话题。绍兴地区有两种生意主要在茶店里谈成，一是锡箔业，货物销售、人力雇佣多以茶店为交易场所；二是请戏班子，主家在茶店里约好戏班子的班主，双方各泡一壶茶，边喝茶边讨论各自的要求，然后达成交易。

The business hours of the tea shops in Shaoxing were particularly long, usually opening early in the morning, and customers gradually left in the late evening. During lunchtime, many members of the Short Gown Gang came to the tea shop to drink tea and relieve their fatigue. In the late period of the Republic of China, there were often notices posted outside tea shops reminding customers not to discuss national affairs to avoid trouble. Therefore, the most discussed topics in tea shops were business or local issues. In Shaoxing, there were two main businesses that were negotiated in tea shops. One was the tin foil industry, where goods and labor sales were often negotiated in tea shops. The other was hiring traveling performance troupes. The host would invite the leader of the troupe to the tea shop, and both would enjoy a pot of tea while discussing their respective demands, then reaching a deal.

旧时，绍兴茶店有一种吃讲茶的风俗。即利用吃茶的场所，在调解下解决民事纠纷的一种民间活动。"朝南衙门八字开，有理无钱莫进来"的俗语在绍兴流传甚广，因此一旦发生民事纠纷，人们大多不愿意对簿公堂，担心落得两败俱伤，而是各自邀请一群亲朋好友、邻里街坊到茶店里吃讲茶。最重要的是请一位在地方上有威望的长者来做最后的仲裁者。吃讲茶时，茶店一般不再接待其他茶客，并给双方各沏一大壶好茶。双方先陈述事情经过、陈述理由，再叙述各自见解、提出处理意见，最后由仲裁者综合大家意见，裁定是非。新中国成立后，随着法制的完善和民事调解组织的成立，吃讲茶的习俗不复存在，但坐茶店的风俗保留至今。

In the past, there was a custom in Shaoxing tea houses that people would eat and drink tea while resolving civil disputes with the help of a mediator. The saying "Although the yamen gate is open wide you still can't go in if you don't have the money" was very popular in Shaoxing. Therefore, when a civil dispute occurred, most people were reluctant to go to court, fearing that both parties would lose, so they would invite a group of relatives, friends, and neighbors to drink tea at a tea house. The most important thing was to invite a respected elder from the local community to act as the final arbitrator. During that moment, the tea house generally did not serve other customers and provided each side with a large pot of good tea. Both sides would first state the facts and reasons behind the dispute, then express their own opinions and propose solutions. Finally, the arbitrator would consider everyone's opinions and make a ruling. After the founding of the People's Republic of China, with the improvement of the legal system and the establishment of civil mediation organizations, the custom of drinking tea to resolve disputes no longer exists, but the custom of sitting in tea houses has been preserved to this day.

曲水流觞
Drinking Wine and Composing Poetry Beside a Meandering Stream

　　曲水流觞，亦称曲水流杯或流觞曲水，该成语出自大书法家王羲之的《兰亭集序》。曲水流觞是旧时三月上巳节的一种饮酒习俗。三月三上巳日被认为是古代民间消除灾祸、祈愿吉福的日子。这一天，人们都去河边清洗身体以求消除凶疾。

The idiom, Qu Shui Liu Shang, with the meaning of drinking wine and composing poetry beside a meandering stream. It is originated from *Preface to the Collection of Poems Composed at the Orchid Pavilion* by the famous calligrapher Wang Xizhi. It refers to a traditional drinking custom during the Shangsi Festival in March. The third day of the third month in the lunar calendar was considered a day for the ancient people to eliminate disasters and pray for good luck. On this day, people went to the riverbank to wash their bodies in order to ward off diseases.

　　曲水流觞是上巳节派生出来的一种民俗活动，"觞"是古代盛酒的器皿，通常为木制，小而轻，底部有托，可浮于水面。曲水流觞指一群人围坐在弯曲回折的溪水边，将酒杯置于水的上游，任其顺着曲折的水流缓缓漂浮，酒杯漂到谁的跟前，谁就取杯饮酒。如此循环往复，直到尽兴为止。

Qu Shui Liu Shang is a folk activity derived from the traditional festival of Shangsi. "Shang" refers to the vessel used to hold wine in ancient times, usually made of wood, small and light, with a bottom holder that can float on the water surface. Qu Shui Liu Shang refers to a group of people sitting around a winding and bending stream, placing wine glasses upstream and letting them slowly float along the twists and turns of the water flow. Whoever the wine glass floats to takes the glass and drinks. It continues until everyone is satisfied.

历史上最有名的一次曲水流觞活动，就属东晋王羲之的兰亭集会了。公元353年三月初三，时任会稽内史的王羲之与包括谢安在内的41位朋友一起前往兰亭曲水流觞、饮酒赋诗，成为流传至今的一段佳话和儒风雅俗。按照古俗，王羲之等人围坐在兰亭清澈的溪水边，约定酒杯在谁面前打转或停下，谁就得即兴赋诗，不然就得罚酒三杯。据记载，在这次游戏中，作诗两篇者11人，作诗一篇者15人，另外有16人因为作诗无果，各自罚酒三杯。正是乘此酒兴，王羲之为诗集作序，成就了举世闻名的《兰亭集序》。王羲之被后人尊为"书圣"，兰亭也成为书法圣地。

The most famous event of Qu Shui Liu Shang in history is the Orchid Pavilion gathering of Wang Xizhi in the Eastern Jin Dynasty. On the third day of lunar March of 353 AD, Wang Xizhi, who was then the internal envoy of Kuaiji, went to Orchid Pavilion with 41 friends including Xie An, to drink, compose poems and have a good time, becoming a well-known story and promoting Confucian values of elegance and propriety to this day. According to ancient customs, Wang Xizhi and his friends sat around the clear stream at Orchid Pavilion

图37 绍兴兰亭 郑红莲摄 Shaoxing Orchid Pavilion PHOTO: Z.H.L.

and agreed that whoever the wine cup passed to had to compose a poem, or else they would be punished by drinking three cups of wine. According to the records, among the participants, 11 composed two poems, 15 composed one poem, and the remaining 16 were penalized for failing to compose a poem by drinking three cups of wine each. It was on this occasion that Wang Xizhi, inspired by the wine, composed a preface for the poetry collection, creating the world-renowned *Preface to the Collection of Poems Composed at the Orchid Pavilion*. Wang Xizhi was later revered as the "saint of calligraphy", and Orchid Pavilion became a sacred place for calligraphy.

这次兰亭集会突出饮酒赏景、赋诗作文，为三月三的民俗赋予了新意。上巳赋诗的习俗由此而起，盛传不衰，甚至东传到日本。如在公元958年，日本福冈县太宰府天满宫，就效仿兰亭永和盛会，举办了"曲水宴"。1981年夏历三月初三，江浙沪两省一市著名的书法家共27人集会兰亭，倡议建立兰亭书会。1985年，确立每年夏历三月初三为绍兴市书法节，把这一会稽儒风发扬光大。从此，每到这一天，中外书法家、书法爱好者，多在兰亭聚会，仿照当年永和盛事，曲水流觞，饮酒赋诗，泼墨挥毫，交流书艺。

The Orchid Pavilion Gathering, which highlighted drinking wine and appreciating the scenery, as well as writing poetry and essays, gave new meaning to the folk customs of the third day of the third lunar month. The custom of composing poetry on the occasion of the Double Third Festival originated from this event, and has been passed down through the ages, even spreading to Japan. In 958 AD, for example, the Tenman Palace, Dazai Prefecture in Fukuoka, Japan, held a "drinking wine and composing poetry banquet" modeled on the Orchid Pavilion Gathering. In 1981, 27 well-known calligraphers from Jiangsu, Zhejiang and Shanghai gathered at Orchid Pavilion to establish the Calligraphy Society of Orchid Pavilion. In 1985, the Shaoxing Calligraphy Festival was established on the third day of the third lunar month every year, in order to promote the literary traditions of Kuaiji. Since then, on this day, calligraphers and enthusiasts of calligraphy from China and abroad gathered at Orchid Pavilion to drink wine, write poetry, splash ink, and exchange literary skills in emulation of the grand event at Yonghe Period.

水龙会
Water Dragon Association for Firefighting

　　防火灾，保一方平安，明清时期，绍兴各村落都置木制水龙，并成立水龙会。在火灾时，水龙奔赴现场扑救。水龙会为了加强对"龙兵们"的训练，常备不懈，使救火龙拉得出、用得上，每年农历六月廿三日，俗传为火神菩萨生日，举行赛龙会，又叫"分龙口"。火神以火为灾，人们以"水龙"抗御。也有一说，古人以为龙主水，而盛夏常有"夏雨隔牛背"的现象，传说龙的上司这天命令下属各自分头行雨，以便"察看而治之"，由此有"分龙"之说。"分龙口"可以说是绍兴人结合地方传统节日开展的消防演习活动，主要是通过竞技让水龙会之间进行较量和比赛实力，是一项带有传统体育特色的群体竞技项目。

　　Fire prevention is important for safety. In the Ming and Qing dynasties, every village in Shaoxing had a wooden water dragon and established a Water Dragon Association for firefighting. During a fire, the water dragon rushed to the scene to put out the fire. To enhance the training of the dragon troops, the Water Dragon Association was always prepared to ensure the water dragon could be used when needed. Every year on the 23rd day of the sixth lunar month, which is commonly known as the birthday of the Bodhisattva of Fire, a dragon boat race, also known as "Fen Long Kou" was held. The God of Fire caused disasters with fire and people defended against them with water dragons. Some people believe that the ancient Chinese thought that dragons were masters of water, and in midsummer, there were often thunderstorms as if dragons ordered their subordinates to rain. It was said that this was done to "observe and handle". Hence, the phrase "Fen Long" was derived. "Fen Long Kou" can be considered as a firefighting demonstration activity that Shaoxing people developed based on local traditional festivals. Through competition and strength testing in the form of a sports event, it is a traditional group competitive project.

"水龙"是旧时绍兴城乡普遍使用的一种木制杠杆式消防器具，其形状像特大号的腰圆木水桶，桶的中间装有一个压水器具，一支圆木杠杆横贯其上，左右按压杠杆，由"龙头"手执铜瞄子，用大拇指捺住瞄子口，等到水压增至一定程度就迅速移开拇指，水便从铜制龙头嘴激射而出。比赛胜负取决于射程远近。整个过程不仅考验关键的"把瞄子"的技巧，也检阅了团队的体力状况、动作敏捷和配合默契的程度。

Water Dragon is a wooden lever-type fire extinguisher commonly used in urban and rural areas of Shaoxing in ancient times. Its shape is like an oversized waist wooden water bucket, with a water pressure device in the middle, and a round wooden lever across it. The lever can be pressed left and right. The dragon head holds a copper sight, presses the thumb on the sight port, and when the water pressure increases to a certain degree, quickly removes the thumb, and water will shoot out from the mouth of the copper head. The winner of the contest is determined by the range of the water. The whole process not only tests the key skill of aiming, but also examines the team's physical condition, agility and cooperation.

在干燥的夏季到来之前，进行一次灭火救灾演习，既起到了防患于未然的作用，也使群众得到了娱乐。大家通过比赛，切磋了技艺，增进了友谊。"分龙口"是一种寓教于乐的传统体育竞技活动，深受绍兴老百姓的喜欢。民国期间，绍兴城区有义龙局20所，水龙会员1200人左右。农村的青壮男子更是以参加"水龙会"为荣。水龙会作为民间的一种自发消防组织，对保护当地百姓的生命财产安全，发挥过积极的作用。

Before the dry summer season arrived, a fire-fighting and rescue drill was carried out to prevent any potential disaster, which also provided entertainment for the masses. Through the competition, participants were able to showcase their skills and develop friendships. "Fen Long Kou" was a traditional sports competition that combines education with entertainment, and it was very popular among the people of Shaoxing. During the Republic of China period, there were about 20 dragon bureaus in the urban area of Shaoxing, with around 1,200 members of the water dragon association. Participating in the water dragon association was considered a great honor for the young men in rural areas. As a self-organized firefighting organization in the folk, the water dragon association played an active role in protecting the lives and property of the local people.

现在没有哪个村再用水龙来灭火了，它已被现代化的高压水泵代替，而村民保存下来的水龙，则成了历史的见证。近年来，随着非物质文化遗产保护的开展，绍兴的一些乡镇在一些旅游点恢复了"分龙口"这个传统的体育竞技项目，组织村民进行表演，不仅丰富了旅游项目，也愉悦了群众的精神文化生活。2008年11月，水龙会被列入第二批绍兴市非物质文化遗产名录。

Currently no village uses water dragons to extinguish fires anymore. The old method has been replaced by modern high-pressure water pumps, and the water dragons preserved by the villagers have become a witness to history. In recent years, with the development of intangible cultural heritage protection, some towns in Shaoxing have revived the tradition of "Fen Long Kou" as a sports competition in some tourist sites, organizing villagers to perform. This not only enriches the tourism industry and but also enhances the spiritual and cultural life of the people. In November 2008, The Water Dragon Festival was listed as the second batch of intangible cultural heritage in Shaoxing City.

施茶会
Tea Offering Association

几百年来，施茶作为一种广为称赞的传统习俗流行于绍兴各地，民间将其组织称为施茶会。为了让路人可以解渴歇脚，施茶地点一般都设在交通要道，并建有一个简单的亭子，以躲避雨淋日晒。亭子两侧放有长条石凳，人们称其为茶亭。

For hundreds of years, tea offering has been a widely praised traditional custom in various parts of Shaoxing, and its organization was known as tea offering association among people. Tea offering locations were usually set up at transportation junctions to quench the thirst and rest of passersby, and a simple pavilion, called tea pavilion, was built to provide shelter from the rain and sun. Long stone benches were placed on both sides of the pavilion for people to sit on.

绍兴最早的茶亭是建于明万历年间的城东广福庵茶亭。到嘉庆年间，绍兴境内有十多处茶亭。这些茶亭，大多地处要道，远离村庄，所以长年施茶。茶亭的开支除了临时募捐外，多数靠田产收入，有的田产是个人捐赠，有的是用募捐款项购置。例如，天王寺茶亭的20亩田产，是由该寺僧人捐献。田产收入用于每年茶亭的茶叶、柴火等开支。捐赠者的姓名和捐赠金额以及田亩数量，均刻在立于茶亭内的石碑上，既是对捐赠者善举的赞许，也体现施茶会成员的清正。

The earliest tea pavilion in Shaoxing was Guangfu Temple Tea Pavilion in the eastern city, built during the Wanli period of the Ming Dynasty. By the Jiaqing period, there were more than ten tea pavilions in Shaoxing. Most of these tea pavilions were located on major highways and far from villages, so they served tea all year round. In addition to temporary donations, the tea pavilions' expenses were mostly covered by income from land. Some of the land was donated by individuals, while others were purchased with donated funds. For example, the 20-acre land owned by the Tianwang Temple Tea Pavilion was donated by monks in the temple. The income from the land was used to cover the annual expenses of the tea pavilion, such as tea leaves and firewood. The names of donors and the amount of their donations and land were all engraved on the stone tablets inside the tea pavilion, praising their contributions and reflecting the integrity of the tea offering association members.

施茶会的成员虽然没有一分钱工资，但工作都很认真负责。到商铺、住户人家劝募茶资时，都很耐心热情，捐募以自愿为原则，数额不论多少。有的人手头一时无现金，也可捐柴火、茶叶。每年秋后，施茶会都把一年的收支账目公之于众。由于账目清晰、做事透明，施茶会在老百姓心中有较高的威信。

The members of the tea offering association may not receive any earnings, but they were all very diligent and responsible in their work. When visiting shops and households to solicit tea funds, they were patient and enthusiastic. Donations for tea offering were voluntary and the amount of money did not matter. Some people may not have cash on hand, but they can also donate firewood or tea leaves. After each year's harvest season, the tea offering association makes its income and expenditure account public. Due to clear accounting and transparent operations, the tea offering association has a high level of credibility among the people.

民国时期，绍兴城里的福缘茶会比较出名，其成员大多是月池坊、斜桥直街的商户。福缘茶会在每年农历六月十九专门在香炉峰脚下南镇殿前设点施茶，还有仁丹、十滴水等降暑药物免费发送给上山的香客。开元寺东首的同善局，每年夏天也都在开元寺对面的广场上设大棚子施茶，每天都有上千个来往的茶客。

During the era of the Republic of China, the Fu Yuan Tea Club in Shaoxing City was quite famous, with most of its members being merchants from Yuechi Lane and Xieqiao Straight Street. Fu Yuan Tea Club set up a tea station in front of the Nanzhen Temple at the foot of the Xianglu Peak on the 19th day of the sixth lunar month every year, serving tea and distributing free heat-relief medicine such as Rendan and 10 drops to the pilgrims going up the mountain. Additionally, during every summer, the Tongshan Bureau on the east of the Kaiyuan Temple also set up a tea offering station on the square opposite the temple, serving thousands of tea lovers every day.

施茶会在民国时数量最多，当时绍兴各地加起来共有50多个。其中影响较大的，有平水等施茶会。平水地处会稽山麓，一直是茶叶的集散地，一年到头，来平水买卖茶叶的客商很多。以前平水大多为山道，都只能靠双脚步行。夏天天气炎热，当地的茶商和热心人士，出钱办起施茶会。从清晨到傍晚，在平水镇上行人必经的茶亭施茶。不仅路人可以取茶饮用，附近的农民在田头劳动口渴时，也可以喝茶解渴。一直到秋天凉爽下来，才停止施茶。

During the period of the Republic of China, there were over 50 tea-offering associations in Shaoxing, with the largest number in history. One of the more influential association was located in Pingshui, which was situated at the foot of Kuaijishan and served as a hub for tea collection and distribution throughout the year, attracting a large number of tea merchants. Pingshui was mostly connected by mountainous paths in the past, which could only be traveled on foot. In the hot summer weather, local tea merchants and enthusiastic individuals would sponsor a tea offering association that lasted from morning to evening at the tea house in Pingshui town, which was a must-visit spot for passersby. Not only could pedestrians take tea to drink, but nearby farmers laboring in the fields could also take a break to quench their thirst. The tea offering activity only ceased when the weather cooled down in the fall.

施茶作为一种传统的施善举动，在绍兴地区广为流传。如今，在夏天仍然可以见到各种自发组织的免费供应茶水的地方。

As a traditional act of benevolence, tea offering is widely spread in Shaoxing. Nowadays, various spontaneously organized places of free tea supply can still be seen in summer.

Chapter 5 第五章

生产商贸篇
Production, Commerce and Trade

养蚕
Sericulture

　　在绍兴，养蚕具有悠久的历史。早在新石器时代，越人就开始养蚕，河姆渡遗址出土文物上的蚕纹雕刻可以为证。据史料记载，从越王勾践把"劝农桑"作为国策，越地的采桑养蚕生产技艺和蚕事习俗延续了很久的时间，特别是在绍兴诸暨养蚕成为一大农事。到唐朝时，诸暨几乎家家户户养蚕织丝，他们所生产的蚕丝作为贡品年年敬贡朝廷。明朝的《嵊县志》也有"农桑衣食之本"的记载。清朝时，新昌、诸暨、嵊县以及绍兴南部山区都有着众多的养蚕户，桑树成林。在两千年的养蚕历史中，绍兴形成了特有的养蚕习俗。

In Shaoxing, sericulture has a long history. As early as the Neolithic Age, the Yue people began to raise silkworms, as evidenced by the silkworm pattern carvings on relics unearthed in Hemudu Site. According to historical records, since the Yue King Goujian made "promoting agriculture and sericulture" as a national policy, the sericulture production techniques and customs have been continuing for a long time in the Yue area, especially in Zhuji, Shaoxing, where sericulture has become a major agricultural activity. By the Tang Dynasty, almost every household in Zhuji raised silkworms and wove silk, and the silk they produced was presented as tribute to the court every year. The Ming Dynasty's *Sheng County Annals* also recorded that "agriculture and sericulture are the foundation of clothing and food". During the Qing Dynasty, there were numerous silkworm farmers in Xinchang, Zhuji, Shengxian, and the southern mountainous area of Shaoxing, and mulberry trees grew into forests. In the two thousand years of sericulture history, Shaoxing has formed unique sericulture customs.

图38　蚕房 郑红莲摄 Silkworm room PHOTO: Z.H.L.

祭祀蚕神是绍兴养蚕的一件大事。蚕神，也叫蚕花娘娘，"马头娘娘"。蚕花娘娘是一位美丽的女仙子，她身穿红衣，头戴蚕茧，手持橄榄枝，是蚕茧的守护神和保佑者。在每年的蚕花娘娘诞辰日、蚕茧出丝日等重要节日，人们会在神坛前燃香、献花，向蚕花娘娘祈求健康、平安和产业兴旺。

Worshiping the Silkworm Goddess is a significant event for

sericulture in Shaoxing. The Silkworm Goddess, also known as the Silkworm Flower Goddess or the "Horse-Headed Goddess", is a beautiful female fairy. She wears a red dress, a silk cocoon on her head, and holds an olive branch. She is the protector and guardian of silkworm cocoons. On important festivals such as the birthday of the Silkworm Flower Goddess and the day when silkworm cocoons produce silk, people burn incense and offer flowers at the altar to pray for health, peace, and prosperous sericulture.

相传，南宋年间，当时的绍兴地区因为盐业兴盛而富庶，当地百姓都以养蚕织丝为生，蚕花娘娘也就被尊为蚕茧的守护神。而在这个蚕业兴盛的年代，有一个朴实善良的女子，她每天都带着自己的马去干活，务农的同时也来祭拜蚕花娘娘，她非常虔诚。有一年，她的马突然死去，女子十分悲伤。在她悲痛万分的时候，蚕花娘娘在她梦中出现了，告诉她马的灵魂已经逝去了。然而，蚕花娘娘也告诉她，在这个特殊的祭拜日，马的灵魂会重归马体，重返人间，因此女子要准备一些饲料，等待马头娘娘的归来。

According to legend, during the Southern Song Dynasty, the Shaoxing area was prosperous due to the thriving salt industry. The local people made a living by raising silkworms and weaving silk, and the Silkworm Flower Goddess was revered as the guardian goddess of the silkworm cocoons. In this prosperous era of sericulture, there was a simple and kind woman who went to work every day with her horse. She farmed and also came to worship the Silkworm Flower Goddess very devoutly. One year, her horse suddenly died, and the woman was very sad. In her grief, the Silkworm Flower Goddess appeared in her dream, telling her that the horse's soul already passed away. However, the Silkworm Flower Goddess also told her that on this special day of worship, the horse's soul would return to the horse's body and return to the human world, so the woman should prepare some feed and wait for the return of the Horse-Headed Goddess.

女子认真地置办好马儿最爱的食物，当作重要的客人那样恭敬迎接。当天晚上，蚕花娘娘的祭拜活动结束后，女子才收工回家、生火、煮饭。就在她开心地吃东西的时候，一个她不认识的中年妇女出现了，自称是马头娘娘，自己是因为蚕花娘娘的祝福而赐予了新生的。她为蚕茧业运送了许多蚕茧和蚕豆，受到当地百姓的爱戴。而马头娘娘就被认为是这匹马的化身，成为蚕茧业的重要守护神。

The woman carefully prepared the favorite food of her horse, welcoming it respectfully like an important guest. It wasn't until after the ceremony to worship the Silkworm Flower Goddess was over that night that the woman went home to start a fire and cook her meal. Just as she was happily eating, an unfamiliar middle-aged woman appeared, claiming to be Horse-Headed Goddess and that her new life was granted by the blessing of the Silkworm Flower Goddess. She delivered many silkworm cocoons and beans for the local sericulture, earning the love of the people there. Horse-Headed Goddess was regarded as the incarnation of the horse and became an important guardian deity of the sericulture industry.

另一种说法是，马头娘娘是蚕茧业的一位得力助手，她拥有一匹神马，马背上坐着御史，每年检查蚕茧销售利润。在一次检查中，御史对马头娘娘和她的马产生了兴趣，就要求马头娘娘献出马作为礼物。然而，马头娘娘不忍心将自己的伴侣送走，就干脆将自己化作了一匹神马来献礼。御史大为惊异，就决定尊她为马头娘娘，将她作为蚕茧业的守护神继续保护着蚕农和蚕茧生产。

Another version of the story is that Horse-Headed Goddess was originally a capable assistant in the silk industry. She owned a divine horse that carried a magistrate who inspected the profits from silk sales each year. During one inspection, the magistrate became interested in the assistant and her horse, and asked her to present the horse as a gift. However, the assistant did not want to part with her companion, and thus transformed herself into a divine horse to offer as a gift. The magistrate was amazed and decided to honor her as Horse-Headed Goddess, the goddess who protected the silk farmers and silk production.

无论马头娘娘的起源如何，她都成为了蚕茧业的重要信仰对象之一，为当地农民和商贾带来了祈福和助力。到了今天，当地民众在蚕花娘娘和马头娘娘的圣诞日举行的祭祀活动也更加隆重和热闹。历史上，绍兴的蚕茧业得到了皇帝和官方的重视，称为"蚕都"，而蚕花娘娘也成为了地方文化里不可缺少的一部分，为当地人民提供了重要的精神支持。

No matter what the origin of Horse-Headed Goddess is, she has become one of the important objects of worship for silk reeling industry, bringing blessings and benefits to local farmers and merchants. Today, the local people hold more grand and lively sacrificial activities on the birthday of the Silkworm Flower Goddess and Horse-Headed Goddess. In history, the sericulture industry in Shaoxing received attention from the emperor and officials, and Shaoxing was known as the Silk Capital, while the Silkworm Flower Goddess has also become an indispensable part of the local culture, providing important spiritual support for the local people.

诸暨一带，元宵佳节还有"抢蚕花"的习俗。就是在元宵舞龙环节，人们争抢掉落在地上的龙须、龙鳞，然后把它们贴在蚕房的墙上，认为可以保蚕房平安。有些地方是用糯米粉制作"蚕茧果"祭祀龙王，俗称"龙王斋"。诸暨姚江、湄池等地，每年农历二月十三日，还举行"踢蚕花"庙会。养蚕户聚集在祠堂，点香燃烛，摆上贡品，进行祭祀，以求养蚕顺利。

In Zhuji, there was a custom called snatching silkworm flowers during the Lantern Festival. During the dragon dance, people competed to grab the dragon's beard and scales that fell on the ground, and then pasted them on the walls of the silkworm room, believing that this can keep the silkworm room safe. In some places, a sticky rice ball called Dragon Paste was made to worship the Dragon King, also known as Dragon King's Fasting. In places such as Yaojiang and Meichi in Zhuji, a temple fair called kicking silkworm flowers was held on February 13th of the calendar second month. Silkworm farmers gathered in the ancestral temple, lighted incense and candles, offered tribute, and prey for smooth silkworm rearing.

养蚕过程中还有很多禁忌。例如，属鼠的妇女不能养蚕；外来客人和产妇不能进出蚕房；养蚕妇女不能涂抹胭脂香粉，不能抽烟喝酒，不能吃姜蒜及重口味的食物。此外，蚕房要保持绝对安静，忌讳拍门敲窗等弄出很大声响的行为。绍兴俗称蚕作茧为"上山"，这时，旁边必须放置镜子、剪刀等物，认为可以辟邪驱毒。现在绍兴已实施现代化科学养蚕模式，以前养蚕过程中的一些含有迷信色彩的旧俗已经消失不见。

There were many taboos in the process of raising silkworms. For example, women born in the Year of the Rat cannot raise silkworms. Guests and puerpera cannot enter or leave the silkworm room. Women raising silkworms cannot apply rouge, powders, smoke or drink alcohol, eat ginger, garlic or heavy-flavored food. In addition, the silkworm room must be kept quiet, and it was taboo to slam doors or windows or make loud noises. Silkworm cocoon production was known as going up the mountain in Shaoxing. During this period, a mirror, scissors, and other items must be placed nearby, which was believed to dispel evil and drive away toxins. In modern times, Shaoxing has implemented a modern scientific silkworm-rearing model, and some of the old customs containing superstitions in the past have disappeared.

稻作文化
Rice-Planting Culture

　　绍兴地区的稻作生产可以追溯到7000年前，这里是世界和亚洲水稻栽培的起源地之一。根据出土的原始痕迹可以证明，越地古代的人们已经掌握了从耕种、种植、收割、保存种子到烹饪米饭的全套稻作生产和加工工艺流程。越地的稻作文化既有河姆渡文化的基础，也融合了良渚文化的影响。传说帝尧时期，禹受舜命令以开辟水道的方式治理洪水13年，三次造访家门口都没有进去，他完成了溪流整治的任务，之后在越北平原领导人们开垦土地、种植水稻，并且拓展到随陵陆地耕种，使水稻种植范围得到了扩大。

　　Rice-planting culture in the Shaoxing region can be traced back to 7,000 years ago and it is one of the origins of rice cultivation in the world. According to excavated primitive traces, the ancient people in the Yue area had mastered the entire set of rice farming and processing procedures, from cultivation, planting, harvesting, seed preservation, to cooking rice. The rice culture of the Yue area has its foundation in the Hemudu culture and also incorporates the influence of the Liangzhu culture. Legend has it that during the reign of Emperor Yao, Yu was commanded by Shun to manage floods for 13 years through opening waterways. Despite visiting his doorstep three times, he did not enter.

He completed the task of stream rectification and then led the people to cultivate land and plant rice in the northern plains of Yue, expanding rice cultivation to the land of Suiling.

在春秋战国时期，绍兴曾是越国的首都，稻作文化在这里得以传承与发展，比其他地区更加繁荣丰富。根据出土的农具考证，从用途上可以分为起土、除草和收割等三类，这些工具能够深耕、增厚熟土层，实现精细化耕作，提高耕种效率。有些工具则用于修建水利设施、开凿沟渠、施肥灌溉等，为农作物的生长提供保障，促进了稻作生产技术的广度和深度发展，提高了生产率，奠定了技术发展的基础。到了唐代后期，插秧法被广泛应用于水稻种植，这种方法能够调节季节，充分利用阳光和温度，促进单位面积产量提高，标志着水稻栽培技术的逐渐完善。

During the Spring and Autumn period and the Warring States period, Shaoxing served as the capital of the Yue State, where the rice-planting culture was inherited and developed, and it was more prosperous and abundant than other regions. According to the archaeological evidence of farming tools, they can be divided into three categories: land preparation, weeding, and harvesting. These tools can deeply till and thicken the fertile soil layer, achieve fine farming, and improve farming efficiency. Some tools were used for building water conservancy facilities, digging ditches, fertilizing and irrigating, providing guarantees for crop growth, promoting the development of rice-planting technology in breadth and depth, and improving productivity, laying the foundation for technological development. By the late Tang Dynasty, the transplanting method was widely applied to rice cultivation. This method could adjust the season, make full use of sunlight and temperature, promote the increase of unit yield, and mark the gradual improvement of rice cultivation technology.

图39　稻穗 郑红莲摄
Ears of rice PHOTO: Z.H.L.

越地先民在历经沧海桑田的变迁后，绍兴的水稻生产占据了人民生活和生产的重要地位。这对于稻区的社会生活的方方面面都产生了影响。越地的民间文化传承，是由一代又一代先民的辛勤劳动和聪明才智创造出来的。它反映了当时当地人民的价值观念、审美情趣、宗教意识、俗神信仰等心态文化，并包含了涵盖广泛的稻作文化系统的范围。这些民间文化还体现了人民的传统生活习惯和生活方式。

After going through the vicissitudes of history, the indigenous people of the Yue area have come to rely on rice-planting culture in Shaoxing as an important aspect of their lives and production, which has had an impact on all aspects of their social life in the rice-growing regions. The folk culture of the Yue people has been passed down from generation to generation through their hard work and cleverness. It reflects the attitudes and cultural traits of the local people at that time, including their values, aesthetic taste, religious consciousness, and belief in folk deities, and encompasses a wide range of the rice-planting culture system. The folk culture of rice-planting also embodies the traditional way of life and habits of the people.

在农村地区，人们有许多祭祀活动和习俗，其中包括敬拜土地神，牵引迎春牛，春分祈愿迎接新年，清明时节祈求五谷丰收和祭祀祖先，立夏时开启种田季节的大门，夏至时祭奉田神，农历十月尝新米以庆祝丰收，在遇到旱灾、虫灾等的困难时，进行祭祀仪式以驱除灾难。农家还习惯在新购置的农具上刻写字号，旨在表现户主对丰收的祈望和期望，字号内容一般针对该农具的使用功能。

In rural areas, people have many worship activities and customs, including worshiping the God of Land, leading the Spring Ox to welcome the new year, praying for a bountiful harvest during the Spring Equinox, performing ancestral worship during the Qingming Festival, opening the door to the farming season during the Beginning of Summer, offering sacrifices to the Field God on the Summer Solstice, tasting new rice in October to celebrate the harvest, and conducting worship rituals to ward off droughts, pestilence, and other afflictions. Rural families also have a tradition of inscribing characters on newly purchased farming tools, expressing the head of the household's hopes and expectations for a bountiful harvest. The characters are generally tailored to reflect the tool's intended use.

绍兴的稻作文化不仅在古代文献和考古发掘中得到了有力印证，而且从上世纪80年代以来的民族民间艺术资源和全市"非遗"普查中所采集的大量口头文学资料中，得到了直接或者间接的证实。这些口头文学资料包括瑰丽多彩的稻作起源神话、神奇的稻米传说、有趣的稻米故事，以及大量的歌谣、谚语等，充分体现了稻区民众的社会生活方式和传统思想理念，反映了绍兴民众温和善良、思想丰富、细腻的性格和情感。绍兴的稻作文化具有传承价值、史学价值、经济价值、人文价值、民俗学价值以及学术研究价值，是一份极为珍贵的非物质文化遗产。

The rice-planting culture in Shaoxing is not only strongly corroborated by ancient literature and archaeological excavation, but also directly or indirectly confirmed by a wealth of oral literature resources collected from ethnic and folk arts resources since the 1980s and the city-wide intangible cultural heritage survey. These oral literary materials include vivid and colorful myths about the origin of rice cultivation, fascinating legends about rice, interesting stories about rice, as well as a large quantity of folk songs, proverbs, etc., fully reflecting the social life style and traditional ideological concepts of local people in rice-planting areas and reflecting the gentle, kind, rich in thought, and emotional character and temperament of Shaoxing residents. The rice-planting culture in Shaoxing has inheritance value, historical and academic value, economic value, cultural value, folklore value, and academic research value, making it an extremely precious intangible cultural heritage.

幌子招牌青龙匾
Signboards, Banners and Dragon Plaques

　　幌子、招牌和青龙匾是旧时绍兴店铺招揽顾客的主要宣传手段，路人只要看到它们，就马上知道这家店铺经营的商品。积年累月，挂幌子、挂招牌和安放青龙匾，成了绍兴城里沿街店铺的一种商贸习俗。

　　Signboards, banners, and dragon plaques were the primary means of attracting customers for business in old Shaoxing. Passers-by could immediately recognize the type of goods sold when they saw them. Over the years, hanging banners, putting up signboards, and displaying dragon plaques have become a commercial tradition for stores along the streets of Shaoxing city.

　　幌子又称帷幔，是一种用来展示商店售卖物品或提供服务项目的标志，即古时店铺门外的招牌或标志物。幌子作为中国的一种商业民俗，其起源可以追溯到战国时期，最初专指酒店门前用来招揽顾客的布帘。这些布帘被缀在竿顶上，悬于门前，以吸引游客，也被称为"幌子"。唐代陆龟蒙的《和袭美初冬偶作》中便有"小垆低幌还遮掩，酒滴灰香似去年"一句，幌子指的就是酒店门前的招牌。后来这个词逐渐引申至凡商店招揽顾客门面上展示的标志都被统称为"幌子"。绍兴的街头巷尾，都挂有各式招幌，一块一尺多宽，二尺来长的黄色或者青色的布帘上，写着大大的文字，顾客一看便有了消费的冲动。

A hanging signboard, also known as a curtain, is a type of logo or symbol used to display items for sale or services offered by a shop, often seen in front of shop entrances. This tradition originated in the Warring States Period and originally referred to the cloth curtains used outside of hotels to attract customers. These curtains were hung on poles, suspended outside of entrances, to attract tourists. Later on, the term hanging signboard gradually extended to cover all kinds of signs displayed on the front of stores to attract customers. In famous shopping districts of Shaoxing, various signboards of different colors and sizes can be seen

图40 绍兴街头的幌子
郑红莲摄 Signboards on the streets of Shaoxing PHOTO: Z.H.L.

hanging in the streets, with large letters written on yellow or blue curtains that are over one foot wide and about two feet long, inducing customers to purchase by just a glance.

在绍兴这座手工业见长的城市，繁华城里，各类商铺、饭馆、酒肆林立，有各式各样的招牌争奇斗艳，吸引着人们的眼球，招牌不仅体现着绍兴城的烟火味，还凝聚着书法艺术和设计上的巧思。绍兴的招牌以艺术性极强和鲜明的特点，被誉为"东方招牌艺术的珍品"和"江南招牌之最"。例如"文信阁"招牌是一个木质结构的大屏风式标志，上绘有"文信阁"三个大字和各种艺术图案，这个招牌在绍兴市最为著名。据说，文信阁的主人每次换招牌，都会专门请书法家和画家制定设计方案，以展现其门店的地位和文化内涵。

In the bustling city of Shaoxing, known for its proficiency in handicrafts, various shops, restaurants, and pubs can be found lining the streets, all with eye-catching signs vying for people's attention. These signs not only reflect the lively atmosphere of the city, but also showcase the art of calligraphy and clever design. Shaoxing banners are renowned for their artistic qualities and distinctiveness, and are considered to be "treasures of eastern sign art" and "the finest examples of sign art in Jiangnan". For instance, the banner for Wenxin Pavilion is a wooden screen-like structure, with the three characters Wenxin Pavilion and various artistic designs painted on it. This banner is one of the most famous in Shaoxing city. It is said that the owner of Wenxin Pavilion always hires calligraphers and painters to create a custom design for their banner every time they change it, in order to convey the status and cultural connotation of their storefront.

"金稻荷"招牌则是以金色的稻穗和绿色的荷叶为主题，表现了农荣商显的时代特征。"双龙"招牌由两只龙头和龙眼组成，寓意着商铺生意兴旺，财源广进。"天平斧行"招牌以一个手持天平秤和斧头的小孩为主题，表现了主营砍柴采伐和木器销售的特点。"梦松堂"招牌是一个四角梦松纸的标志，上面印有门洞镶嵌古玉的装饰，表现了梦松堂的文化底蕴和专业性。这些绍兴旧时的招牌不仅是商店标志，更成为城市文化艺术的展示。虽然已经过去了很多年，但这些招牌仍然是文化遗产中的珍品，也是深受人们喜爱和追捧的历史文化。

The banner of Gold Rice and Lotus is themed with golden rice ears and green lotus leaves, showcasing the characteristics of the era of combined agriculture and commerce. The banner of Twin Dragons consists of two dragon heads and eyes, wishing the shop business prosperity and financial abundance. The banner of Tianping Woodcutter features a child holding a balance scale and a hatchet, representing the main business of woodcutting and wooden goods sales. The banner of Dream Pines Hall is a logo of a square dream pine paper with decorations of ancient jade inlaid in the doorways, demonstrating the cultural heritage and professionalism of Dream Pines Hall. These old banners in Shaoxing are not only store logos, but also an exhibition of urban culture and art. Although many years have passed, these banners are still treasures in local cultural heritage and are deeply loved and pursued by people as historical and cultural relics.

青龙匾是旧时南方地区流行的一种广告牌，通常用于在店堂内表明经营范围和商品特征。青龙牌通常位于曲尺形柜台的终端，它是店面装潢的重要组成部分之一。青龙牌上通常写着四个斗大的汉字，这些汉字表明了店铺的业务性质。不同的行业通常使用不同的字样来表明自己的业务性质，如米行用的字样有"民食为天""长路粮食"，水果店用的字样为"南北果品"，调味品店用的字样为"调和鼎乃"，锡箔庄则用的字样为"洪武遗风"等。

The Dragon Plaque was a type of advertisement popular in southern China in the past. It was usually used to indicate the scope of business and characteristics of the goods in the store. The Dragon Plaque was usually located at the end of the curved counter, and it was an important part of the store's decoration. There are usually four large Chinese characters written on the Dragon Plaque, which indicate the nature of the store's business. Different industries typically use different characters to indicate their business nature. The Chinese characters used in rice shops include "民食为天" (the people's food is heaven) and "长路粮食" (food for the long journey). The characters used in fruit shops include "南北果品" (fruit from the north and south). The characters used in seasoning shops include "调和鼎乃" (the harmony of flavors). The characters used in a tin foil shop are "洪武遗风" (the legacy of the Hongwu era).

青龙匾在绍兴地区的酒店也很常见。这些青龙牌上的文字非常含蓄典雅，同时也别具一格。这些字样既生动有趣，又富含意义，如"太白遗风""刘伶停车""闻香下马""杏花深处""曲水流觞""斗酒百篇"等等。这些字样不仅让人一目了然地了解了店铺的业务性质，而且也很能引起人们的共鸣，激起他们探寻更多美好的体验的欲望。通常，在这些青龙牌的后面就会是顾客独酌或对饮的雅座所在。如今，绍兴咸亨酒店的布局就完全依照鲁迅笔下的描述，当街一个曲尺形的柜台，柜台顶端就竖有一块青龙匾，匾上写有"太白遗风"四个大字，来绍兴的游客仍可领略到咸亨酒店当年的风采。

The Dragon Plaque is also very common in hotels in Shaoxing. The wording on these plaques is very implicit and elegant, and at the same time unique. These phrases are both vivid and interesting, and rich in meaning, such as "the legacy of Li Bai" , "Liu Ling's parking", "dismounting to smell the fragrance" , "deep in the apricot blossom", "drinking and toasting by the winding river" , "a hundred poems on wine", and so on. These phrases not only enable people to understand the nature of the store's business at a glance, but also resonate with them, arousing their desire to explore more beautiful experiences. Typically, behind these Dragon Plaques are elegant seats for customers to drink alone or with companions. Today, the layout of the Xianheng Hotel in Shaoxing is completely in accordance with the description by Lu Xun, with a curved counter on the street, and a Dragon Plaque standing atop the counter with the phrase "the legacy of Li Bai" , allowing visitors to still experience the charm of the Xianheng Hotel of the past.

酒业会市
Wine Industry Fair

　　酒业会市，俗称"酒神会"，是绍兴独有的一种古越文化的印记，也是绍兴黄酒节习俗的前身。绍兴酿酒业自古以来十分发达，历史悠久，很早就出现"恭请酒菩萨"这种乡风习俗，旧时酿造者也只有完成这一风俗的程序，才会在心里面感到这一年的酿酒能平平安安、万事顺意。后来又逐步演变成以迎奉酒仙菩萨为主要内容的各类"酒神会"，从此奠定了绍兴酒文化史册中的一个重要民间习俗。

　　The wine industry fair, commonly known as the Wine God Festival, is a unique imprint of Shaoxing's Yue culture and the predecessor of the Shaoxing Huangjiu Festival customs. Shaoxing's wine-making industry has been well-developed since ancient times with a long history, and the custom of "inviting the wine Bodhisattva" has been around for a long time. In the past, only after completing this custom's procedure could the brewer feel that the year's brewing had been safe and smooth. Later, it gradually evolved into various Wine God Festival events, with the main focus being on welcoming and serving the Wine God Bodhisattva, thus laying an important folk custom in the chronicles of Shaoxing's wine culture history.

绍兴各地酿酒坊都会举行酒神会，但以绍兴东浦镇上的"酒神会"最出名。东浦镇位于绍兴越城区，以酿酒闻名。该镇形成于南宋，繁荣于明清，镇内河流纵横、户户通舟。当年的东浦沿河两岸店铺林立，其中光酒楼、酒店就有四五十家。自清代起，这里就开始形成每到冬季家家户户酿酒的习俗。20世纪30年代，东浦镇上大大小小的酒作坊有400多家。

Various breweries in Shaoxing hold wine deity ceremonies, but the Wine Deity Ceremony in Dongpu Town, Shaoxing, is the most famous. Dongpu Town is located in Yuecheng District of Shaoxing and is famous for its brewing. The town was formed in the Southern Song Dynasty and flourished in the Ming and Qing dynasties. The rivers run through the town and every household has a boat. Shops lined both sides of the river in Dongpu and more than forty or fifty restaurants and hotels could be found. Since the Qing Dynasty, it has been a custom for every household to brew wine in the winter. In the 1930s, there were more than 400 wine breweries large and small in Dongpu Town.

每年农历七月初六至初八的这三天中，东浦各酒坊都会举办"酒仙神诞庆神会"。最初，这些活动由民间酒坊单独举行，后来则由几个主要酒坊大户牵头举行迎神祭拜的活动。主要活动是迎奉酒仙菩萨。菩萨为女像，头挽发髻，身着唐代衣衫，两侧侍立两个僮儿，左边的手持酒耙，右边的手捧酒坛。

Every year from the 6th to the 8th day of the lunar calendar in July, various distilleries in Dongpu hold "Divine Ancestor Festival to celebrate the birth of the wine deity". Initially, these activities were held separately by folk distilleries, but later, several major distillery proprietors took the lead in organizing the worshiping and welcoming ceremony. The main activity is to worship the wine deity Bodhisattva. The Bodhisattva is a female statue with hair in a bun, dressed in Tang Dynasty clothes, and is flanked by two attendants, with one holding a wine rake and the other holding a wine jar.

1936年，绍兴地方乡绅陈子英为振兴东浦酿酒业，提议将酒神会改称"酒业会市"，举办会市邀请海内外酒商参加，并同时展示酒坊新生产的酒品。酒业会市改变了原先单一祭拜酒神的模式，而有文体活动、行业交流、产品推广、业务洽谈、沟通情况、扩展影响等方面的内容，成为绍兴黄酒业的一种展销集会，创新和提升了传统酒俗。

In 1936, Chen Ziying, a local gentry from Shaoxing, proposed to rename the Wine God Association to Wine Industry Fair in order to revitalize the Dongpu brewing industry. The fair invited wine merchants from home and abroad to attend, and also showcased the new wine products produced by the distillery. The Wine Industry Fair changed the previous single model of worship the Wine God, and included content such as cultural activities, industry exchanges, product promotion, business negotiations, communication, and expanding influence, becoming a promotional event for the Shaoxing yellow wine industry, innovating and improving traditional wine customs.

农历七月初六是酒业会市的第一天，东浦赏村戒定寺是主会场，寺前热闹非凡，各地善男信女和游客酒商纷至沓来，大家点烛

敬香，诵经念佛，人声鼎沸，昼夜不息。直到第二天（七月初七）
拂晓，庙祝为酒仙菩萨装扮一新，炮仗频频点燃，锣鼓唢呐齐鸣。
在村民们的簇拥下，酒仙菩萨塑像被送上神舟。舟上各种祭品齐
备，在烛光照耀下，香烟袅袅，突显仪式的庄重神圣。等到酒仙菩
萨安坐完毕，会市总指挥一声令下，各路乐队鼓乐齐奏，炮仗再次
鸣放。队伍分水陆二路行进，神州、龙船浩浩荡荡出发，所过之处
各村都在宽阔空地搭棚迎神，万人空巷恭候酒仙菩萨的到来，以求
得菩萨赐福。

The first day of the fair is on the sixth day of the lunar seventh
month. The main venue is the Jieding Temple in Dongpu Shangcun.
The front of the temple is bustling with activity. People from various
places, including devotees, tourists, and wine merchants, come in droves.
Everyone lights candles and incense, recites sutras and chants, and it is
noisy day and night. It continues until the dawn of the second day (July
7th) when the temple priest dresses up the Wine Immortal Bodhisattva
anew, sets off firecrackers, and the sound of gongs, drums, and suona
horn fills the air. With the crowd of villagers, the statue of the Wine
Immortal Bodhisattva is sent up to the divine ship. On the ship, all kinds
of sacrificial offerings are ready, and under the candlelight, incense smoke
curls up, highlighting the solemnity and sacredness of the ceremony.
When the Wine Immortal Bodhisattva is seated, the commander of the
fair orders the bands to play in unison again, and the firecrackers explode
once more. The procession advances by water and land. The divine ship
and dragon boat set out in a grand manner. Every village sets up tents
on open spaces to welcome the deity, with eager crowds waiting for the

arrival of the Wine Immortal Bodhisattva, hoping to receive blessings from the deity.

酒业会市共有三天，每天各村的青壮年都会组队赛龙舟。晚上村村都有戏班子演戏，通宵达旦，高亢的绍兴大板、婉约的越剧戏曲让人如痴如醉。一些大的酒坊都是宾客好友盈门，每天宴席不散。酒业会市凝聚了众酒坊的力量，表达了酿酒人对神明的敬畏，诚信酿酒丰富了绍兴黄酒文化的内涵，也有益于绍兴酿酒业的规范和健康发展。

The Wine Industry Fair takes place in the city for three days, during which young adults from each village form teams to compete in dragon boat races. At night, every village has theater troupes performing plays until dawn, while the reverberating Shaoxing Daban music and soft and graceful Yue Opera leave people mesmerized. Some of the large wineries are teeming with guests and friends and host banquets each day. The Fair harnesses the power of various wineries, demonstrates wine makers' reverence for the gods, and enriches the cultural connotation of Shaoxing Huangjiu, which is beneficial for the normative and healthy development of the Shaoxing wine industry.

锡箔锻制
Production Process of Tinfoil

相比于"没有围墙的博物馆"和"老绍兴，醉江南"等称号，绍兴曾经有一个更为响亮的名号：锡半城。 锡箔，也称作锡箔纸，最初是用于祭祀的物品，追溯到明太祖时期，至今已有六七百年的历史。

Compared with the titles "The Museum Without Walls" and "Old Shaoxing, Drunken Jiangnan", Shaoxing once had a more famous title: the Half City of Tin. Tinfoil, also known as tinfoil paper, was originally used for worship and dated back to the Ming Dynasty over six or seven hundred years ago.

关于锡箔的起源没有确切的记载。据说刘伯温在绍兴待了三年，了解当地的风俗。绍兴民间在祭祀祖先时，会向神龛投掷一些碎银子，这些银子一般不会再取用。后来，协助朱元璋打天下时，军饷匮乏，难以筹集资金。刘伯温提出向百姓借用神龛里的银子，并承诺等到财政充足时会归还。然而，天下未定，财政仍然困难，因此刘伯温教导百姓用锡箔代替银子进行祭祀，这样既增加了祭祀活动的内容，又解决了一部分人的经济来源，锡箔因此逐渐成为冥钱使用的材料。

There is no exact record regarding the origin of tinfoil. It is said that Liu Bowen stayed in Shaoxing for three years and learned about local customs. In Shaoxing, people would throw some silver pieces into the ancestral shrine when worshiping their ancestors, which were usually not used again. Later, when he helped Zhu Yuanzhang to conquer the world, funds were difficult to raise due to a shortage of military salaries. Liu proposed borrowing the silver from the people's ancestral shrines, promising to repay them when the finances improved. However, the world was not yet settled and the financial situation remained difficult. Therefore, Liu taught people to use tinfoil instead of silver for worship, which both added content to the worship activities and solved part of the people's economic source. Tinfoil gradually became the material used for hell bank note.

锡箔的制作过程极其繁琐，且全部依靠手工完成。其工艺流程包括以下几步：首先将锡块放入坩锅中熔化，称为"烊"，然后注入夹层模型中，铸造成长三寸、宽一寸的"叠箔"，工序称为"浇箔"。接下来由上间司和下间司进行锤打，直至不能再锻打为止。每块锡铸件一般可以打造三千两百张锡箔纸，称为"一脚"。锤打完成后，通过扑上一层揩粉，再由箔头工人按照不同的样式进行裁剪，这个工序叫作"页子"。接下来的步骤是"褙纸"，即将锡箔贴在大小相称的"鹿鸣纸"上。最后进行"矸纸"工序，将已经完成的锡箔牢牢地黏在纸上。然后就可以将矸好的锡箔使用于制作元宝形状的纸锭，整个锡箔制作工序就完成了。

The production process of tinfoil is extremely complicated and all done by hand. The technical process includes several steps: First, the tin block is melted in a crucible, called wax. Then it is poured into a sandwich model and cast into a stacked foil that is three inches long and one inch wide, a process called casting foil. Next, the upper and lower smiths use hammers to forge it until it can no longer be hammered. Each tin casting can generally produce 3,200 sheets of tinfoil paper, called one foot. After forging, a layer of ground powder is applied, and the foil head worker cuts it into different styles, which is called pages. The next step is mounting the paper, which is sticking the tinfoil on Luming paper that matches its size. Finally, the grinding paper process is performed to firmly stick the finished tinfoil on the paper. Then the tinfoil can be used to make paper ingots and the entire tin foil production process is completed.

图41　锡箔制品 郑红莲摄 Tinfoil products PHOTO: Z.H.L.

绍兴的锡箔制作精湛，品种繁多，适应各地的习俗。在民国时期，绍兴的锡箔业达到了盛衰交替的高峰。然而随着历史的发展，该行业在建国后逐渐衰落。但在90年代后期，这一传统产业得以重新被挖掘和振兴。锡箔制作的工艺师傅们通过不断的修行，已经掌握了一流的制作技术。现在，他们已经能够制作古时绍兴锡箔业中最受欢迎的产品，这些产品不仅畅销杭州、上海等地，还远销东南亚各国。绍兴市在2006年6月把锡箔锻造技艺列入第一批非物质文化遗产名录中。

The tinfoil production in Shaoxing is exquisite, with a wide variety to adapt to various customs across the country. During the Republic of China period, the tinfoil industry in Shaoxing reached its height of glory and decline. However, with the development of history, the industry gradually declined after the founding of the country. But in the late 1990s, this traditional industry was revived and explored. Master craftsmen of tinfoil production have gained first-class production technology through continuous practice. Now, they are able to produce the most popular products in ancient Shaoxing tinfoil industry, which are not only sold well in Hangzhou, Shanghai and other places, but also exported to Southeast Asian countries. In June 2006, Shaoxing City listed tinfoil forging techniques as the first batch of intangible cultural heritage.

市集
Markets

绍兴市集的历史可以概括为"唐代起源，宋代繁荣，民国发展，至今延续……"。早在春秋战国时期，绍兴就有"村民社赛"的记载，这一传统一直延续至今。在传说中的菩萨生日或忌日，绍兴村民会举行"迎神赛会"或"庙会"，以演戏、杂技等形式祭祀神灵，吸引周边乡村居民前来观看，同时也吸引了各种商贾云集，向游客推销商品，从而形成了市集。久而久之，举行市集的场所形成了一定的市场。

The history of Shaoxing's market can be summarized as "originated in the Tang Dynasty, prosperous in the Song Dynasty, developed during the Republic of China, and continues to this day...". As early as the Spring and Autumn and Warring States period, there were records of "village social competitions" in Shaoxing. This tradition has been passed down to this day. On the legendary birthday or anniversary of bodhisattvas, Shaoxing villagers will hold welcoming god competitions or temple fairs to worship gods with performances such as plays and acrobatics, attracting nearby rural residents to come and watch, as well as various merchants who gather to sell goods to tourists, thus forming a market over time in the place where the market is held.

据记载，早在秦汉时，山阴县的治所，即现在的绍兴老城区，就已经有了集市。到了唐代，绍兴各地都出现了集市，比如会稽县的平水、诸暨县的枫桥等。据《嘉泰会稽志》和《万历绍兴府志》等志书记载：南宋时，绍兴府城内已有照水坊市、清道桥市、大高桥东市、大高桥西市、龙兴寺前市、释地市和江桥市。此外，山阴县还有钱清镇、梅市；会稽县有车城、三界、平水等镇。

According to records, as early as the Qin and Han dynasties, there were already markets in what is now the old city area of Shaoxing, which was the capital of Shanyin county. In the Tang Dynasty, markets appeared all over Shaoxing, such as Pingshui in Kuaiji county and Fengqiao in Zhuji county. According to records in books such as *Jiatai Kuaiji Annals* and *Wanli Shaoxing Prefecture Annals*, during the Southern Song Dynasty, there were already several markets within the city of Shaoxing, including Zhaoshui Fang Market, Qingdao Bridge Market, Dagaoqiao East Market, Dagaoqiao West Market, Longxing Temple Front Market, Shidi Market, and Jiangqiao Market. In addition, there were Qianqing Town and Meishi in Shanyin county, as well as Checheng, Sanjie, and Pingshui in Kuaiji county.

到了明代，会稽县已经有了七个集市，山阴县则有五个集市。清代乾隆年间（1736—1795），这些市集进一步增加，如山阴县废除了隆兴寺前市，但新增了东浦、下方桥市；会稽县废除了纂风市，但新增了皋埠、汤浦等市。这样，到民国时期的1949年3月，绍兴府城内已经有了大江桥、大云桥、长桥、北海桥等市集。城区周围也已有偏门、西郭门、五云门、昌安门市集。绍兴县区的柯桥、安昌、平水、东关则已经成为四大集镇。此外还有20多个乡村市集。

By the Ming Dynasty, there were already seven markets in Kuaiji County and five in Shanyin County. During the reign of Emperor Qianlong in the Qing Dynasty (1736—1795), these markets further increased. Shanyin County abolished the Longxing Temple market and added Dongpu and Xiafangqiao markets; Kuaiji County abolished the Zuanfeng market, but added Gaobu, Tangpu and other markets. By March 1949, there were already markets such as Dajiangqiao, Dayunqiao, Changqiao, Beihaiqiao, etc. in the city of Shaoxing. There were also markets such as Pianmen, Xiguomen, Wuyunmen, and Chang'anmen around the city. Keqiao, Anchang, Pingshui, and Dongguan in Shaoxing County have become the four major market towns. In addition, there are more than 20 village markets.

据地方史志记载，绍兴府（地区）最早的市集可能要算是平水的茶市。早在唐代，平水就已经成为有名的茶叶集散地。尤其是在越州成为南宋的临时国都之后，平水茶叶中被称为"龙团""凤团"者，更是成为当时地方政府向南宋小朝廷进贡的物品。其他县市比较有名的市集如诸暨县娄家荡的牛市，曾有学者撰文描述道："牛市设在浦阳江边，占地二三百亩，日上市量少至五六百亩，多则千头以上……"。

According to the local historical records, the earliest market in Shaoxing Prefecture (region) could possibly be considered as the Tea Market of Pingshui. As early as the Tang Dynasty, Pingshui had become a well-known tea gathering place. Especially after Yu Zhou became the temporary capital of the Southern Song Dynasty, the tea leaves from Pingshui known as Dragon Ball and Phoenix Ball became items that the local government offered as tribute to the Southern Song imperial court. Other famous markets in other counties and cities include the Cattle Market in Loujiadang, Zhuji County, where scholars once wrote that the cattle market was located on the banks of the Puyang River, covering an area of two to three hundred acres. The daily market volume ranged from as low as five to six hundred acres to over a thousand heads of cattle.

绍兴府城内通过长年累月举行的各种市集，逐渐形成了很多有固定场所的专业市场。到了清末民初，形成了米市、鱼市、菜市、锡箔、茶市等专门集市。旧时绍兴的米市多集中于偏门、西郭等水陆门头，绍兴城东的五云门更是绍城重要的米市之一。这里的米市除收购本地所产之粮以外，还有不少粮商远赴江苏的无锡、安徽的芜湖、江西的九江等地贩运粮食。那时，绍兴府的萧山、山阴、会稽、上虞的棉农和茶农常年去那里购粮。久而久之，五云就以米行街而闻名，那里也成了绍兴的粮食集市。

In the city of Shaoxing, various markets have gradually formed within the city walls, which have been held regularly for many years. By the end of the Qing Dynasty and the beginning of the Republic of China, specialized markets with fixed locations such as rice markets, fish markets, vegetable markets, and tinfoil, tea markets had formed. In the past, the rice market in Shaoxing was mainly concentrated in the peripheral gates such as the Pianmen and Xiguo Gate. Wuyun Gate in the east of Shaoxing City was one of the important rice markets in Shaoxing. In addition to purchasing local grains, many grain merchants from places such as Wuxi in Jiangsu, Wuhu in Anhui, and Jiujiang in Jiangxi also came here to trade grain. At that time, cotton farmers and tea farmers from Xiaoshan, Shanyin, Kuaiji, and Shangyu in Shaoxing Prefecture often went there to buy grain. Over time, Wuyun became famous for its rice shops, and it also became a grain market in Shaoxing.

在绍兴城北的昌安门外，地近海涂，从前那里水域广阔，水产丰富。昌安又处于城郊，离府城不远。城外渔民来此出售鱼虾，城内鱼贩在此进货，城乡附近的百姓在此购买水产都十分方便。久而久之，这里也就成了水产的自由交易区。直到上世纪八九十年代，昌安的鱼市依然非常热闹、壮观。

Outside the Chang'an Gate in the north of Shaoxing, the land is close to the tideland, which used to have a vast water area and abundant aquatic resources. Chang'an is also located on the outskirts of the city, not far from the downtown. Fishermen from outside the city come here to sell fish and shrimp, while fish dealers inside the city come here to purchase goods. It is very convenient for people from nearby towns and villages to buy aquatic products here. Over time, this area has become a free trade zone for aquatic products. Even in the 1980s and 1990s, the fish market in Chang'an was still very lively and spectacular.

城区广宁桥东面的龙王塘，位于城乡结合部，正好兼具水路便利，城郊的菜农很容易把自己种植的瓜果蔬菜运到这里来批发销售，城内百姓也很方便每日前来购买。随着时间推移，这里逐渐成为远近闻名的蔬菜集市。

Longwangtang on the east side of Guangning Bridge in the urban

图42　昌安鱼市 郑红莲摄 Chang' an fish market PHOTO: Z.H.L.

area is located at the juncture of urban and rural areas, which has the advantage of being easily accessible by waterway. It is a popular vegetable market where suburban farmers can easily transport their produce to wholesale and sell here, and urban residents can conveniently come to buy daily. With the passage of time, this place has gradually become a famous vegetable market.

关于绍兴上大路的"锡箔茶市"究竟起始于何时，地方史志上虽然没有准确的记载，但据1996年版的《绍兴市志》和前辈老人的口述，推测可能源于绍兴生产的锡箔纸。以前是通过箔庄收购后运销到外埠的，绍兴生产锡箔纸的店铺、坊主及箔庄之间会在茶店洽谈生意。绍兴百姓一般称其为"茶市"。

Regarding when the Aluminum Foil Tea Market on Shangda Road in Shaoxing originated, although there is no accurate record in local historical materials, according to the 1996 edition of *Shaoxing Chronicle* and the narration of previous generations, it is speculated that it may be related to the production of tinfoil paper in Shaoxing. Previously, it was purchased and distributed to other places through the purchase of foil factories. Shops, communities and foil factories involved in tinfoil paper production in Shaoxing would negotiate business deals in tea shops. Shaoxing citizens generally refer to it as the tea market.

绍兴市集按时间分，通常可以分为常年存在和季节性存在两类。季节性集市一般以庙会的形式每年定期举行。例如在诸暨娄家荡举行的牛市，分别在每年阴历二月十五和十月十五，非常有名。另外，还有农历三月初二在稽山门外南镇集市，以出售小孩玩具为主，比如竹笼、纸鹞、二胡、箫、笛等。

In Shaoxing, markets can be divided into two categories based on time: those that are open year-round and those that are seasonal. Seasonal markets are often held in the form of temple fairs on a regular basis every year. For example, the famous cattle market in Loujiadang, Zhuji is held on the 15th day of the second and tenth lunar months. In addition, there is also a market held outside Jishanmen in Nanzhen on the second day of the third lunar month, mainly selling toys for children, such as bamboo cages, paper kites, erhus, Xiaos, flutes, and so on.

当铺与当票
Pawnshops and Pawn Tickets

　　旧时，绍兴城乡遍布着当铺。光绪二十九年（1903）的调查显示，当时共有64家当铺，府城开元寺还设有当业公所。当铺主要透过压低当物价值来获取高额利润。当票字迹潦草，而不论当物（俗称"当头"）的品质如何，都会被标上"破旧"这个字样。即使是完好无损的衣服也会被写成"虫吃鼠咬"，狐皮袍子也常常被描述为"烂板羊皮袄"，金戒指也往往被标注为"淡金戒"等等。过期未赎回的当头称为"死当"，当铺就有权利对其进行处理。所以有一句俗语说："穷死莫去当，屈死莫告状。"

　　In the past, pawnshops were prevalent in both urban and rural areas of Shaoxing. According to a survey in the 29th year of the Guangxu period (1903), there were a total of 64 pawnshops, and even a pawnshop association was established in the Kaiyuan Temple in the downtown. Pawnshops mainly gained high profits by lowering the value of pawned items. The handwriting on pawn tickets was often sloppy, and regardless of the quality of the pawned items (commonly known as the head of the pawn), they would be labeled with the words "old and worn out". Even clothes in good condition would be described as "ravaged by bugs and nibbled by mice". Fox fur coats were often called tattered sheepskin jackets, while gold rings were typically labeled as pale gold rings, and so on. Pawned items that have not been redeemed after their due date are known as "dead pawns", and pawnshops have the right to dispose of them. Therefore, there is a saying that goes, "Don't go to pawn when you're poor, and don't file a lawsuit when you're wronged."

绍兴当铺的历史源远流长，早在明代初年就有在绍兴设立的当铺。当时，绍兴的当铺主要出售粮食、丝绸、布匹等货品。到了清代，当铺的营业范围逐渐扩大，开始代理典当、金银首饰、字画、古董等物品。在古代，当铺是城市中极为重要的商业机构。在绍兴，许多当铺都是百年老字号，声誉和地位非常高，人们因此会选择信誉良好的当铺去典当物品。同时，在当铺工作的文化人也相对较多，许多当铺成为文人雅集的聚集地，为文化人提供了一个交流的场所。

The history of pawnshops in Shaoxing can be traced back to the early Ming Dynasty, when they mainly sold goods such as grain, silk and cloth. In the Qing Dynasty, the scope of business gradually expanded to include pawnbroking, gold and silver jewelry, calligraphy and paintings, antiques and other items. In ancient times, pawnshops were extremely important commercial institutions in cities. In Shaoxing, many pawnshops are century-old brands with high reputation and status, and people would choose pawnshops with good reputation to pawn items. Meanwhile, there are relatively more cultural people working in pawnshops. Many pawnshops become gathering places for literati, providing a place for cultural exchanges.

　　绍兴的当票就如同今天银行的支票或借记卡一样，被视为一种经济交易工具。当票上会附上担保人的姓名和印章等信息。在典当物品时，当票上通常会印有"宝"字。这是因为在古代，"宝"被认为是吉祥之物，既象征着典当物品的珍贵，也寓意着人们借助当铺得以摆脱贫困，而"宝字当头"也成为许多人的祈求之语。在绍兴的当铺里，金银首饰、古董字画、书画、玉器、名表等物品的典当比例较高，这也代表了当时绍兴的商业发展和文化特色。在典当时，人们通常会携带质押物品的证明，这同样成为当票上的一个重要内容。当人们在当铺典当物品后，如果想要赎回来，一般需要按时支付一定的利息，如期赎回物品即可。如果赎当时间过期，或者没有支付利息，当铺就有权将物品出售。

　　The pawn tickets in Shaoxing were regarded as a kind of economic transaction tool, similar to today's checks or debit cards. The pawn ticket would include information such as the name and seal of the guarantor. The Chinese character for "treasure" would usually be printed on the pawn ticket when an item was pawned. This is because in ancient times, treasure was considered a symbol of auspiciousness, representing the value of the pawned item and the hope that people who were in need would be able to obtain assistance from pawnshops. In Shaoxing's pawnshops, the pawned items with a higher proportion were generally gold and silver jewelry, antique calligraphy and paintings, jade, watch, and other cultural items, which also represented the commercial development and cultural characteristics of Shaoxing at that time. When people pawned items, they usually carried a certificate of the pledged item, which became an important content on the ticket. If people wanted to retrieve their items, they generally needed to pay a certain amount of interest on time, and if they succeeded, they can redeem their items before the due date. If the redemption period was over or the interest was not paid, the pawnshop had the right to sell the items.

供奉行业祖师
The Worship of Ancestral Masters of Various Professions

　　绍兴旧时有供奉各行各业祖师爷的传统，例如建筑工匠供奉鲁班，酿酒师傅供奉杜康，绍剧戏班供奉唐明皇，等等。供奉的方式不尽相同，有的在作坊或工地设置牌位，有的悬挂画像，祭拜时间和方式也因行业不同而各异。

There was a tradition in the old days of Shaoxing to worship ancestral deities of various professions, such as the worship of Lu Ban by builders, the worship of Du Kang by winemakers, and the worship of Tang Ming Huang by Yue Opera troupes, etc. The ways of worship varied, some set up plaques in the workshop or on the construction site, while others hanged pictures. The time and manner of worship also varied depending on the profession.

　　鲁班是中国古代著名的木匠大师，被后世木工、泥瓦匠等建筑行业奉为祖师爷。在绍兴，流传着鲁班出谋划策造荷湖桥和北海桥的故事。据说很早以前，荷湖附近的老百姓很想建造一座石桥，但接连造了好几年，都是造一次，塌一次，让所有的工匠都束手无策。

Lu Ban is a famous ancient carpenter in China. He is regarded as the ancestor of carpenters and bricklayers industries by later generations. In Shaoxing, there is a story that Lu Ban provided ideas for the construction of both Hehu Bridge and Beihai Bridge. It is said that a long time ago, the local people near Hehu Lake wished to build a stone bridge. However, after several years of construction, the bridge collapsed every time it was built, leaving all the craftsmen at a loss.

这时，来了一位短衫老者，他在造桥的位置转了几圈，然后来到附近的茶店坐下，拿出一小包木块，一边慢慢品茶，一边摆弄着木块，过了一会儿，他就对着发愁的工匠们说道："我已经找到建造石桥的办法啦！"大家纷纷围过来，只见老者用小木块搭了几个不同形状的桥墩，然后拿起一块木板在桥墩上一放，让大家去推，看会不会塌掉。奇妙的是，这个模型桥果然很扎实。于是，在老人的指点下，工匠们把荷湖桥建好了。桥落成之时，人们想感谢老人，但却找不到人影。原来这位老人就是大名鼎鼎的鲁班。

At this point, an old man in short shirt arrived, and after walking around the bridge construction site for a while, he went to a nearby tea shop, sat down, and took out a small package of wooden blocks. As he slowly sipped his tea, and fiddled with the wooden blocks. After a while, he said to the worried craftsmen, "I have found a way to build a stone bridge!" Everyone gathered around, and saw that the old man had built several different shaped bridge piers with the small wooden blocks, and then he picked up a wooden board and put it on top of the piers and asked everyone to push and see if it would collapse. Amazingly, the model bridge was very solid. So, under the guidance of the old man, the craftsmen built the Hehu Bridge. When the bridge was completed, people wanted to thank the old man, but he was nowhere to be found. It turned out that the old man was the famous Lu Ban.

相传农历五月初五是鲁班的生日，这一天，木工、泥工需要供奉祭品，点烛焚香，然后所有工匠按照大小依次跪拜鲁班，以求得到祖师爷的庇佑。在绍兴，有的木工业还专门设有鲁班会，筹划每年的祖师祭祀活动。

According to legend, the fifth day of the fifth lunar month is the birthday of Lu Ban. On this day, carpenters and bricklayers need to offer sacrifices, light candles and incense, and then all the craftsmen kneel and bow to Lu Ban in order to seek his protection. In Shaoxing, some woodworking industries also have a special Lu Ban Association to plan the annual ancestor worship activities.

在绍兴，酿酒行业供奉的祖师是夏朝的杜康。相传，杜康采用独特的工艺，加入黄米、大麦、豌豆等多种粮食和野菜来酿酒，使得酒的品质和口感得到极大的提升，酿出当时颇受欢迎的美酒。此后，杜康的酒被很多人所称道，酿酒师傅将他视为中国酿酒业的祖师。旧时，绍兴酒坊在每年冬酿开始之前，都要先祭祀杜康，以求酿出好酒来。

In Shaoxing, the patron saint of the brewing industry is Du Kang from the Xia Dynasty. Legend has it that Du Kang used a unique process and added a variety of grains and wild vegetables, such as yellow rice, barley, and peas to brew wine, greatly improving the quality and taste of the wine, and producing popular wine at that time. Since then, Du Kang's wine has been praised by many people and brewing masters consider him as the ancestor of China's brewing industry. In the past, before the winter brewing began in Shaoxing wineries, Du Kang was always first offered sacrifice in order to brew good wine.

在绍兴，绍剧戏班子有供奉唐明皇的独特习俗。唐明皇热爱音乐和戏曲，对戏曲的发展起到了重要的推动作用，因而被绍剧戏班的演员们视为祖师爷般尊崇。他们有的在戏班后台设置唐明皇的神位，在演出前或者特定的日子里，怀着敬畏之心进行祭拜。他们献上鲜花、果品，燃香祈祷，期望唐明皇能保佑演出成功、戏班兴旺。

In Shaoxing, Shaoju opera troupes have the unique custom of worshiping Tang Ming Huang. Tang Ming Huang, who loved music and opera, played an important role in promoting the development of opera. Therefore, he is respected by the actors of Shaoju opera troupes as an ancestor. Some of them set up the shrine of Tang Ming Huang in the backstage of the troupe. Before a performance or on specific days, they worship with reverence. They offer flowers and fruits, burn incense and pray, hoping that Tang Ming Huang can bless the success of the performance and the prosperity of the troupe.

Chapter 6

游艺娱乐篇

Entertainment and Amusement

社戏
Community Opera

　　"社"是古代的乡村组织，古时"百姓二十五家为一社，其旧社及人稀者不限"，至今绍兴还有不少带有"社"字的乡村名称，如谷社、阮社等。各地在社庙里还供奉有社神，这就是民间的土地庙、城隍庙和山神庙。社庙定期有演戏谢神的习俗，民间俗称"社戏"或"年规戏"。

　　A community, is an ancient rural organization in China. In ancient times, twenty-five families make up a community, and there is no limit to the number of old communities and sparsely populated areas. There are still many village names with community in Shaoxing, such as community Gu and Ruan. Local people also worship the gods of the community in the temples there, which are equivalent to the Earth God temple, Town God temple, and Mountain God temple in folk culture. There is a custom of performing operas in the community temple to thank the gods, which is called community opera or New Year's regular opera in Chinese folk culture.

　　根据旧俗，凡是村里有社戏表演的，家家户户都要邀请七大姑八大姨所有亲戚前来观看。清朝陶星驰在《竹枝词》写道："可怜妇女不胜忙，接眷邀亲似发狂。寄语吾家姑奶奶，千万代唤汝家郎。"正因为亲朋好友都要赶来看戏，所以每家每户都要增加一大笔接待开支，有些贫困人家甚至典当首饰或贵重物品，以用来接待来看戏的亲戚。那几天，码头埠船的生意也会特别兴隆，不仅上上下下的乘客多，还有捎带东西的活儿也特别多。村里的小河边，全是忙着杀鸡宰鹅的妇女，河水也泛着一圈圈的油光。

According to the old tradition, whenever a village held a performance of community operas, every household was expected to invite all their relatives and friends to watch. In the Qing Dynasty, Tao Xingchi wrote in his *Bamboo Branch Song*, "Poor women can't handle the busy preparations, inviting relatives and friends as if they were crazy. I would like to address my grandmother from my family and ask for your help for generations to come." Because of the number of guests coming to watch, each household had to increase their spending on hospitality, and some even had to pawn their jewelry or valuable items to entertain relatives and friends. During those few days, the business at the dock and port area was also particularly prosperous, and not only were there many passengers, but there were also lots of goods being transported. At the small riverbank in the village, women were busy slaughtering chickens and geese, and the water was covered in circles of oil slicks.

请戏班子的费用主要由社庙的田产收入承担。有时小村庄人太少，单独请戏班子不划算，便出钱与邻村一起请。还有的是"头家先生"主动到各家各户筹钱请戏班子，他筹好钱后，到绍兴城内的茶店去找戏班主订好戏、演出时间和费用价格。成交后，双方不得反悔。头家先生回村后就张贴告示，通知村民某月某日某戏班子来村里演戏。

The cost of hiring a performance troupe was mainly borne by the income from the land owned by the temple in the village. Sometimes, when there were not enough people in the village, it was not cost-effective to hire a performance troupe alone, so they may combine with neighboring villages to raise money for a shared performance. In other cases, the leader of the village took the initiative to raise money from each household to invite a performance troupe. After the funds were raised, the leader went to a tea shop in Shaoxing city to negotiate the performance details and the cost with the troupe leader. Once the deal was made, neither party can back out. The leader would then post a notice in the village, informing villagers of the date and time of the performance by the specified troupe.

演出当天，一大早就有各种商贩来到戏台附近抢地摆摊，俗称"摆台下摊"。这种台下摊卖的商品有吃的、用的、穿的、玩的，琳琅满目、应有尽有，比如瓜果、糖饼、粽子、馄饨、绸缎、五色布、西洋镜、布娃娃，等等。整个社庙就像一个小集市。

On the day of the performance, various vendors arrived near the stage early in the morning to grab a spot to set up their stalls, commonly known as setting up stalls beneath the stage. The merchandise sold at these stalls included food, daily necessities, clothing, and toys. There were a wide variety of goods, such as fruits, pastries, rice dumplings, wonton, silk, colorful fabrics, mirrors, cloth dolls, and so on. The entire temple fair was like a small market.

根据演出的目的，社戏分为平安戏、大戏和目连戏三类。吃过午饭，就开始敲锣演戏，先闹头场、二场。这是发给观众的信号，告诉大家好戏马上上演，赶紧就位看戏。好戏一般集中在晚上演出，武打戏一般作为开台戏。这类戏一开始，前场演员赶进赶出，后场乐队紧锣密鼓，人人忙得不可开交。

According to the purpose of the performance, community operas are divided into three categories: peace operas, grand operas, and Mulian operas. After lunch, the actors started to beat the gongs and played the drums, and performed the first and second acts. This was a signal to the audience, telling everyone that a good show was about to start, so hurry up and take your seats. The best performances were generally held at night, and martial arts dramas were usually performed as the opening act. At the beginning of this type of drama, the actors in the front rushed in and out, and the musicians in the back were busy with the drums and cymbals.

作为水乡，绍兴的戏台一般搭在土地庙前的小河里，俗称"万年台"和"水台"。观众既可以站在岸上看戏，也可以坐在船上看戏，还有请人在陆地上搭建的草台，上面蒙着篷布，可以遮阳避雨。草台面积小，演大戏不够用，还必须在台边搭个耳台，俗称"个半台"。晚上，灯火阑珊，弦歌悠扬，水上陆上挤满了看戏的人们。

As a water town, the stages of Shaoxing's theaters are generally built in shallow rivers in front of local temples, commonly known as Ten-thousand-year Stage and Water Stage. Spectators can either stand on the shore to watch the show, or sit on boats to watch it. There are also temporary grass stages built on land, covered with canopies to provide shade and shelter from the rain. However, these grass stages are often not big enough to accommodate large-scale performances, so an additional semi-stage, also called half stage, must be built next to it. At night, with dim lights, melodious music, the audience, both on the land and on the water, are packed together to enjoy the show.

社戏中最难得的是看对台戏。1946年七月初七，从三脚桥到官塘桥，相距不到30米，在临街小河上竟然搭了两个戏台，一边演的是《凤仪亭》，另一边演的是《钓金龟》，两边的演员都很卖力，互争观众。观众挤来挤去，这边听听，那边瞧瞧，兴奋不已。虽然现在绍兴农村已经没有演戏谢神的风俗，但邀请戏班或剧团下乡演戏，或剧团主动送戏下乡，依然非常流行，甚至场面比以前还热闹。

The most difficult part of community operas is watching the performance on two separate stages. On the seventh day of the seventh lunar month, 1946, the distance between the Three-Legged Bridge and the Guan Tang Bridge was less than 30 meters. Yet, two stages were set up over the small river by the street, with one side performing *Phoenix Pavilion* and the other performing *Fishing for Golden Turtle*. Both sides of the performers were very enthusiastic, competing for the audience's attention. The excited audience moved back and forth to listen to one side, then watch the other, enjoying themselves immensely. Although the tradition of performing opera to thank the Gods no longer exists in the rural areas of Shaoxing nowadays, inviting opera troupes to perform in the countryside, or troupes actively sending their performances to the countryside, remains very popular, and even more lively than before.

赛龙舟
Dragon Boat Race

绍兴赛龙舟的习俗，自宋以来至明清，一直盛行不衰。但与别处不同，绍兴赛龙舟很少在端午这一天，而是农村迎神赛会的固定活动。根据《越谚》记载，四月初六青甸湖、六月初七章家弄桥、六月十四、十五、十六等日在许多村的会市中，都有赛龙舟的项目。全年下来，绍兴各地的赛龙舟举办次数达到30余次。

The tradition of dragon boat race in Shaoxing has been prevalent since the Song Dynasty till the Ming and Qing dynasties. However, unlike other places, dragon boat race in Shaoxing is rarely held on the Dragon Boat Festival, but a regular event for rural ceremonial activities. According to *Yue Proverbs*, dragon boat race was held on the 6th day of the 4th lunar month at Qingdian Lake, on the 7th day of the 6th lunar month at the Zhangjia Lane Bridge, and on the 14th, 15th, and 16th days of the 6th lunar month in many village markets. Throughout the year, dragon boat race was held more than 30 times in various parts of Shaoxing.

在绍兴，赛龙舟的起源有不同的说法，有的认为源于越王勾践在复国时操练水师；有的认为是源于吴王夫差与西施的娱乐活动。比较公认的说法是为了纪念楚国大夫屈原。据说，古时赛龙舟场面非常壮观，不论达官贵人，还是平民百姓，都去河边观看，就连平时很少出门的大家闺秀，也有前往观看的。唐代诗人张建封以《竞渡歌》生动描绘了当年赛龙舟的热闹场面，"……鼓声三下红旗开，两龙跃出浮水来。棹影斡波飞万剑，鼓声劈浪鸣千雷。鼓点渐急标将近，两龙相望目如瞬"。

In Shaoxing, there are different opinions about the origin of dragon boat racing. Some believe that it originated from the practice of water warfare when King Goujian of Yue was reestablishing his country. Some believe it originated from the entertainment activities of King Fuchai of Wu and his favorite concubine Xi Shi. The most widely accepted theory is that it was created to commemorate the nobleman Qu Yuan of the Chu State. It is said that the dragon boat racing scene was very spectacular in ancient times. Both government officials and ordinary people went to the riverbank to watch, even the rarely seen noble women would also come to watch. Tang Dynasty poet Zhang Jianfeng vividly depicted the lively scene of dragon boat racing in *Competition and Boat Song*, "... the drum sounds three times and the red flag opens, two dragons leap out of the floating water. The shadow of the oars flies like ten thousand swords, and the drum sounds like thunder crashing waves. The drumbeat gradually accelerates as the finish line approaches, and the two dragons face each other with eyes like lightning flashes".

绍兴龙舟一般有十来米长，船身的中部较宽，前后可坐10至12名水手，头尾部较窄，只能坐下一名鼓手和舵手。船头雕刻昂首龙头，船尾雕刻龙尾，船身两侧则彩绘龙鳞。当所有的水手奋力划桨时，整条船就像一条劈波斩浪的游龙。赛龙舟时，所有的水手都统一着装,上穿对襟无领短袖上衣,下穿短裤,打赤脚。船头的鼓手是整条船的总指挥,水手按照鼓点声用力划桨;船尾的舵手手握一支长橹,站在船尾把握方向。

A typical Shaoxing dragon boat is about ten meters long with a wider middle section for seating 10-12 rowers, and narrow front and rear sections that accommodate one drummer and one steersman respectively. The boat features a dragon head carving at the bow, a dragon tail carving at the stern, and dragon scale paintings on both sides of the hull. When all the rowers vigorously paddle, the whole boat looks like a dragon moving forward through the waves. In dragon boat races, all rowers wear matching outfits consisting of a short-sleeved, collarless top and shorts, and go barefoot. The drummer at the front of the boat serves as the commander, and the rowers follow the drumming rhythm to paddle hard; the steersman at the rear of the boat holds a long wooden oar and stands to steer the boat's direction.

在龙舟比赛开始前,每条船一般要到附近的村庄巡游一圈,村里的一些大户人家常常给参赛的选手们一些赏赐。绍兴本地谚语"龙船转转头,买田买地勿断头"指的就是龙船带来的好运,所以一些有钱人家会特地在江面较宽、可供龙舟转身的岸边,准备老酒、果品等物,等到龙舟开过来送给水手们。龙舟接受赠物之后,便在河上掉头转身,为这些人家讨个吉利。

Before the dragon boat race began, each boat usually paraded around the nearby villages, and some wealthy households in the village often gave rewards to the participating athletes. The local proverb in Shaoxing, "When the dragon boat turns its head, don't cut off your purchase of land and property", refers to the good luck brought by the dragon boat. Therefore, some wealthy families prepared old wine, fruits and other items on the banks of the river where the dragon boat can turn around, and wait for the sailors to pass by to give them these gifts. After accepting the gifts, the dragon boat turned around on the river to bring auspiciousness to these households.

由于绍兴水域广阔，江河纵错，赛龙舟既是民间喜爱的一种娱乐民俗，也是一项体育运动项目。20世纪80年代，很多乡村重新恢复赛龙舟活动，例如1984年国庆节，马山区举行了首届龙舟比赛，沿河两岸，观者如潮。此后，在瓜渚湖上，多次举办绍兴赛龙舟活动，特别是以绍兴姑娘组成的女子龙舟队，英姿飒爽，曾获得两届冠军。

Due to the vast water area and winding rivers in Shaoxing, dragon boat race has become both a popular folk entertainment and a sports activity. In the 1980s, many villages resumed dragon boat race activities. For example, during the National Day in 1984, the first dragon boat race was held in Mashan District, attracting a large number of spectators. In the following years, Shaoxing dragon boat race events were held many times on Guazhu Lake. Especially, the women's dragon boat team composed of Shaoxing girls won two championships with their heroic and cool looks.

斗鸡
Cockfighting

斗鸡是指让两只公鸡在一起进行搏斗，以比较它们的力量和勇气。在绍兴，斗鸡被视为一项传统的娱乐活动，深受当地人民的喜爱。斗鸡也是中国传统的民俗游戏，起源于农耕社会。据《左传》记载，春秋战国时期就有斗鸡的记录，并且已经十分盛行。斗鸡的比赛时间通常从清明开始，一直持续到夏至。

Cockfighting refers to the activity of two roosters fighting each other to compare their strength and bravery. In Shaoxing, cockfighting was considered a traditional form of entertainment and was greatly beloved by local people. Cockfighting was also a traditional folk game in China, originating from the agricultural society. According to *Zuo Zhuan*, records of cockfighting dated back to the Spring and Autumn and Warring States period and cockfighting was already popular at that time. The cockfighting season usually started from Qingming Festival and lasted until the Summer Solstice.

唐朝时期，斗鸡活动达到了巅峰，不仅在民间设立鸡场，就连皇帝也喜欢斗鸡。在那时，斗鸡之戏是清明节俗的一项重要内容。李隆基当上皇帝后，在宫内建鸡坊，"索长安雄鸡，金毫、铁距、高冠、昂尾千数，养于坊中"，并有500人专司驯鸡。结果上行下效，有钱的倾家荡产买鸡，没钱的就以假鸡为戏。在长安有个名叫贾昌的少年，驯鸡有一套办法，博得唐玄宗李隆基欢心，一下子就荣华富贵，成了闻名天下的"神鸡童"。唐代斗鸡驯鸡发达，社会却为此付出了世风靡废的巨大代价。斗鸡使人如痴如狂，也使一些"斗鸡小儿"恃宠骄横，不可一世。李白在《古风》诗中有云："路逢斗鸡者，冠盖何辉赫。鼻息干霓虹，行人皆怵惕。"

During the Tang Dynasty, cockfighting reached its peak. Not only did common people establish chicken farms, even the emperor enjoyed watching cockfights. At that time, cockfighting was an important part of the Qingming Festival festivities. After Li Longji became emperor, he built a chicken coop in the palace and sought out thousands of roosters with gold combs, iron spurs, high crowns and upswept tails to be raised in the coop. 500 people were responsible for raising and training the chickens. As a result, those who could afford it spent their fortune on buying roosters, while those who couldn't afford it used fake roosters to participate in the fights. There was a young man named Jia Chang in Chang'an who had a special ability to train the cocks, who won the favor of the emperor Li Longji and became the famous Rooster Whizz-kid. However, this prosperity came at a great cost as cockfighting made people obsessed and even led some cockfighting youngsters to become arrogant and unruly. Li Bai once wrote in his poem *Ancient Style*, "Whoever meets a cockfighting, will be awed and intimidated by its grandeur. Its breath is like that of a rainbow, making passersby tremble with fear."

明朝时期，绍兴民间也十分盛行斗鸡。据说，著名的散文家张岱因为喜欢斗鸡，在龙山设立了一个斗鸡社，经常邀请朋友一起以斗鸡为乐。张岱有一位叔叔，也很喜欢斗鸡，经常拿一些字画古玩和他打赌斗鸡，但每次都输给了张岱。现在绍兴城区新市场附近，还留有一处叫斗鸡场的地方，据说这里就是当年绍兴斗鸡的场合。

During the Ming Dynasty, cockfighting was also very popular among the common people in Shaoxing. It is said that the famous essayist Zhang Dai, because of his love for cockfighting, set up a cockfighting club in Longshan and often invited friends to enjoy cockfighting together. Zhang Dai had an uncle who also loved cockfighting and often bet on some calligraphy, paintings, and antiques with him, but he always lost to Zhang Dai. Now, near the new market in the downtown area of Shaoxing, there is still a place called the Cockfighting Arena, which is said to be the venue for cockfighting in Shaoxing in the old time.

斗鸡场一般设在空阔的地方，占地大约半亩，周围是一米来高的围墙，人们站在围墙外观看。斗鸡时，鸣锣击鼓，气氛热烈，不时有观众呐喊助威。过去，因为没有钟表，人们主要以滴水计时。具体方法是在桌上放两只木桶，一个桶底有小洞，比赛时开始滴水到另一个空木桶中。比赛的顺序按照参赛鸡的重量排列，由轻到重。

The cockfighting arena is usually located in an open area, covering an area of about half an acre, surrounded by a one-meter-high wall, and people stand outside the wall to watch. During the cockfight, drums and gongs are sounded, and the atmosphere is lively, with occasional shouts of encouragement from the audience. In the past, because there were no clocks, people mainly used water drops to time the fights. The specific method was to place two wooden barrels on the table, one of which had a small hole in the bottom. During the match, water dripped from the barrel with the hole to an empty wooden barrel. The order of the matches was arranged according to the weight of the participating roosters, from light to heavy.

两鸡相斗时，如果一只鸡先退后，另一只没有追逐，算违规。如果一只鸡先退后，另一只仍然继续追赶搏斗，先退的鸡一直不还击，就算输了。工作人员将败鸡拿走，留下获胜的鸡继续和下一只鸡搏斗。每斗完一局，就记一次分，最后累积分数最多的鸡获胜。

When two chickens engage in a fight, if one chicken retreats and the other does not pursue, it is considered a violation of the rules. If one chicken retreats and the other continues to pursue and fight but the retreated chicken does not fight back, it is considered a loss. The staff will remove the defeated chicken and leave the winner to continue fighting the next chicken. A point is recorded after each round and the chicken with the highest accumulated score at the end wins.

通常人们认为体格粗大、羽毛光亮、鸡爪强壮的鸡为上品，但也有体格瘦小的鸡出奇制胜。绍兴民间，就流传绍兴小白鸡大败琉球大公鸡的故事。据说，明朝时期琉球国使节带了一只高大威猛的大公鸡来到我国，他在京城摆下斗鸡擂台，果然百战百胜，琉球使节得意地宣布，他的鸡天下无敌。后来他听说绍兴斗鸡很出名，于是带着大公鸡来到绍兴。绍兴府挑选善斗的公鸡来应战，但最后都败下阵来。

People usually consider chickens with large bodies, shiny feathers, and strong claws to be superior, but there are also small and thin chickens that can win unexpectedly. In Shaoxing folklore, there is a story about how the Shaoxing little white chicken defeated the Ryukyu large cock. It is said that during the Ming Dynasty, a Ryukyu envoy brought a tall and strong cock to China, and set up a cockfighting arena in the capital. The large cock won all the battles, and the Ryukyu envoy proudly declared that his rooster was invincible in the world. Later, he heard that Shaoxing was famous for its cockfighting, so he brought the rooster to Shaoxing. Shaoxing selected good fighting roosters to challenge it, but in the end they all lost.

就在这时，绍兴城里的徐老头带着他的小白鸡前来应战。这只小白鸡全身羽毛雪白，十分机灵勇猛。琉球使者看到小白鸡只有大公鸡的一半高，不由得哈哈大笑。可是小白鸡一上场就巧妙地躲过了大公鸡的正面攻击，并且腾空一跃跳到大公鸡的背上。当大公鸡想扭头啄小白鸡时，小白鸡不慌不忙，对准大公鸡的眼睛，狠狠地啄了几下，大公鸡的眼部马上血流不止，痛得落荒而逃。场外的看客们欢声雷动，为小白鸡喝彩。琉球使者只能灰溜溜地走了。当地老百姓为了纪念这次斗鸡的胜利，把这个斗鸡的地方叫作斗鸡场，尊称徐老头为斗鸡爷爷。

At that moment, Xu, an old man from Shaoxing, arrived with his little white rooster to challenge it. The small white cock had snow-white feathers, was exceptionally clever and valiant. The Ryukyu envoy couldn't help but burst out laughing when he saw that the small white rooster was only half the height of the big rooster. However, as soon as the small white chicken entered the arena, it skillfully evaded the big rooster's frontal attack and jumped onto its back in a swift motion. When the big rooster tried to turn its head to peck at the small white cock, it calmly aimed at the big rooster's eyes and pecked viciously a few times, causing blood to flow from the big rooster's eyes and consequently the big rooster fled in pain. The spectators outside the ring cheered and applauded for the small white cock, and the Ryukyu envoy left with shame. To commemorate this victory in cockfighting, the local people named the place where it took place Cockfighting Arena and revered Xu as Cockfighting Master.

尽管斗鸡习俗在民间已经不常见，但一些旅游景点推出了斗鸡娱乐项目，例如在绍兴会稽山的百鸟乐园仍能观看到斗鸡的精彩场面。

Although cockfighting tradition is no longer common among the public, some tourist attractions still introduce cockfighting entertainment programs. For example, at Paradise of Hundreds of Birds in Kuaijishan, one can still watch exciting cockfighting scenes.

猜谜
Riddle-Guessing

　　绍兴是中国著名的文化古城，也是猜谜习俗的发源地之一，绍兴的猜谜习俗可以追溯到唐代，历史悠久、风靡一时。谜语是一种常见的文学形式，通常由一段文字、一幅图画或一段音乐组成，通过隐晦、含蓄的描述或提示，让人去猜测其真正的意义或答案。谜语的出现可以追溯到古代，是一种传统的文化娱乐方式，也是一种考验智力和想象力的文字游戏。旧时，绍兴民间流行猜谜，特别是夏天晚上乘凉的时候，不论老少都以猜谜为乐。

　　Shaoxing is a famous cultural ancient city in China and one of the birthplaces of riddle-guessing customs. The tradition of riddle-guessing in Shaoxing can be traced back to the Tang Dynasty, which has a long history and was popular at that time. Riddles are a common form of literature, usually composed of a passage of text, a picture, or a piece of music that uses subtle and implicit descriptions or hints to challenge people to guess its true meaning or answer. The appearance of riddles can be traced back to ancient times and is a traditional cultural entertainment, as well as a word game that tests intelligence and imagination. In the past, riddle-guessing was popular among the people of Shaoxing, especially in the evenings when they enjoyed a cool summer breeze. People of all ages and backgrounds enjoyed the game of riddle-guessing.

　　谜语的表述通常比较隐晦，需要通过一些提示或线索来引导猜谜者去思考、推断。其次，谜语的构成通常采用一些双关语或多义词，使得谜底能够有多种解释和理解。再者，谜语的章法通常比较独特，有时会采用一些排比、反复、倒叙等修辞手法。最后，谜语是一种娱乐性强、趣味性十足的文学形式，能够激发人们的智力和想象力，增强人们的文化素养和生活情趣。猜谜的形式多种多样，有文字谜、画谜、音谜、字谜、动物谜，等等。谜面通常是由作者用诗、歌、故事、成语、俚语等方式表达出来，而猜谜者则需要根据谜面的提示，通过联想、推理、猜测等方式来猜出谜底。

Riddles are usually phrased obscurely and require some hints or clues to lead the guesser to think and infer. Secondly, riddles are usually composed of some puns or homophones so that the answer can have multiple interpretations and meanings. Furthermore, riddles have a unique structure, sometimes using rhetorical devices such as parallelism, repetition, and inversion. Lastly, riddles are a highly entertaining and amusing literary form that can stimulate people's intelligence and imagination, enhance their cultural literacy and life interest. There are various forms of riddles, such as word riddles, picture riddles, sound riddles, character riddles, animal riddles, and so on. The riddle face is usually expressed by the author in the form of poetry, song, story, idiom, or slang, and the guesser needs to use association, reasoning, guessing and other methods to solve the answer based on the riddle face hints.

　　绍兴的猜谜形式多种多样，以字谜和画谜为主。其中，字谜是指通过字形、音、义、结构等方面的变化来表达谜底的谜语；画谜则是用图画或图形来表示谜底的谜语。绍兴的猜谜题材丰富多样，有历史人物、古诗词、成语、俚语、故事传说等等，既考验了猜谜者的智力和想象力，也让人们更好地了解中国传统文化。

There are various forms of riddles in Shaoxing, mainly including character riddles and picture riddles. Character riddles refer to the riddles that express the answers through changes in the character's shape, sound, meaning, structure, etc.; picture riddles use pictures or graphics to represent the answers. The riddle themes in Shaoxing are rich and diverse, including historical figures, ancient poetry, idioms, slang, stories and legends, etc., which test not only the intelligence and imagination of the riddle solvers, but also help people to better understand traditional Chinese culture.

绍兴名人徐谓善于设计谜语，例如，"但见争城以战，不见杀人盈城，是气也而反动其心。"谜底为"走马灯"。另有一则为"开如轮，敛如槊，剪纸调胶护新竹。日中荷盖影亭亭，雨里芭蕉声簌簌。晴天则阴阴则晴，晴阴之说诚分明。安得大柄居吾手，去覆东西南北之人行。"谜底为"伞"。

Xu Wei, a famous person from Shaoxing, is proficient in designing riddles. For example, "There is a battle in the city, but no one is killed. It's just an atmosphere that makes people rebellious." The answer is "carousel". Another one goes like this, "Open like a wheel, fold like a spear, paper-cutting, glue-tuning and protecting new bamboo. In the middle of the day, the lotus cover casts a shadow, and the banana leaves rustle in the rain. It's sunny and then cloudy, and the difference between them is clear. If I had a large handle in my hand, I could cover people traveling in all directions." The answer is "umbrella".

绍兴的猜谜习俗以"元宵猜谜"最为盛行，每年农历正月十五元宵节期间，在绍兴市内的各大公园、广场、文化场所等地，都会举行盛大的猜谜活动。在这一天晚上，参与者们会聚集在一起，互相交流猜谜心得，共同寻找谜底，增进彼此之间的友谊。清朝诗人戴春波在《越中新年竹枝词》中写道，"几辈斯文费苦思，灯谜悬处立多时。偶然猜着唐诗句，青果三枚笔一枝。"

The guessing riddle tradition in Shaoxing is most prevalent during the Lantern Festival on the 15th day of the first lunar month. Large-scale guessing riddle events are held in various parks, squares, cultural venues and other places in Shaoxing city during the Lantern Festival. On this evening, participants gather together to exchange their guessing riddle experiences, and work together to find the answers to increase friendship between each other. Dai Chunbo, a poet of the Qing Dynasty, wrote in *New Year Bamboo Branch Poetry of Yuezhong*, "Several generations of scholars have racked their brains. Standing for a long time in front of the lantern riddles. Occasionally one guessed a Tang Dynasty poem, he could get three green fruits and one pen".

斗蛐蛐
Cricket Fighting

斗蛐蛐，也叫斗蟋蟀，即用蟋蟀相斗取乐的娱乐活动。蟋蟀从原先的听其声，发展至今的观其斗，从这一微小的侧面，也反映了社会历史的变化。至于斗蛐蛐这一活动起源于哪个朝代，至今仍没有资料可以证明，但宋代朝野内外大兴斗蟋蟀之风，并将"万金之资付于一啄"已有史料证明。

Cricket fighting, also known as cricket duel, is a recreational activity in which crickets are pitted against each other for entertainment. From initially just listening to their chirping sounds to now watching them fight, this tiny aspect reflects the changes in social history. There is no evidence to prove which dynasty the activity originated from, but in the Song Dynasty, cricket fighting became popular among both the court and the common people, and there are historical records of large amounts of money being spent on them.

绍兴民间的斗蛐蛐纯属娱乐，很少有赌博性质的。喜欢蛐蛐的一般深更半夜听声音找到蛐蛐的洞穴。白天的时候翻砖掀瓦，或者用热水冲浇，等到蛐蛐跳出来，赶忙用网罩住。带回家后，先在盆里静养几天，用毛豆等喂食，然后，把新抓来的与以前的做比较，留下体长腿壮、威武犀利的蟋蟀，取名叫大将、二将、三将等。在比赛中被斗败的蟋蟀，要么送给小孩子玩，要么放走，甚至用来喂鸡。

The folk cricket fighting in Shaoxing is purely for entertainment and rarely involves gambling. Those who love crickets usually listen to their sound to find their caves in the middle of the night. During the day, they turn over bricks and tiles or pour hot water to force the crickets to jump out and quickly catch them with a net. After bringing them home, they rest in a basin for a few days and are fed with green beans before being compared to the ones caught before. The strong and powerful crickets with long legs are kept and named the general, second general, third general, etc. The crickets that lose in the competition are either given to children to play with, released, or even used as food for chickens.

装蟋蟀的盆大多用瓦烧成，当年买的不能马上用，得放在阴凉处盖上一两年后，成为旧盆、老盆才能使用。喂蟋蟀的饲料，不能用饭粒，否则蟋蟀容易长胖变得没有力气，也就没有斗志。引蟋蟀打斗的植物叫"蛐蛐草"，在三伏天采摘，然后蒸饭时一起蒸熟，再把它晒干就可以使用了。

The pots used for keeping crickets are mostly made of fired clay, which cannot be used immediately after purchase. It needs to be stored in a cool place and covered for one or two years to become an old pot or a vintage pot before use. The food for feeding crickets should not be rice grains, otherwise the crickets will easily become overweight and lose their strength and fighting spirit. The plant used to lure crickets for fighting is called "cricket grass", which is harvested during the dog days of summer and then steamed with rice, dried in the sun and can be used for crickets fighting.

斗蛐蛐的时间从白露开始，随着天气变冷，到重阳时节就结束了。这时，蟋蟀的生命即将结束，自然没有力气继续争斗。捉蛐蛐、养蛐蛐、斗蛐蛐，作为一种民间娱乐，流传到现在依然还广受欢迎。每年秋天，绍兴花鸟市场的一些摊位上还有蛐蛐出售。

The time for cricket fighting starts from the White Dew period and ends with the Double Ninth Festival as the weather turns cold. At this time, the life of crickets is coming to an end, so they naturally do not have the energy to continue fighting. Catching, raising, and fighting crickets, as a kind of folk entertainment, is still popular today. Every autumn, some stalls in the Shaoxing flower and bird market still sell crickets.

猜拳
Finger-Guessing Game

猜拳是绍兴民间的一种社交习俗，一般在酒宴上进行，这一活动可活跃酒席气氛，提升宾客酒兴，所以在旧时的酒宴中经常看到喝酒猜拳的。

Finger-guessing game is a folk social custom in Shaoxing, which is usually played at banquets. This activity can liven up the atmosphere of the banquet and enhance the guests' drinking mood, so it was often seen at old banquets where people drank and played finger-guessing game.

猜拳一般在两人之间进行，在一桌酒席上，有时也会出现有数对同时猜拳的热闹场面。猜拳时，两人同时出拳比划，并在出拳时，喊出从一到十的某一个数字，如某人喊出的数字，正好与两人所伸出的手指数之和相同，就是获胜方。这个时候，输的那方就必须罚酒一杯，有的甚至罚酒一碗。也有的以三次为一局，具体来说，就是在猜拳前，在酒杯上放三根筷子，每获胜一次，就拿筷子一根，以三战两胜为一局，即凡是取得两根筷子的为胜方，输的一方罚酒一杯。

Finger-guessing game is usually played between two people, but sometimes it can be a lively scene where several pairs of people play at a table during a dinner party. During the game, both players simultaneously make a gesture with their hand and shout out a number from one to ten. If the number shouted by one person is exactly the same as the total number of fingers extended by both players, that person wins. The loser then has to drink a glass of wine, or sometimes even a bowl of wine. Some people play three rounds to determine a winner. Before the game, three chopsticks are placed on the wine glass, and each time a person wins, they take away one chopstick. The person who takes two chopsticks is the winner of the game, and the loser must drink a glass of wine.

猜拳的数字只限于一到十，叫拳的时候，一般都是把数字组成含有吉利意义的短句，二个字，三个字，但一般都是四个字。例如，数字"一"，叫"一定发财""一举夺魁"。数字"二"则叫"两相好"或"双双发财"。旧时绍兴把福星、禄星、寿星称作"三星"，把科举会考殿试中的状元、探花、榜眼称作"三元"，所以当叫数字"三"时，多用"三星高照""三元及第"。"四"一般叫"四季发财"或"四季平安"。因相传五代时有燕山窦禹钧者，五个儿子先后登科，故遇到数字"五"常叫"五子登科"。

The numbers for playing Finger-guessing game are limited to one to ten. When calling out the number, people usually use a short phrase that contains lucky meanings, usually with two, three, or four characters. For example, The number one is called "one is sure to get rich" or "one wins the championship". The number two is called "double happiness" or "both get rich together". In ancient times, the people of Shaoxing referred to the gods of fortune, prosperity, and longevity as the Three Stars, and the top three scholars in the imperial examinations as the Three Top Scorers.

Therefore, when the number three is called, it is often accompanied by "three stars shining brightly" or "obtain the highest honors in three imperial examinations". The number four is generally called "four seasons of wealth" or "four seasons of peace". According to legend, during the Five Dynasties period, there was a man named Dou Yujun from Yanshan, whose five sons all passed the imperial examinations. Therefore, when the number five is called, it is often accompanied by "may your five sons pass the imperial examinations".

　　"六"在中国传统文化中有"君义、臣行、父慈、子孝、兄爱、弟敬，所谓六顺也"的说法，因此猜拳常叫"六六大顺"或"六六顺风"。数字七则与七夕乞巧有关，一般叫"七巧"或"七巧玲珑"。数字八常叫的是"八仙过海"或"八面威风"。九与"久"同音，常叫"九九长寿"。数字十则叫"十全十美""十全如意"或"全如意"，含有福寿齐全的意思。有时人们也用同一桌人的姓名谐音来即兴组词，妙趣横生，常赢得满桌的人哄堂大笑。

In traditional Chinese culture, the number six is associated with the concepts of loyalty, filial piety, brotherly love, and respect for elders. Therefore, finger-guessing game is often referred to as "everything goes smoothly" or "have favorable winds all the way". The number seven is associated with the Qixi Festival, also called the Chinese Valentine's Day, and is often referred to as Qi Qiao or "exquisitely delicate and clever". The number eight is associated with the legendary Eight Immortals crossing the sea, or associated with "commanding presence and prestige". The number nine has the same pronunciation as long-lasting in Chinese, so it is often called "longevity at ninety-nine". The number ten is often referred to as "be perfect in every respect", representing the wish for a full and happy life. Sometimes, people use the homophones of the names of people sitting at the same table to create funny words, which often result in laughter and amusement.

猜拳不仅需要头脑灵活、反应迅速，而且还需要一定的酒量，不是每一个人都敢轻易上场较量。现在绍兴农村还保持着酒席上猜拳的习俗，但城里的酒宴已经看不到这种习俗。除了用数字外，绍兴民间还流传着用"剪刀石头布"来进行猜拳游戏的，这种猜法在儿童之间仍广泛流行。

Finger-guessing game is not only a game of quick wit and reflexes, but also requires a certain amount of alcohol tolerance, which not every person would dare to participate in. While rural areas in Shaoxing still keep the tradition of playing finger-guessing game at banquet tables, this practice has largely disappeared from urban areas. In addition to using numbers, people in Shaoxing also commonly play rock-paper-scissors games, which is still widely popular among children.

目连戏
Mulean Opera

　　绍兴目连戏是一种传统戏剧，流传于中国浙江省绍兴市地区，是国家级非物质文化遗产之一。该戏剧的主题是目连救母，因此得名。在绍兴水乡以及整个民间戏曲中，绍兴目连戏是主要的剧种之一，被誉为"戏剧始祖"和"戏剧活化石"。演出绍兴目连戏的戏班被称为目连班，这些班自发组织，盛行于清末至抗日战争前。目连班专门演出目连戏，将戏剧、民间音乐和民间舞蹈融合在一起，也被称为大戏。

　　Shaoxing Mulean Opera is a traditional drama popular in the Shaoxing region of Zhejiang Province, China. It is one of the national intangible cultural heritages. The play is named after the story of Mulean saving his mother. Shaoxing Mulean Opera is one of the main drama genres in Shaoxing Water Town and folk drama, hailed as the ancestor of drama and living fossil of drama. The performance team of Shaoxing Mulean Opera is called Mulean Troupe, which is organized spontaneously and prevailed from the end of the Qing Dynasty to the Anti-Japanese War period. Mulean Troupes specialize in performing Mulean Opera, integrating drama, folk music and folk dance, and are also known as the grand opera.

与国内其他地区流行的目连戏相比，绍兴目连戏在出目、唱腔、表演风格等方面都有独特的鲜明特色。例如《男吊》（又名《男红神》）、《女吊》（又名《女红神》）、《白神》（又名《调无常》或《跳无常》）、《出鹤》和《收鹤》等，这些出目是其他地区的目连戏中所没有的，只有在绍兴目连戏中才能看到。其中，《男吊》《出鹤》和《收鹤》等在表演风格上尤为突出，演员仅凭借表情、舞蹈、武术、杂技等表演形式来表现角色的情感和故事情节的起伏变化，相当于哑剧表演。

Compared with the popular Mulean Opera in other regions of the country, Shaoxing Mulean Opera has unique and distinct features in terms of repertoine singing and performance style. For example, *Male Hanging* (also known as *Male Red God*), *Female Hanging* (also known as *Female Red God*), *White God* (also known as *Diao Wuchang* or *Jumping Wuchang*), *Chuhe* and *Shouhe*, these performances are unique to Shaoxing Mulean Opera and cannot be seen in other regional Mulean Operas. Among them, *Male Hanging*, *Chuhe* and *Shouhe* are particularly outstanding in terms of performance style, and the actors rely solely on expressions, dances, martial arts, acrobatics and other forms of performance to express the emotions of the characters and the ups and downs of the story plot, similar to a silent play.

绍兴市东部的上虞地区一直有演出《哑目连》的传统，一场演出长达三个多小时，没有唱和念的部分，全凭演员的表情、身段、武术、特技等来表现故事情节。这些"哑剧"表演在民间演出中备受观众喜爱。绍兴目连戏中的"哑剧"表演形式十分丰富，大致可分为以下几种类型：技巧性的杂耍表演、舞蹈化的身段表演、诙谐式相互挑逗的肢体表演，此外还有一些特技表演等。这些表演形式既可以单独呈现，也可以相互渗透、交织在舞台上共同呈现。可以说，绍兴目连戏中的"哑剧"表演是多种艺术门类表演手段融合的综合性艺术呈现。

The Shangyu area in the east of Shaoxing city has a tradition of performing *Ya Mulean* (*the Mute Masked Play*). The performance, lasting over three hours, does not involve singing or recitation, but relies entirely on the actors' facial expressions, movements, martial arts, acrobatics, and other techniques to convey the story. These mime plays are beloved by audiences in folk performances. The mime play forms in Shaoxings Mulean drama are diverse and can be roughly divided into several types: skillful acrobatics, dance-like movements, humorous teasing through body language, as well as special effects. These performances can be presented separately or intertwined and integrated on stage. It can be said that the mime play in Shaoxing's Mulean drama is a comprehensive art form that integrates various performing techniques.

《无常》是绍兴目连戏中最受民众喜爱的剧目之一，创作于1926年6月，讲述了绍兴民间迎神赛会中的"勾魂鬼"，其职责是在阴间惩罚未能在现实中受到应有惩罚的恶人，是阴间"真正主持公理的角色"。他的主要职责是在人寿命终结时，将其魂魄由阳间带入阴间。与人类一样，他也有自己的家庭。在迎神赛会上，他的家庭成员也会出现，比如"无常嫂"，她看起来像个村妇；还有"无常少爷"，戴着小高帽，穿着小白衣，但大家都叫他"阿领"，似乎没有太多的敬畏之意。鲁迅曾经说过，这是因为"无常和我们是同辈"，所以并不存在太多敬畏之情。

Wuchang is one of the most popular plays in the Shaoxing Mulean Opera, created in June 1926. It tells the story of the soul-catching ghost in the Shaoxing folk-worshiping festival, whose duty is to punish evil-doers who have not received their due punishment in the mortal world. He is the true role that presides over justice in the underworld. His main responsibility is to take the soul into the underworld when the person's life is over. Like humans, he also has his own family. During the festival, his family members will also appear, such as Wuchang Lady, who looks like a village woman, and Wuchang Young Master who wears a small top hat and a small white coat. However, everyone calls him A Ling, and there seems to be little awe. Lu Xun once said that this is because Wuchang is of the same generation as us, so there is not much awe.

周作人把绍兴目连戏称为"纯民众"的戏剧，因为演员所用的语言是地道的绍兴方言。所穿服装和所用道具都是粗制简陋，至今绍兴人还叫那些衣冠不整、器具破烂的人为"目连行头"。演员也都是业余的，有农民、吹敲道士、豆腐司务、泥水工、打铁匠等等。大家都是农历七月你邀我、我邀你凑成一个目连班到各地演出。等到七月一过就散伙回去做各自的本行。

Zhou Zuoren referred to the Shaoxing Mulean Opera as a purely folk drama because the language used by the actors is the authentic Shaoxing dialect. The costumes and props used are also simple and crude, and to this day, Shaoxing locals call people who are shabbily dressed and use worn-out tools as Mulean actors. The actors are also all amateur, including farmers, Taoist musicians, tofu caregivers, bricklayers, blacksmiths, etc. They form a Mulean troupe in July every year, and perform in various places. Once the month is over, they will disband and return to their original occupations.

放风筝
Kite Flying

"草长莺飞二月天，拂堤杨柳醉春烟。儿童散学归来早，忙趁东风放纸鸢。"说的是春分前后，民间有放风筝的习俗，这个活动在绍兴传承至今。风筝在我国南方称为鹞，在北方称为鸢，绍兴人称作"放鹞"。春分期间，大人带着孩子到野外放鹞，找寻乐趣。"正月灯，二月鹞，三月上坟船里看姣姣"，这是绍兴流传很广的一句谚语。农历二月，东风劲吹，正是放风筝的好季节。

"Grass grows long, birds fly in February sky, and willows by the banks sway in the spring breeze. Children return home from school early, hurrying to fly kites in the east wind." This describes the tradition of flying kites during the spring season, which has been passed down in Shaoxing. Kites are called Yao in the south and Yuan in the north, while people in Shaoxing call it Fang Yao. During the Spring Equinox, adults take their children to the countryside to fly kites and find joy. "Lanterns in the first month, kites in the second month, and visiting ancestors' tombs in boats in the third month" is a widely spread proverb in Shaoxing. In the second lunar month, when the east wind blows strongly, it is a great time to fly kites.

放风筝流行于中国各地，历史悠久，至今已有2000余年的历史，被称为人类最早的飞行器，原用于军事上。相传春秋时期，著名的建筑工匠鲁班曾制木鸢飞上天空。后来，以纸代木，称为"纸鸢"；汉代起，人们开始将其用于测量和传递消息；唐代时，风筝传入朝鲜、日本等周边国家；到五代时期，又在纸鸢上系以竹哨，风入竹哨，声如筝鸣，因此又称"风筝"。至宋代，放风筝逐渐成为一种民间娱乐游戏；元代时，风筝传入欧洲诸国。唐以前的风筝用丝绸制作，晚唐时改用纸制。品种繁多，结构有硬翅、软翅、伞形、桶形、长串等。题材广泛，形式多样。

Kite flying is a popular game throughout China, with a long history of over 2,000 years, and kite is known as the earliest flying object of mankind. It was originally used for military purposes. Legend has it that during the Spring and Autumn Period, the famous architect Lu Ban made a wooden kite fly up to the sky. Later, paper replaced wood and it became known as a paper kite; from the Han Dynasty onwards, people began using it for measurement and message transmission. During the Tang Dynasty, kites spread to surrounding countries such as Korea and Japan; in the Five Dynasties period, bamboo whistles were attached to paper kites. The wind entering the bamboo whistle produced sounds like those of a zither, hence the name "kite". By the Song Dynasty, kites flying gradually became a popular folk entertainment game; during the Yuan Dynasty, kites were introduced to European countries. Kites before the Tang Dynasty were made of silk, but during the late Tang Dynasty, paper was used instead. There are many types of kites with various structures, including hard wings, soft wings, umbrella shapes, barrel shapes, long strings, etc. They cover a wide range of themes and have diverse forms.

图43　放风筝 郑红莲摄 Flying a kite PHOTO: Z.H.L.

明清后，风筝的工艺愈加精巧，成为一种可供赏玩的工艺品。在绍兴，风筝制作是先把竹片扎成"王"字形骨架，然后在骨架上糊上棉纸。还有蜈蚣、老鹰、蝴蝶、金鱼等各种形状的风筝，制作精美、形态逼真、颜色艳丽，放上天空后，非常好看。这些风筝大多是商铺从外地购买来销售的。放风筝的习俗，至今在绍兴各地青少年中仍广泛流传。每年春季，风和日丽，老鹰、蝴蝶等各式风筝在蓝天下互争高低，既锻炼身体，又增添不少乐趣。

After the Ming and Qing dynasties, the craftsmanship of kites became more sophisticated and developed into a type of artwork for appreciation. In Shaoxing, the process of making a kite involves fastening bamboo pieces into the shape of the Chinese character "Wang" as the frame, then sticking cotton paper onto the frame. Kites of various shapes including centipedes, eagles, butterflies, and goldfish are created with exquisite craftsmanship, vivid shapes, and vibrant colors. These kites are mostly purchased from other regions and sold in local shops. The custom of flying kites is still widely spread among young people in Shaoxing. Every year in spring, when the weather is fine, kites in the shape of eagles, butterflies and other kinds fly in the blue sky, oftentimes competing with each other for height and creating both physical exercise and a lot of fun.

Chapter 7 第七章

民间信仰篇
Folk Beliefs

大禹祭典
The Ceremony of Worshiping Dayu

　　大禹祭典是一项流行于绍兴市的民俗活动，也是国家级非物质文化遗产之一。禹是中国古代传说中的一位治水英雄，据传他是黄帝的后代、颛顼的孙子。

　　The ceremony of worshiping Dayu is a popular folk activity in Shaoxing City and is also one of the national intangible cultural heritages. Dayu is a legendary hero in ancient Chinese mythology who was believed to be the descendant of the Yellow Emperor and the grandson of Zhuanxu. He was known for his efforts in flood control.

　　幼年时，禹随父亲鲧东迁至中原，并被封于崇。当时，中原洪水泛滥，百姓生活异常艰苦。帝尧命令鲧治水，但鲧采用的障水法并未奏效，治水九年未果。接着，禹被任命为司空，继任治水之事。禹与伯益、后稷等人一起召集百姓协助治水，视察河道并检讨鲧治水失败的原因。禹总结了父亲治水失败的教训，改革治水方法，以疏导河川为主导，利用自然趋势疏通河道。他带领民工测量地形高低，树立标杆，规划水道，翻山越岭，趟河过川，逢山开山，遇洼筑堤，费尽心力治水。经过13年的艰苦努力，禹成功地治理了中原洪水泛滥的灾害，成为一位治水英雄，被尊称为"大禹"。

In his childhood, Yu followed his father Gun to migrate eastwards to the Central Plains, and was enfeoffed in Chong. At that time, the floodwaters in the Central Plains were severe and the people were living in extremely difficult conditions. Emperor Yao ordered Gun to manage the flood, but Gun's strategy of blocking the water did not work, and the flood was not controlled for nine years. Then, Yu was appointed as the Minister of Public Works to take over the flood control work. Yu, together with Boyi, Houji, and others, convened the people to assist in flood control by inspecting the rivers and reviewing the reasons for Gun's failure. Learning from his father's failure to control the flood, Yu reformed the flood control methods, mainly focusing on dredging the rivers and using natural trends to guide the watercourses. He led the laborers to measure the heights and elevations of the land, set up benchmarks, planned the waterways, crossed mountains and rivers, built dams in the hollows, and worked tirelessly to control the flood. After 13 years of hard work, Yu successfully controlled the floodwaters in the Central Plains, becoming a hero of flood control and being revered as Dayu.

大禹去世后葬于会稽，从此开始有了守禹陵、奉禹祀的活动，并传承至今。据史书记载，祭禹之典始于夏王启，公元前2059年左右，夏王启首创祭禹祀典，祭会稽大禹陵，成为国家祭典的雏形。公元前210年，秦始皇曾亲自前往会稽祭禹。历代以来，皇帝派遣使者赴会稽祭禹的情况更加普遍。宋太祖在960年颁布诏书，保护禹陵，并将祭禹正式列为国家常典。到了明代，遣使特祭成为制度，清代康熙、乾隆也曾亲临绍兴祭禹。民国时期，祭禹改为特祭，每年9月19日举行，一年一次。

After the death of Dayu, he was buried in Kuaiji. This initiated the activities of guarding the tomb of Yu and offering sacrifices to him, which has been carried on till today. According to historical records, the tradition of sacrificing to Yu originated in the Xia Dynasty, around 2059 BC. Xia King Qi established the tradition by holding a sacrifice at Yu's tomb in Kuaiji, which became the prototype of national sacrificial ceremonies. In 210 BC, Emperor Qin Shi Huang personally went to Kuaiji to hold a sacrifice to Yu. In subsequent dynasties, it became increasingly common for emperors to send envoys to hold sacrifices at Yu's tomb. In 960 AD, Emperor Taizu of the Song Dynasty issued a decree to protect Yu's tomb and formally designated the sacrifice to Yu as a national ceremony.

图43 大禹陵 郑红莲摄
The tomb of Dayu PHOTO:
Z.H.L.

During the Ming Dynasty, sending envoys for the purpose of holding sacrifices became an established practice. In the Qing Dynasty, Kangxi and Qianlong personally visited Shaoxing to hold sacrifices to Yu. During the Republic of China period, the sacrifice to Yu was changed to a special ceremony held once a year on September 19th.

1995年4月20日，浙江省人民政府和绍兴市人民政府联合举行了"1995浙江省暨绍兴市各界公祭大禹陵典礼"，继承了中华民族四千年来尊禹祀禹的传统，开启了中华人民共和国新的祭禹典章。公祭活动每五年举行一次，地方民祭和后裔家祭则每年一次，历久弥新。这是中华人民共和国成立以来对大禹陵的第一次公祭，也是20世纪30年代停止祭祀以来的第一次公祭。自2005年起，公祭活动改为每年举行一次。2006年4月2日，来自海内外的三千余名各界人士在绍兴市大禹陵祭祀广场参加公祭大禹典礼。

On April 20th, 1995, the Zhejiang Provincial People's Government and the Shaoxing Municipal People's Government jointly held the Memorial Ceremony for Emperor Yu's Tomb. It inherited the tradition of venerating Emperor Yu that has been passed down by the Chinese nation for four thousand years and opened up a new chapter of sacrificial rites in the People's Republic of China. The public memorial ceremony is held every five years, and local and descendants' family sacrifices are held once a year, remaining evergreen. This was the first public memorial ceremony for Emperor Yu's Tomb since the founding of the People's Republic of China, and the first public memorial ceremony since the 1930s when the sacrificial ceremony was stopped. Since 2005, the public memorial ceremony has been held once a year. On April 2nd, 2006, more than 3,000 people from all walks of life at home and abroad participated in the Emperor Yu's Tomb memorial ceremony on the square in Shaoxing City.

2007年，祭禹典礼成为国家级祭祀活动，标志着中华民族祭祀先祖形成了"北有黄帝陵，南有大禹陵"的格局。同年，浙江绍兴举行了公祭大禹陵典礼，这是公祭大禹陵典礼成为国家级非物质文化遗产之后的首次祭祀活动。该年的公祭大禹陵典礼主题为"祭祀华夏之祖、弘扬大禹精神、建设和谐社会"，邀请了海外侨胞、港澳同胞、台湾同胞、大禹后裔代表及社会各界代表4000多人参加，人数为历年之最。

In 2007, the ceremony of worshiping Dayu became a national-level sacrificial activity, marking the formation of the pattern "the Yellow Emperor's Mausoleum in the north and the Great Yu Mausoleum in the south" in the Chinese nation's ancestor worship. In the same year, a public sacrifice ceremony was held at the Great Yu Mausoleum in Shaoxing, Zhejiang, marking the first sacrificial activity after the public sacrifice ceremony of the Great Yu Mausoleum became a national-level intangible cultural heritage. The theme of the public sacrifice ceremony was "worshiping the ancestor of the Huaxia race, carrying forward the spirit of Dayu, and building a harmonious society". More than 4,000 representatives from overseas Chinese, Hong Kong, Macao, and Taiwan, as well as descendants of Dayu and representatives from all walks of life, participated in the ceremony, which was the largest in history.

大禹祭典仪式包括13项议程：肃立雅静、鸣铳、献贡品、敬

图44　大禹铜像
郑红莲摄 The bronze
statue of Dayu PHOTO:
Z.H.L.

香、击鼓、撞钟、奏乐、献酒、敬酒、恭读祭文、行礼、唱颂歌献
祭舞、礼成。自大禹去世以来，大禹陵庙历经几千年的祭典相继，
是后人学习大禹明德、弘扬大禹精神的明证，也是弘扬民族精神的
重要举措，对中华民族起着无可替代的凝聚作用。大禹陵祭典的制
度和礼仪，包括祭品、祭器、祭乐、祭舞和祭文等，蕴含了十分丰
富的民族传统文化信息。大禹祭典是一种"复兴的传统"，融合了
传统元素与现代元素，经过多年的发展，大禹祭典活动促进了大禹
文化向社会日常生活的渗透，推动了大禹文化的海内外交流，并提

升了绍兴市历史文化的海内外影响力。

The ceremony of Dayu Sacrifice includes 13 items on the agenda: standing silently, firing guns, offering tribute, offering incense, beating drums, striking bells, playing music, offering wine, showing respect with wine, respectfully reading the sacrificial text, performing ritual gestures, singing and dancing in praise of the sacrifice. Since the passing of Dayu, the Dayu Mausoleum has hosted thousands of years of sacrifices, serving as proof of Dayu's virtue and spirit, as well as a significant measure to promote national spirit. The system and etiquette of the Great Yu Sacrifice, including sacrificial offerings, ceremonial vessels, sacrificial music, sacrificial dance, and sacrificial texts, contain rich traditional cultural information. Dayu Sacrifice is a "revival of tradition", blending traditional and modern elements. After years of development, Dayu Sacrificial activities have promoted the penetration of Dayu culture into everyday life and facilitated the exchange of Dayu culture at home and abroad, enhancing the historical and cultural influence of Shaoxing.

祭祖
Ancestral Worship

　　在绍兴，祭祖是民间的一件大事。倘若有人走上仕途，被封了个一官半职，必定要回乡祭祖，感谢祖宗的庇佑。所以家家户户都延续着祭祖的习俗。祭祖时间，一般为祖先的生辰、逝世的日子，以及一年中的清明、夏至、七月半、冬至、除夕等岁时节气。还有部分名门望族固定在春分、秋分举行祭祖仪式。

　　In Shaoxing, ancestral worship is a big event among the people. If someone enters officialdom and is granted an official position, they must return to their hometown to pay respects to their ancestors and thank them for their blessings. Therefore, every household continues the custom of ancestral worship. Ancestral worship is generally held on the ancestors' birthdays, death anniversaries, and during the seasonal festivals such as Qingming, Summer Solstice, the Ghost Festival, Winter Solstice, and Chinese New Year's Eve. Some prestigious families also hold ancestral worship ceremonies on the Spring and Autumn Equinoxes.

　　在绍兴，旧时祭祖有"横神直祖"的讲究，具体来说，就是祭祀神灵时放贡品的桌子应该横着放，而祭祖时放贡品的桌子应该竖着放。桌子的上首和左右摆放木凳。祭品是各式菜肴，可荤可素，酒盅和筷子一般摆放六副或八副，酒盅内倒入少许酒，桌子四角供热饭四碗。祭祖时只点蜡烛，不燃香。所有家庭成员依次叩拜。期间还需要倒酒一次，然后焚烧锭箔等物，等到火烛快要熄灭时，全体成员还须叩拜一次，然后吹灭蜡烛，结束祭祖活动。

In Shaoxing, there is a tradition of "horizontal gods and vertical ancestors" when worshiping ancestors. Specifically, the table for offerings to gods should be placed horizontally, while the table for offerings to ancestors should be placed vertically. Wooden stools are placed at the top and sides of the table. Offerings include various dishes, both vegetarian and non-vegetarian, with six to eight sets of wine cups and chopsticks placed on the table. Four bowls of hot rice are placed at the four corners of the table. Only candles are lit for ancestor worship, and no incense is burned. All family members take turns kneeling and kowtowing. During the ritual, wine is poured once, followed by the burning of gold foil and other offerings. When the candle is about to go out, all family members must kowtow again before blowing out the candle to end the ancestor worship activity.

对于祭祖，绍兴民间有祭祖宗、祭地主和祭外客的区分。祖宗是直系亲属祖先，俗称"祖宗大人"；地主指的是当地亡灵，俗称"地主阿太"；外客指的是旁系的宗族祖先，俗称"外客祖宗"。在祭祀时，不仅需要分开祭祀，就连祭品也不一样，并且锭箔之类的需要分别焚烧。绍兴谚语"快菩萨，慢祖宗"就是强调祭祖的时间宜长，意思是让祖宗慢慢享用。

For ancestor worship, there are distinctions between worshiping ancestors, landlords, and visiting ancestors in the folk tradition of Shaoxing. Ancestors refer to direct bloodline ancestors, commonly known as "ancestral gods"; landlords refer to local spirits, commonly known as "landlord aunties"; and visiting ancestors refer to ancestors of lateral clans, commonly known as "visiting ancestor gods". It is not only necessary to worship separately, but also to offer different offerings, and to burn separate items such as gold and silver foil. The Shaoxing proverb "fast bodhisattva, slow ancestors" emphasizes that the time for ancestor worship should be long, meaning that ancestors should enjoy it slowly.

官宦人家的祭祖规格则高很多，不仅仪式隆重，而且还传有祝文，以供后代在祭祀时诵读。例如绍兴齐贤镇韩氏家族祭祖时，祝文有特定的格式。祭祀的时间不同，祝文的内容也随之变化。在绍兴，祭祖不仅是一种向祖先祈求平安和福祉的传统仪式，更是一种家族文化的传承和弘扬，也是一种道德观念和家庭价值观的体现。

The ancestral worship rituals in aristocratic families are much more elaborate and grand, and are accompanied by well-versed blessings that descendants recite during the worshiping ceremony. For instance, during the ancestral worship ceremony in the Han family of Qixian Town in Shaoxing, there is a specific format for the blessing, and the content of the blessing changes depending on the time of the worship ceremony. In Shaoxing, ancestral worshiping is not only a traditional ritual to pray for the peace and well-being of the ancestors, but also a way to pass on and promote family culture, as well as to embody moral and family values.

炉峰香市
Lufeng Incense Market

旧时，绍兴各处寺庙众多，据记载，南宋时期绍兴有116座寺院。至清末民初，开元寺、能仁寺、大善寺、平阳寺、光相寺、石佛寺、长庆寺、炉峰禅寺等著名寺院仍留存于世间。其中，炉峰禅寺的香火最旺。

In the past, there were many temples in Shaoxing, and it is recorded that there were 116 temples in Shaoxing during the Southern Song Dynasty. Until the end of the Qing Dynasty and the beginning of the Republic of China, famous temples such as Kaiyuan Temple, Nengren Temple, Dashan Temple, Pingyang Temple, Guangxiang Temple, Shifo Temple, Changqing Temple, and Lufeng Zen Temple still existed in the world. Among them, Lufeng Zen Temple had the most prosperous incense.

香炉峰高约260米，山势陡峭，山路蜿蜒曲折，登上山顶可以俯瞰整个绍兴。山上有许多古建筑和文化遗迹，如唐代的南岳庙、明代的文昌阁等，这些历史建筑与自然景观相得益彰，为香炉峰增添了浓厚的人文气息。现在香炉峰已经重建，新建了三圣殿和观音宝殿。山脊线石壁上，有近现代题刻七处，摩崖中字数最多的是"般若波罗密多心经"。过瘦牛背，右手边满壁的"般若波罗密多心经"刻石,把人引向山顶的观音殿。据记载,炉峰之巅原有天柱山寺。南朝宋时,寺内香火已盛,高僧法慧在此隐居三十年,持律甚严,诵读法华经,不曾离开。

The Xianglu Peak, which is about 260 meters high, has a steep mountain terrain with winding and twisting mountain roads. From the top of the mountain, you can overlook the entire city of Shaoxing. There are many historical buildings and cultural relics on the mountain, such as the Nanyue Temple of the Tang Dynasty and the Wenchang Pavilion of the Ming Dynasty. These historical buildings complement the natural landscape, adding a strong humanistic atmosphere to the Xianglu Peak. Nowadays, the Xianglu Peak has been rebuilt and the Sansheng Hall and Guanyin Hall have been newly built. On the stone walls of the mountain ridge, there are seven inscriptions from the modern and contemporary times, and the one with the maximum characters is the Heart Sutra of the Prajna Paramita. Passing through the Shouniu back and on the right side, there are inscribed Heart Sutra steles that lead people to the Guanyin Temple at the summit. According to records, there was originally a Tianzhu Mountain Temple at the top of the Furnace Peak in ancient times. During the Southern Liu Song Dynasty, incense was already popular in the temple. The eminent monk Fahui lived here for thirty years, adhering to strict Buddhist monastic rules and reciting the Lotus Sutra, who had never left.

唐代诗人刘禹锡与憎灵启上人交情深厚,憎灵启上人在去世后也葬于香炉峰。相传宋朝时,一位僧人在此供奉观音玉像,人们称之为南天竺。明代魏耕的诗中有"昔闻天竺寺,梦想玲珑厓"之

图45 炉峰禅寺
郑红莲摄 Lufeng Zen
Temple PHOTO: Z.H.L.

句，此后南天竺历经兴废。著名教育家蔡元培曾为该寺题写"慈云广被"的横额。观音殿四周山麓，名胜古迹众多，包括显圣寺、表胜庵、天瓦庵、石屋塔院、南镇庙、阳明洞、龙瑞宫等，还有葛洪炼丹井和欧冶子铸剑铺遗址。

The Tang Dynasty poet Liu Yuxi had a close friendship with Monk Zenglingqi, who was also buried at the Xianglu Peak. It is said that in the Song Dynasty, a monk erected a jade statue of Guanyin at this location, which became known as the Southern Tianzhu Temple. The temple's fortunes rose and fell over time, and in the Ming Dynasty, Wei Geng wrote the poem "I once heard about the Tianzhu Temple, and dreamed of a lustrous peak". The famous educator Cai Yuanpei once wrote the inscription "Ciyun Guangbei" for the temple. The Guanyin Hall is surrounded by many famous scenic spots, such as the Xiansheng Temple, the Biaosheng An, the Tianwa An, the Shiwu Tayuan, the Nanzhen Temple, the Yangming Cave, the Longrui Palace, as well as the Ge Hong Alchemy Well and the Ou Yezi Sword Making Site.

现在香炉峰上规模最大的建筑是炉峰禅寺，该寺由华侨出资，在1990年利用峰顶的空地重建而成，占地15.3万平方米，包括观音宝殿、配殿、僧寮和客堂等建筑。观音宝殿坐北朝南，三楹，重檐翘角，四面临风，殿下凌空部分设有僧寮。其东侧为五楹配殿，采用钢筋水泥结构，气势不凡。

The largest building on Xianglu Peak currently is the Xianglu Zen Temple, which was reconstructed on the peak's open space in 1990 with funds from Chinese expatriates. Covering an area of 153,000 square meters, the temple complex includes buildings such as the Guanyin Hall, auxiliary halls, monk dormitories, and guest halls. The Guanyin Hall faces north and sits south, has three beams, double eaves with upturned corners, and it is exposed to winds from all four sides. The lower part of the hall is partly occupied by monk dormitories. On the east side of the hall is a five-beam auxiliary hall, which was built with reinforced concrete and has an imposing presence.

每年的农历二月十九、六月十九、九月十九日是炉峰香市，游客络绎不绝，前来朝拜、进香和观光，非常热闹。俗称二月十九为观音诞生日，六月十九为观音成道日，九月十九为观音涅槃日。香市以六月十九最为旺盛。这个时候已经进入盛夏，有的香客为了赶烧第二天的头柱香，头一天晚上就开始上山，他们或提着灯笼，或打着火把，远远望去，就像在山道上蜿蜒游动的一条火龙，气势壮观。一路上还有商贩设摊供应香烛点心，以及一些慈善团队沿途为香客提供免费的茶水和药品。这些在夜里上山的香客，整夜在观音殿内燃香念佛，俗称"宿山"。也有香客把背上山的糕点水果分给其他人享用，俗称"结缘"。清代诗人有诗为证，"烧饼麻花几大堆，宿山队里结缘来。料知下世投胎去，到处逢人笑口开。"

The 19th of the 2nd, 6th, and 9th months of the lunar calendar are known as Lu Feng Incense Market, a bustling event that attracts many tourists who come to worship, burn incense, and go sightseeing. The 19th of the 2nd lunar month is commonly known as the birthday of Guanyin, the 19th of the 6th month is known as the day of Guanyin's enlightenment, while the 19th of the 9th month is known as Guanyin's Nirvana Day. The market is most prosperous on the 19th of the 6th month, which falls in mid-summer. Some incense burners start climbing the mountain the night before, in order to burn the first incense of the day, carrying lanterns or torches. From afar, it appears like a fiery dragon winding up the mountain path, quite grand in scale. Along the way, vendors sell incense, candles, snacks, and some charitable organizations provide free tea and medicines for incense burners. During the night, these incense burners spend the entire night praying while burning incense in the Guanyin Hall, a practice known as overnight on the mountain. Some incense burners also share their cakes and fruits with others, known as tying fate. A poem from the Qing Dynasty goes, "Cakes and twisted pastries pile up high, made by someone up the mountain side. One could tell, next life, we may meet, and happy smiles would pave the streets."

地方神祇
Local Deity

在绍兴，旧时有很多祠庙供奉当地的一些大善人。他们曾恩泽于地方，得到老百姓的爱戴，因此被当作神仙菩萨供奉，祭祀不断。

In Shaoxing, there were many temples dedicated to the local philanthropists who had helped the community and were beloved by the people. They were worshiped as gods and bodhisattvas and constantly received offerings.

汉代会稽太守刘宠，任职期间秉公执法，精简政务流程，让绍兴政通人和。等到他离职卸任的时候，从山里走来五六位胡须飘飘的老人，他们送给刘宠银两作为路费，并且赞扬自刘宠上任以来"犬不吠夜，民不见吏。"刘宠谦虚地回应道："是老百姓自己努力勤劳的结果。"他从老人手里接过银两，等他走到西小江的时候，把银两丢入水中就离开了。后人为了纪念他，在西小江建了一座"一钱太守庙"。

During the Han Dynasty, Liu Chong served as the governor of Kuaiji. During his term, he enforced the law fairly, simplified government procedures, and promoted harmony among the people of Shaoxing. When he left office, five or six elderly men with long beards came down from the mountains to visit him. They gave Liu Chong silver as travel expenses and praised him for his service saying, "During your tenure, the dogs did not bark at night and the people did not see any officials." Liu Chong humbly responded, "It is the result of the hard work and diligence of the common people." He threw the silver coins into the West Xiaojiang River as he passed by and continued on his way. Later, to commemorate him, a temple was built in the West Xiaojiang River called "The Governor Who Threw Away One Coin".

　　汉朝还有一位会稽太守叫马臻，在他执政期间，绍兴发大水，洪涝灾害严重。马臻制定了一个将会稽山北部三十六水源汇为一湖的宏伟规划。他发动老百姓，主持修建东至曹娥江、西至钱清江，全长127里的鉴湖水利工程。工程竣工后，如果有旱情可以泄湖灌田，如果有洪水可以闭湖泄田水入海。灌溉田地面积达到9000多顷，得到老百姓的称颂。由于马臻造湖淹没了部分豪门冢墓，侵犯了他们的利益，这些豪门联名具状控告马臻，使其蒙冤入狱，被处以极刑。绍兴当地老百姓悲愤不已，在鉴湖边为其建墓立祠。后来，又在跨湖桥南岸为其建马太守庙。

During the Han Dynasty, there was a governor named Ma Zhen in Kuaiji. While he was in office, Shaoxing suffered from a severe flooding disaster. Ma Zhen proposed a grand plan to gather 36 water sources in the north of Kuaiji Mountain to form a lake. He rallied the common people to initiate the construction of the Jianhu water conservancy project, which ran from the east bank of Cao'e River to the west bank of Qianqing River and was 127 kilometers long. The project was designed to drain the lake in times of drought and irrigate the fields in times of flood, and was highly praised by the local residents. However, due to the construction of the lake, some of the tombs of wealthy families were submerged, and Ma Zhen was accused and unjustly imprisoned and then executed for this by these families. The local people of Shaoxing were deeply grieved and irate at the situation, and built a tomb and shrine for him along the Jianhu Lake and a temple for him on the south bank of the Cross-Lake Bridge.

汤绍恩是明代中期的一位知名官员，他曾经担任过绍兴知府。汤绍恩生于嘉靖年间（1522—1566年），是浙江绍兴人。他年轻时就以才华出众和清廉正直而闻名，曾经在明神宗朝（1573—1620年）担任过兵部主事和户部员外郎等职务。后来，他被任命为绍兴知府，并在任期间积极推行改革，努力为民众谋福利，被誉为"清官"。

Tang Shaoen was a well-known official in the mid-Ming Dynasty, who once served as the governor of Shaoxing. Born in the Jiajing period (1522-1566 AD), Tang Shaoen was a native of Shaoxing, Zhejiang province. He was known for his outstanding talents, honesty and integrity from a young age, and had served as a military primary and a Department of Household Affairs official during the reign of Emperor Shenzong (1573-1620 AD). Later, he was appointed as the governor of Shaoxing, where he actively promoted reforms and worked hard for the welfare of the people, earning him the reputation of a clean official.

汤绍恩在担任绍兴知府期间，非常注重整治水利。他采取了一系列措施，来改善当地的水利状况。首先，他加强了对于河道和水库的管理和维护。他下令清理河道，疏通水道，加固堤坝，修建水闸，以保证水流的顺畅，防止洪水灾害。他还规定了水库开闸放水的时间，以避免水库溃坝引发的灾害。其次，他推行节水措施，提倡水资源的合理利用。他鼓励人们修建水井，开挖水渠，提高水利设施的利用率。他还制定了水资源的使用和管理制度，禁止乱排乱倒，保护水源和水环境。最后，他加强了水利工程的建设和维修。他积极推动水利工程的建设，如修建水库、堤坝、水闸等，使得水利设施得到了大力改善。他还组织人员对于水利设施进行了定期的检查和维修，确保水利设施的正常运行。

During his tenure as the governor of Shaoxing, Tang Shaoen paid great attention to water conservancy. He implemented a series of measures to improve the local water situation. Firstly, he strengthened the management and maintenance of rivers and reservoirs. He ordered the clearance of rivers, dredging of waterways, reinforcement of embankments, construction of water gates to ensure smooth water flow, and prevent floods. He also established a schedule for opening reservoir gates to release water to avoid disasters caused by dam break. Secondly, he promoted water conservation measures and advocated for the rational use of water resources. He encouraged people to dig wells, excavate canals, and improve the utilization rate of water facilities. He also developed a system for water resource use and management, prohibiting random dumping and protecting water sources and the water environment. Finally, he strengthened the construction and maintenance of water conservancy projects. He actively promoted the construction of water conservancy projects such as reservoirs, embankments, and water gates, greatly improving water facilities. He also organized regular inspections and maintenance of water facilities to ensure their normal operation.

除了整治水利，汤绍恩还加强治安，改善教育，重视农业生产，大力发展经济，使得绍兴的经济繁荣起来。他还十分注重教育，鼓励民间自学，开设义学，让更多的人接受教育。他在任期间，深得民心，被当地百姓所敬仰和爱戴。汤绍恩去世后，人们为了纪念他，兴建了汤绍恩祠庙，供人祭拜。

In addition to rectifying water conservancy issues, Tang Shaoen also strengthened public security, improved education, emphasized agricultural production, and vigorously developed the economy, making Shaoxing prosperous. He also highly valued education, encouraged self-study among the people, and established private schools, enabling more people to receive education. During his tenure, he won the hearts of the people and was respected and loved by the local residents. After Tang Shaoen passed away, in order to commemorate him, the Tang Shaoen Temple was built for people to worship.

清代还有位叫倪涵初的医生，他出身医学世家，精通医术，救人无数，还做了许多好事。倪医生去世后就被当地村民尊为天医菩萨，并在村前建天医祠庙，四时祭祀。时至今日，许多祠庙已经破败或毁废，但这些清正廉洁、一心为民的事迹故事仍在民间广泛流传。

In the Qing Dynasty, there was a doctor named Ni Hanchu who came from a family of medicine and was proficient in medical skills. He saved countless lives and did many good deeds. After Dr. Ni passed away, he was revered as the Heavenly Physician Bodhisattva by the local villagers and a Heavenly Physician Temple was built in front of the village, where people worshiped him all year round. Today, many temples have fallen into disrepair or ruins, but these stories of integrity, honesty and service to the people are still widely circulated among the people.

请龙晒龙
Praying to and Sun-Drying Dragon

据《绍兴县志》记载，从东汉到民国，绍兴经历的大旱有文字记载的多达70余次。其中，清朝康熙年间，绍兴从四月到九月连续干旱五个多月。由于古时应对自然灾害的能力有限，老百姓面对大旱只能祈求神灵的帮助。于是，绍兴民间形成了大旱时期请龙晒龙的习俗。

According to the *Shaoxing County Annals*, Shaoxing experienced over 70 documented droughts from the Eastern Han Dynasty to the Republic of China era. During the Kangxi reign of the Qing Dynasty, Shaoxing suffered from a drought lasting over five months from April to September. As the ability to cope with natural disasters was limited in ancient times, people could only pray for divine intervention during droughts. Thus, the Shaoxing people formed the custom of praying to and sun-drying dragon during periods of drought.

龙是中国古代神话中生活于海中的神异生物，身躯长有鳞片，司掌行云布雨，是风和雨的主宰。龙王的职责是兴云布雨，为人类消除炎热和烦恼，因此龙王治水成了民间广泛的信仰。以前，专门供奉龙王的庙宇几乎和城隍庙、土地庙一样普遍。每当风雨失调，长时间干旱或连绵不止的雨季，人们都会前往龙王庙烧香祈愿，希望龙王能治水兴云、保佑风调雨顺。

Dragon is a Chinese mythical creature that lived in the sea in ancient mythology. They have scales all over their bodies and have the power to control wind and rain, making them the master of wind and rain. The responsibility of the Dragon King is to create clouds and rain, eliminating the heat and troubles for humans. Therefore, the belief of the Dragon King's ability to control water has become widespread among the public. In the past, temples dedicated to the worship of Dragon Kings were almost as widespread as Town God Temples and Land God Temples. When there were abnormalities in the weather, such as prolonged drought or continuous rainy seasons, people would go to Dragon King Temple to pray, hoping that the Dragon King could control the water, create clouds and rain, and bless them with favorable weather.

在新昌、嵊州和绍兴南部地区，建有许多龙王庙或龙王殿，当地人常年供奉，祈求龙王保佑无涝无旱、雨顺风调。一旦久旱不雨，人们就会进行请龙和晒龙王等仪式。在龙王庙和龙王殿附近，一般都有深潭，民间称之为龙潭。请龙时，村民们敲锣打鼓，举旗打伞，备上三牲祭礼，抬一顶轿子，排着队伍去龙潭。按照风俗，请龙时一律不得戴帽子。嵊州的部分山区，为表示对龙王的虔诚，在请龙前村里禁止屠宰。

There were many Dragon King temples or shrines built in the areas of Xinchang, Shengzhou, and the southern part of Shaoxing, where locals offered year-round worship to pray for the Dragon King's protection against floods, droughts, and good weather for crops. Once a long drought occurs, people would hold rituals such as inviting and sun-drying the

Dragon King. Near the Dragon King temple or shrine, there was usually a deep pond called Dragon Pond. During the invitation of the Dragon King, villagers beat drums, raised flags and umbrellas, made offerings of three animals, and carried a sedan chair while queuing to the Dragon Pond. It was a custom to never wear hats during the inviting ceremony. In some mountainous areas of Shengzhou, slaughtering was prohibited in the village before the invitation as a sign of piety to the Dragon King.

请龙队伍到达龙潭后，要先到附近龙王庙上供祭祀，然后由道士念诵经文一同返回到龙潭，用神鞭击水，捉一条水蛇、黄鳝、泥鳅等物，放入瓦钵中，作为龙的化身，放入轿中抬回。回到村里，先抬轿饶田地走一圈，意思是请龙王察看旱情，村里的年长者必须到村口恭候迎接。装有水蛇、黄鳝、泥鳅等物的瓦钵放到村里的土地庙内，日夜诵经祷告。如果依然不下雨，瓦钵里的水蛇、黄鳝、泥鳅呈现呆滞状态，就得赶紧放回河里，用鲜活的水蛇、黄鳝或泥鳅代替。

After the Dragon team arrived at the Dragon Pool, they were required to first visit the nearby Dragon King Temple to pay respects. Afterwards, a Taoist priest would recite scriptures, and together they would return to the Dragon Pool. The priest would use a divine whip to strike the water and catch a snake, yellow eel, mud loach, or other creatures, which would be placed in a vat as an incarnation of the dragon. The vat would then be carried back in a sedan chair. Upon returning to the village, the sedan chair would be carried around the fields to show respect to the Dragon King and the elders of the village must greet it at the village gate. The vat containing the snake, yellow eel, mud loach, etc. would be placed in the village's land temple and worshiped with scriptures and prayers day and night. If it still didn't rain, and the creatures in the vat became lethargic, they must be immediately returned to the river and replaced with live specimens.

晒龙，顾名思义，是指把龙王从庙里抬出，暴晒于烈日之下。这种习俗流传于绍兴山区的大旱时期。首先，到龙王庙或龙王殿烧香点烛，叩首礼拜。摆动龙王时，还要敲锣打鼓，把龙王抬到已经干涸的河道边，任其暴晒。也有的是在烈日下抬着龙王到各村田头巡游一圈。人们认为，龙王体验了大旱之苦就能降雨救民。如果真的下雨了，就把龙王请回来，并请戏班演戏谢神。随着科学的普及和应对自然灾害能力的提升，请龙和晒龙的习俗在绍兴已经绝迹。

Sun-drying the dragon, as the name suggests, refers to the practice of carrying the Dragon King out of the temple and exposing it to the hot sun during periods of severe drought. Firstly, people visited the temple or shrine of the Dragon King to light incense and candles and paid their respects. When carrying the Dragon King, they also beat gongs and drums, and lifted it to the dried-up riverbank where it would be left to sun-dry. In some cases, people would also carry the Dragon King in the scorching sun to tour around the fields of different villages. It is believed that if the Dragon King experiences the hardship of drought, it will be able to bring rainfall to help the people. If it did rain, the Dragon King was invited back and a theatre performance was held to thank the gods. With the advancement of science and the improvement of disaster response capabilities, the practice of inviting or sun-drying the dragon has disappeared in Shaoxing.

放湖灯
Lantern Floating Festival

绍兴放湖灯是一种古老的民俗活动，起源于唐代。据传，在唐朝时期，当地居民为了祈求平安和丰收，会在每年农历正月十五晚上，在身旁的小河、池塘或湖面上放置灯笼，并在灯笼中放入纸张、香烛等物品，以祭祀祖先和神灵。随着时间的推移，这种放湖灯的活动逐渐形成了一种独特的民俗文化，被称为"放灯节"。

The Shaoxing Lantern Floating Festival is an ancient folk event that originated in the Tang Dynasty. It is said that during the Tang Dynasty, local residents placed lanterns on small rivers, ponds, or lakes on the night of the fifteenth day of the first lunar month each year, and placed paper, candles and other items in the lanterns to worship their ancestors and gods, praying for peace and a bountiful harvest. Over time, this lantern floating activity gradually developed into a unique folk culture known as Lantern Floating Festival.

农历七月十五是中元节，也是中国民俗的三大鬼节之一。这一天，绍兴当地有祭祀祖先的习俗，俗称"做七月半"。如果家中有刚去世的，还必须请和尚、道士诵经超度，所有的亲戚必须赶回来拜灵。这天晚上，绍兴城乡有给鬼魂送灯的习俗，称作放湖灯。

The fifteenth day of the seventh lunar month is known as the Ghost

Festival or Zhongyuan Festival, which is one of the three major ghost-related festivals in Chinese folklore. In Shaoxing, there was a tradition of ancestor worship on this day, known as making offerings on the seventh month. If there were recently deceased members in the family, monks or Taoist priests must be invited to chant scriptures to help them cross over. Relatives were required to return home to worship the deceased ancestor. On this night, there was a custom of releasing lanterns to guide the souls of the dead in the urban and rural areas of Shaoxing, which was called releasing lake lanterns.

绍兴湖灯是用一片大蚌壳作为灯盏，里面装适量的菜油。再剪一段高粱杆，穿一个小洞，贯以灯芯，放入菜油中。接着，有船的坐在船上，没船的趴在岸边，把灯点燃后，外罩一个荷花形的灯笼壳上去，轻手轻脚地把灯漂在河面上，让它随风逐浪漂向远处。这天晚上，整个河面上灯光水光交织梦幻，景色绚丽迷人。等到菜油燃尽，湖灯最终沉入水底，一去不返，因此绍兴人常把要不回来的债务叫作"放湖灯灯债"。

Shaoxing Lake Lanterns were made with a large clam shell as the lampshade, filled with a moderate amount of vegetable oil. Then, a stalk of sorghum was lit and inserted through a small hole to serve as the wick and placed in the vegetable oil. Next, some people sat in a boat while others lay down on the bank. After lighting the lamp, they covered it with a lotus-shaped lantern shell and gently floated it on the river, allowing it to drift off into the distance with the wind and waves. That evening, the interweaving of lamp light and water light on the entire river surface created a fantastic and magnificent view. When the vegetable oil burned out, the lake lantern sank to the bottom of the lake and disappeared forever. As a result, Shaoxing locals often referred to unretrievable debts as "letting the lake lantern go".

因此，在绍兴民间非常忌讳给人送灯，因为只有鬼魂才需要有人送灯，谚语"赵老送灯台，一去更不回"说的就是这个。在欧阳修的《归田录》里有此记载，北宋有位赵老，有一年官运亨通，得到一个留台御史的官职，他自然开心得很。当地的人调侃他，打趣说"赵老送灯台，一去更不回"，赵老听了心里很不舒服，但也奈何不了。最后竟然真的死在官邸，再也没有回来。所以民间认为给人送灯不吉利。

Therefore, in Shaoxing, it is taboo to give someone a lantern, because only ghosts need to be given lanterns. The saying "Zhao Lao sends the lantern tower, and never returns" refers to this. This is recorded in Ouyang Xiu's *Returning to the Fields*. During the Northern Song Dynasty, there was a man named Zhao Lao who was successful in his official career one year and obtained an official position as a left assistant censor in Liutai. Naturally, he was very happy. The locals teased him and said "Zhao Lao sends the lantern tower, and never returns". Zhao Lao felt very uncomfortable after hearing this, but he couldn't help it. In the end, he really died at the official residence and never returned. Therefore, folk belief holds that giving someone a lantern is unlucky.

求签祈梦
Divination and Dream Seeking

　　求签、祈梦是我国古时人们常用来占卜的两种方法。特别是求签，旧时在绍兴各地，只要有寺庙庵堂的地方，必定备有求签的签筒和解签条。长期以来，求签成为善男信女们问吉凶祸福的一种主要习俗。

Divination and dream seeking are two common methods used by ancient Chinese people for fortunetelling. In particular, seeking divination, in various places in Shaoxing in ancient times, there would always be a sign tube and a set of interpretation slips for seekers. Over time, seeking divination has become a major custom for pious followers to ask about good or bad luck and prosperity.

　　求签习俗是绍兴地区的一种传统文化信仰活动，人们在神庙或寺庙里求取签诗以占卜吉凶，这项习俗至今已有数千年的历史。求签的签通常是由竹子制成的，然后再刻上字。在一些寺庙中，签杆还会被涂上红色或黄色，以示吉祥和庄严。在制作签之前，通常需要进行一些仪式和祈福。例如，在制作竹签时，制作者会先向神明祈求保佑，然后在竹子上写上吉祥的词语或经文。每桶签有100支，大致比例是40%的上签，30%的中签，30%的下签，每支签上都刻有一个号数。

The custom of seeking divine guidance through the use of bamboo sticks is a traditional cultural and religious activity in the Shaoxing region. It involves the act of seeking fortunes or misfortunes through the use of bamboo sticks inscribed with characters and symbols, typically found in temples or shrines. This practice has a history spanning several thousand years. The bamboo sticks, which serve as the divination tools, are typically painted in red or yellow to signify good luck and solemnity. Before the production of the sticks, a ritual or prayer is usually performed to invoke the blessings of divine entities. The inscriptions on the sticks usually comprise auspicious phrases or scriptural text, with each stick numbered among a batch of 100, distributed in the proportion of 40% auspicious, 30% average, and 30% inauspicious signs.

求签时，应先向菩萨燃香点烛，向神明祈求保佑，接着双手捧签筒摇晃筛子，让签杆从筛子中滑落，以第一根掉出的签为准，根据竹签上所刻号数，对号领解签条。签条上会写有预言诗，根据预言诗的内容来判断吉凶、祈求健康、平安、幸福等。以上签为吉，下签为凶，所以有人精神抖擞地去求签，一旦求得下下签，便愁眉苦脸、心事重重。也有人本身是因为工作或生活不顺去求签，这样即使得了下下签，反觉得菩萨灵验。在一些重要节日或特殊场合，如春节、清明节、中秋节等时，更是有大量的人前往寺庙求签祈求好运和吉祥。

When seeking a fortune-telling, it is customary to first light incense and candles in front of the Bodhisattva, and then pray for blessings from the gods. Next, one should shake the sign tube with both hands and let the sign stick slip out of the tube. According to the number inscribed on the bamboo stick, the corresponding fortune-telling poem is found on the sign. Depending on the content of the poem, one can determine whether their luck will be good or bad, and pray for health, peace, and happiness. The signs above are considered lucky, while those below are considered unlucky, which is why some people will be in high spirits when they receive good signs and feel disheartened when they receive bad ones. Even when someone is already experiencing difficulties in work or life, if they go to seek a fortune-telling and receive a bad sign, they may still feel that the Bodhisattva is effective. During important holidays or special occasions such as the Chinese New Year, Qingming Festival, and Mid-Autumn Festival, many people flock to temples to seek fortune-telling and pray for good luck and auspiciousness.

祈梦是一种传统的占卜方式，也被称为"求梦"。它是通过在睡眠时将特定的愿望或问题告诉神明，然后期待在梦中得到关于问题或愿望的答案或预示。这种占卜方式在中国古代非常流行。据《周礼》记载，周朝设有专门的占梦官员。祈梦有"正梦律"和"反梦律"两种，一般以"反梦律"作为解释，如梦见被老虎咬，可能有好事发生；如果梦见路上捡到银子，可能要破财消灾。

Divine Dreaming is a traditional form of divination, also known as "soliciting dreams". It involves telling the gods specific wishes or problems during sleep, and then expecting to receive answers or predictions about them in dreams. This method of divination was very popular in ancient China. According to *Rites of Zhou*, the Zhou Dynasty had specialized dream-divination officials. There are two types of Divine Dreaming: positive and negative dream law, but the negative dream law is generally used for interpretation, such as dreaming of being bitten by a tiger may indicate good things happening; if you dream of picking up silver on the road, it may indicate financial loss for disaster avoidance.

祈梦在晚上进行，求梦者首先燃香点烛跪拜菩萨，向神灵诉说所求之事，然后在寺庙一角或殿堂一侧和衣而睡，祈求菩萨托梦。据说绍兴南镇菩萨不但庇佑地方平安，而且是专门司梦的"梦神"，所以当地很多人去南镇祈梦。醒来后，一般请人解释梦境内容来占卜吉凶。如果没有做梦，一般认为心不够虔诚，需要再次燃香礼拜祈求托梦。

Incense is lit, candles are set and the dreamer kneels to pray to the Buddha, asking for a dream. The dreamer then sleeps in a corner or side chamber of the temple, hoping for the Buddha's guidance in their dreams. It is said that in Shaoxing Nan Town, the local Buddha not only blesses the area with peace, but is also a dream god who specializes in interpreting dreams, which is why many people go there to pray for dreams. When they wake up, they usually ask someone to interpret their dreams to determine good or bad luck. If they don't dream at all, it is generally believed that their heart is not pious enough, and they need to light incense and pray again for the Buddha's guidance in their dreams.

在绍兴，解梦的可能是寺庙里的僧人道士，但大多是在庙前设摊的算命先生。这些人根据梦的内容来占卜吉凶。如果是凶相，就会取出一张红纸，在上面写上"夜梦不详，书之高墙，日头一照，化凶为祥"等字，让求梦者拿回去贴在家里的墙上，认为这样可以逢凶化吉。祈梦的风俗至今还出现在绍兴农村的一些寺庙庵堂里。

In Shaoxing, dream interpreters may include the monks and Taoists in temples, but more commonly are the fortune tellers who set up stalls in front of the temple. These people use the contents of the dream to predict good or bad luck. If it is seen as a bad omen, they will write words such as "the dream is not clear, and write it on a high wall, when the sun shines, the bad turns good" on a red piece of paper. They will then ask the dream seeker to take it back and stick it on the wall at home, believing that this will help turn bad luck into good one. The custom of praying for dreams still exists in some temples in rural areas of Shaoxing today.

三茅菩萨
Three Mao Bodhisattvas

民国前，绍兴剧班，也称绍兴大班，每年有祭祀三茅菩萨的习俗。因为绍兴地域水路较多，为方便乡村演出，戏班子都在船上生活，吃喝拉撒都在水面上解决。戏班子认为弄脏了河水是一种罪过，所以为了消灾脱孽，戏班子有请三茅菩萨的风俗。

Before the Republic of China, the Shaoxing Opera Troupe, also known as the Shaoxing Grand Troupe, had the tradition of worshiping the Three Mao Bodhisattva every year. Because the Shaoxing area had many waterways and in order to facilitate performances in rural areas, the opera troupe lived on boats, eating, drinking, and even relieving themselves on the water. The opera troupe believed that polluting the river water was a sin, so in order to dispel disasters and be saved from tribulations, they had the custom of inviting the Three Mao Bodhisattva.

三茅菩萨，是道教茅山派的三位祖师，均在句曲山得道成仙，俗称"三茅真君"。后人将句曲山改名为三茅山，简称茅山。因此后人多称道士为茅山道士，即由此而来。旧时绍兴戏班子有很多道士班，因此尊"三茅真君"为"三茅菩萨"加以供奉。

The Three Mao Bodhisattva are a triad of Taoist patriarchs from the Maoshan School of Taoism, who became immortal after achieving enlightenment and Dao on Mount Juqu. They are commonly referred to as the Three Maoshan Immortals. Later, Juqu Mountain was renamed Sanmao Mountain, also known as Maoshan. As a result, Taoists are often referred to as Maoshan priests. This is why many traveling theatrical troupes in Shaoxing used to have Taoist priests, who revered the Three Maoshan Immortals as Three Mao Bodhisattva.

但绍剧戏班对三茅菩萨供奉的时间和形式不尽相同。通常在农历六七月，演出的空档期间，由戏班班主商定就地祭祀三茅菩萨。首先，在一块木头牌位上写上"三茅真君"字样，由班主率领全体演员来到江河边，供好木牌，点好香烛，依次进行跪拜，意思是请菩萨上岸。接着，由班主捧着神位走在前面，全体演员紧跟其后，一路上敲锣打鼓，吹吹唱唱，将神位请进邻近庙宇。然后，由戏班轮流在神位前演戏谢神，演员们还要把米染成各种颜色，在纸板上粘出各种花样，供奉在神位前，以示赎罪之心。

The timing and form of the offering to Sanmao Bodhisattva differs from troupe to troupe in Shaoju opera. Typically, during the break period of performances in the Chinese lunar sixth or seventh month, the troupe leader will arrange for an on-site ceremony to pay homage to Sanmao Bodhisattva. Firstly, the words "Sanmao Bodhisattva" will be written on a wooden plaque, which will then be presented to the riverbank by the troupe leader and all the actors. Next, incense and candles will be lit and offerings made in a kneeling ceremony, symbolizing the request for the Bodhisattva's blessings. The troupe leader will then carry the plaque while the actors follow, playing music and singing along the way to escort the plaque to a nearby temple. Finally, the troupe takes turns performing in front of the plaque, expressing their sincere gratitude through colorful offerings of dyed rice and patterns made from paper.

也有的绍剧戏班在农历三月十八后半夜进行，他们在河边焚烧纸钱，然后把神牌接到后台，供祭三天。到第三天后半夜将神牌焚烧，把贡品分给所有人吃掉。民国后期，戏班逐渐有了固定场所，演员不用在船上吃住，祭祀三茅菩萨的习俗自然没有了。

There were some Shaoju opera troupes that performed in the latter half of the night after March 18th in the lunar calendar. They burnt paper money by the river, and then took the god's tablet to the backstage to worship for three days. On the third night, they burnt the god's tablet and distributed offerings to everyone to eat. In the later period of the Republic of China, opera troupes gradually had fixed venues, and actors no longer had to eat and live on boats, so the custom of worshiping the Three Mao Bodhisattva naturally disappeared.